# Wisdom of
# Our Mothers

# Wisdom of Our Mothers

## Stories and poems
## by daughters and sons

Edited by
Eric Bowen

Published in the United States by Familia Books

ISBN 978-145-363101-0
Library of Congress Control Number: 2010928815

Printed in the United States of America

Familia Books
PMB 326
1225 East Sunset Drive Suite 145
Bellingham, WA 98226
www.familiabooks.com

# WISDOM OF OUR MOTHERS

# Contents

**Chapter Title / Theme**

# Introduction and Acknowledgments

Nearly two decades have passed since the idea for this book first came to me. At a junction in my life when I was taking stock of my career and relationships, much of what my mother had tried to teach me as a boy and young man (which, naturally, I had discounted or ignored) suddenly made sense.

As I began listing her terse words of wisdom on topics from ethics to health to relationships, it occurred to me that a wealth of spoken wisdom from other mothers is out there, waiting to be written down.

Eventually I set about gathering some of those words of wisdom. As sons and daughters sent their stories, I was struck by the amazing variety of experiences and lessons.

Our mothers were our first teachers. We all learned different lessons, but for nearly all of us, they had a profound impact, laying the foundation for our feelings, values, self-image, and personalities.

This is not to idealize motherhood. We were taught by human beings, and the lessons carried with them all the flaws of which humans are capable. Sometimes they brought distress, resentments, and estrangement, as well as wisdom.

But they came from what is the most demanding task which most humans could ever face: bringing into this world another human being, nurturing, caring for that life, for as long as the mother or child lives.

No one can ever define fully what this means either to mothers or their children. But in this anthology, we have a sampling.

**Giving back:** "We do well by doing good," is one of my mother's lessons. In that spirit, I have pledged half of my profits from the sale of this book to shelters for women and their children escaping from abusive relationships – to support and honor women being mothers under the most trying of circumstances.

Though I began work on this book long before the publication of Tim Russert's *Wisdom of Our Fathers*, I would like to acknowledge

Russert and his book for inspiration and guidance in the completion of this anthology.

And of course my own mother, Rachel Christensen, offered the inspiration and example without which I would never have undertaken this project.

*--E.B.*

# Chapter 1

# DEDICATION:

## Mothers protecting and nurturing their children

# FDR (Winter of 1937)
## Myrna McKee

*Mother calls the President to save her daughter's life*

Even though I was just nine years old, and it was the spring of 1945, I will always remember what I was doing the day our president died. It was Thursday evening, April 12, and I was upstairs listening to my radio program, when right in the middle of Tom Mix the announcer broke in.

His voice was so solemn, that you could almost hear the tears, when he announced that Franklin Delano Roosevelt, our 32nd president, had just died in Warm Springs, Georgia, of a cerebral hemorrhage. The airwaves were then filled with the sounds of mournful music. I ran to the edge of the stairs and called to my mother, "Mama! Mama! Come quick – the president is dead. The man said so on the radio."

My mother ran up the stairs, her hair askew, her apron tied around her waist, and with a dishtowel in her hands. "What did you say? Who is dead? No! Not the President!"

"Yes, Mama," I replied. "Come listen. The radio announcer will speak again."

Mama came into my room and sank down on the edge of the bed. The music stopped and the announcer again repeated his sad message. FDR was indeed dead.

Mama started to cry. With tears streaming down her cheeks, she said softly over and over, "We have lost our best friend. The nation has lost its best friend."

The sad music filled the air as commentators continued to interrupt with further news bulletins.

The whole country was in shock. FDR had been president for four terms. It seemed like forever. What were we going to do? The nation had lost its father.

There was a deep sense of loss in the country, but for our family it was really a personal loss, for FDR had saved my life. It was during the winter of 1937. There was a bad epidemic of strep throat. I was only a few months old when I got very sick with it. Finally after fighting the infection for two weeks, my parents put me in the hospital. I was running a low-grade fever of 100 degrees and ran it for over 30 days. My little body was fighting, but I was losing the battle. The doctors told Mama there was very little hope for my survival. The rabbis, priests, and ministers were praying and the nuns were lighting candles in the churches. My mother's family was very important in our town, but in spite of all their money and influence I was dying.

One night Mama was listening to the news on the radio when they announced that President Roosevelt's son, John Aspenwall, had strep throat and was very ill in the infirmary at Harvard University in Cambridge, Massachusetts.

There was a new experimental drug called prontalin that had been discovered in Germany in 1936. The doctors were flying in this new miracle drug to Boston for FDR's son.

It didn't take Mama but a second to get on the phone. She called the White House and asked to speak to FDR. After speaking to numerous people and answering many questions Mama got to speak to FDR himself. This wasn't surprising if you knew Mama. She explained that her baby was dying and she needed medicine. She said to him, "You are a father and I am a mother. My baby is dying. Please help."

FDR had a big heart. He told Mama not to worry; he would help her. When the medicine arrived by airplane in Boston, it was divided into two batches. One batch went to Cambridge, the other to Worcester, by police escort.

My doctors told Mama they wanted nothing to do with the experimental medicine. Mama said, "You have given her less than 24 hours to live. What difference does it make? Let her have a chance."

I was given the medicine that night and the next morning my temperature was normal for the first time in over six weeks. I was on the road to recovery. It is stated in the medical history books that FDR's son,

John Aspenwall, and an infant, Baby Green, were the first in New England to be given the then-new drug prontalin, what we today commonly call sulfa.

Indeed, FDR had saved my life. I will be ever so grateful to him and my mother's determination that I'd have a chance, all the days of my life.

G/D IS GOOD

*Myrna McKee is a transplanted Yankee who has lived in the south for 30 years. She is a nationally published journalist, syndicated columnist, and comedic storyteller; member and co-founder of new guild, Upstate Story Tellers 2009; co-founder of new guild Clemson Area Story Tellers (CAST) 2009; National Organization of Woman Writers; "Prime Time" Senior Advocate; Inspirational Speaker. Her columns include "A Slice of Life" and "How to Live life Lower on the Hog" in the* Seneca Journal, Clemson Messenger, *and* www.UpstateToday.com. *National Blog:* PainlessPennyPinching.com. *E-mail mmyrnamckee@bellsouth.net.*

---

# Mother Bear
## Kathy Krisko

*A protective mother's surprising transformation*

When I was a child, I lived with my parents in the deep woods in a valley in the mountains. We lived in a small house, with a big picture window in the front that looked out over the rest of the tiny neighborhood and a big picture window in the back that looked out into the shady woods. The trees, tall, dark pines and lop-topped hemlocks, came right down to the back of the house, and marched around the side, almost into the neighborhood. They leaned over the rooftop, their roots drinking from a little brook that ran along near the side of the house.

Right where the pines ended and the lawn began was one small, bright maple tree.

I had no brothers or sisters. I really wanted a pet, perhaps a cat or a dog or a pony, but my parents told me pets were too much trouble. Still, I thought it wise to ask for one every birthday and every winter holiday time.

One day in the early fall, I walked home after school to find my parents not at home. They had gone shopping in town while I was in school. Town was two hours away, and they had warned me at breakfast that they might be home late, and not to worry, but to go inside and read a book until they returned. They trusted I could take care of myself for a short time. I put up my school things, changed into play clothes, and settled down on the couch with a book. But it wasn't long before I heard the powerful engine of the big station wagon as it hauled up the hill into the driveway.

"There's something for you in the back seat," my mother told me. "It's in a cardboard box. But open it carefully. It's fragile."

I ran outside and opened the back door of the station wagon. There it was, the box flaps slightly askew. I gently pulled the flaps open and peered in, but at first all I saw was shredded paper.

Then something moved.

Wide-eyed, I parted the shreds of paper and revealed the gift: a small, black-and-white guinea pig, with a peevish expression, huddled in the corner of the box.

The guinea pig quickly took center stage in my life. My mother helped me build a guinea pig house from a big, waxed cardboard chicken box lined with newspaper. My mother and I cut shelters from cookie boxes, sliced carrots, and peeled the skins from grapes for treats. My father never came in from work without a handful of grass plucked from the front yard. Soon his footsteps on the front walkway would elicit squeals of excitement from the guinea pig.

Of course, besides the fun to be had, there was a lot of responsibility. I had to change the newspaper in the box every day after school and even on weekends. I had to remember to feed the guinea pig every morning and every evening and give it fresh water. I could never skip these chores, even when I felt sick or tired or upset. My mother explained that when you accept responsibility for something, you can never shirk that duty. That thing, whether it's a plant or a guinea pig, depends on you for its needs, its safety, its very life. I understood that, but sometimes it was difficult to remember or accept how important I had become to another living thing.

On bright, fall days, I would take the guinea pig outside in the cool of the early evening. I would place it on the grass under the shady little maple tree in the side yard. The guinea pig's entire focus became that fantastic expanse of green: an edible world, incredibly covered with food.

My job was to scan the sky for airborne predators, to make sure the guinea pig was not swept away from above. There were hawks in the valley, circling on the rising currents, and crows as well, and even jays might take a small rodent. A coyote or bobcat might turn up, too.

One day, as I relaxed under the maple, with the guinea pig contentedly munching around my legs, I heard the front screen door slam. My mother, who was short and somewhat heavy, came whirling out of the house huffing and puffing. Her arms waved and her face was red. For a moment, I thought I might be in trouble for something.

But that was not it. "Grab the guinea pig and go inside!" my mother shouted. "There's a big, black bear coming down out of the woods, and it's headed right for the house!"

Now, I knew quite a bit about bears. After all, I had grown up around them. I knew how to behave and what to do should I come across one in the woods. My mother, however, was not raised around bears. She was raised in Birmingham, Alabama, and Brooklyn, New York. Her parents were actors, and she had belonged to a college drama society and received a degree in English Literature from William and Mary. She was a fair sculptural artist, played classical guitar, and could sing a substantial selection of the Child Ballads. She also stood barely five-feet-four.

Both of us knew that the black bears in the area were not usually dangerous to human beings. They were much more interested in garbage. But we also knew that a small, docile animal obliviously grazing on grass might be too much for a bear to resist. And we knew that bears are quick enough to catch small animals, and that a bear might unkindly move a little girl out of the way in order to get to such a treat.

I jumped up and dove for the guinea pig. With an instinct born of survival as a small animal, the guinea pig deftly evaded me as if I was one of the big birds I kept one eye cocked for, and scooted under the nearest azalea. Around and around the azalea I went, arms extended. Around and around the azalea the guinea pig went, tiny legs pumping furiously. If I changed direction, so did the guinea pig, the two of us like some flock of birds, some school of fish, somehow invisibly connected and able to precisely mirror each other's movements. All the time, my mother screamed for me to get in the house, and all the time I screamed that I hadn't caught the guinea pig.

After an eternity, it seemed, I laid hands on that pig and swept it up into my arms. At that moment, I noticed how strangely silent things had become. I turned to see my mother standing along the stone walkway, near the back of the house. In her hand she held a tiny piece of broken fence slat.

Just then, the bear popped around the corner of the house and they met, face to face, just feet from one another. The bear pulled up short, surprised. They stood there for an agonizing moment. I clutched my guinea pig to my chest. I could not move, nor take my eyes away.

Then I saw something astonishing happen.

My mother changed.

She was no longer a woman at all. She was a bear, an angry mother bear with cubs to protect. She rose up, shook her claws, and roared.

Now, there is only one thing a big male bear fears, and that is another bear, a mother bear protecting her young. He backed up slowly, then turned and took off back into the woods. At that very same moment, I turned and ran for the front door. I could hear my mother coming behind me. Inside, with doors slammed and, for good measure, locked, we stood panting, watching the retreating rear of the bear disappear into the gloom of the overgrown pine forest through the big picture window.

I turned slowly to my mother. My mother was not a bear after all. She was only a woman, a short, heavy woman with a red face.

I carefully put my guinea pig down into its chicken-box home.

"You chased that bear away with a fence slat," I said shakily.

"Well," my mother said casually, "I certainly wasn't going to let it get your guinea pig."

And by that I understood that she meant me.

# Love Overpowers All
## Rose Marks

*A mother protects her daughter from an unhealthy father*

"Don't do that," Mom screamed to me across the room. "The bowl will fall off the unsteady table and we will lose our brownie mix." Like any other fourth grader, I thought I knew everything and was too good for anyone. "Just listen to me, Ro." Of course, I rolled my eyes after she spoke like always. I guess you could say that she and I can't live with each other, and can't live without each other.

Mom poured the brownie mix in a pan and put it in the oven. "C'mon sweetie, go get dressed for school while I prepare your lunch today. Daddy is coming over today to talk to me about something. Now, when you are home from school, I want you to help me set the dinner table. Everything as far as the meal and dessert is done for tonight. I'll just heat up the dinner in the microwave before we eat." I wanted to think positively because I love my daddy to death, but deep down inside I *knew* something unpleasant was going to happen tonight.

Once I was done brushing my teeth, I began to wander around in search of my backpack. "Mom, do you know where my backpack is?"

Thinking for a few moments, she replies "Downstairs, baby. Anyway, I am believing in you tonight. Please behave, help me with dinner, and don't do anything to get Daddy angry, ok?" I don't think that she could have said that any nicer. But telling me to not get Daddy angry is like telling me to eat shrimp. It clearly won't happen.

In deep thought, I whispered, "Everything will be fine tonight. It's 8 a.m., we need to leave." Truth is though, all day at school I couldn't seem to take my mind off of tonight. It's like I was painting a picture in my head of what could be going on tonight. I no longer wanted to think about it anymore. Every time I did, the more my smile seemed forced. I don't think that the school day could have passed any slower, and that made me know that tonight would seem like forever. I still told myself that I was ready for whatever was going to happen, still hoping for the best. I had to stay by my mom tonight.

The next time I looked at my watch, it was almost time to leave school. For the time being, I jumped rope with Diana, until my mom arrived to pick me up. When she came, I knew by the look on her face that something was already bothering her. I glanced over at her and asked what happened.

"Your father says he'll be an hour late tonight and refuses to tell me why. He's just playing his game."

I tried to think positively and said, "At least he is still coming over since the fight you guys had on Monday."

Mom cleared her throat. "I know, he is just so stubborn. Everything has to be his way. Hey, how about we go to the movies and watch what you've been dying to see since we have the time now?" I couldn't say no to that because that might be the only peace I would get to enjoy today. Right after we stuffed our faces with popcorn at the movies, there was just enough time to heat up dinner before Daddy would be over.

While I was shooting hoops outside, there was a light that nearly blinded me near my driveway. It was Daddy. All I could notice is how he was ridiculously losing weight faster than normal. Healthy was not the word, he looked confused, worn down, deprived of energy, and depressed. But somehow nothing seemed to get to me once I saw my Daddy because just seeing him and spending time with him made me grateful, no matter what we did. A minute later and I heard the door slam. It was my mom, who looked furious. Next thing I knew she sat in his truck and they had a twenty minute conversation. The conversation ended, and so did dinner with Daddy tonight; as soon as my mom slapped him I knew so. He stormed off out of rage. He was in such a rush that he forgot all about his little princess that he once again let down.

I ran inside where my mom went and instantly knew why she was crying and why the family was getting torn apart. Daddy had picked up his old habits. Sniffing coke was obviously more important to him than being a family. And then I thought to myself that this must have been going on for a while now. That was why I lost sleep at night. That was why there was fighting for hours at night to where even if I tried to sleep,

I couldn't. The more I heard them scream, yell, and argue, the more I felt emotionally drained. Too many nights there were filled with tears. How could one man make me have so much hate and heartbreak, while at the same time be a dad that I will never stop loving? My family was feeling the same pain as I, because we all felt we were losing life. Everything now was clear. My mom was protecting us. Just by having to see her falling apart made me realize the seriousness and importance of life. She had taught me how to love from the love she showed me. She had taught me life, the right way to live in which she showed me by keeping harm out of my way.

---

# Take It or Leave It
## Anne-Marie Hood

*Don't complain about what you allow*

Being a parent is no easy job. I'm sure our own parents would agree; they too, probably had their moments. I question my own parental skills as I shake my head and lament, why did I do that? I think back to the times when I allowed situations to continue, that never would have been tolerated in my family home growing up. Have you had a similar experience?

I have two daughters; one is thirty-five and the mother of two adorable little boys and the other is nineteen, attending university and living at home. Someone once commented, "Wow, there is quite an age difference between your children?" I just grinned and replied, "Yes, there sure is. I lost the recipe for a few years and it took me awhile to find it again."

Raising my older daughter taught me a thing or two but when my second child was born, I must have lost a few brain cells somewhere during that pregnancy. There's one area which I now acknowledge was a big mistake: I would ask my younger child what she wanted to eat. Imagine!

When I was growing up, you had two choices concerning the menu, take it or leave it. You could ask what was for dinner but that would be it. You didn't say, "I don't want that. Can I have something else?" Even today, I can envision the look on my mother's face, if such a question were asked. Without a moment's hesitation, the response would be, "What you see is what you get." A smart person would choose to eat it. Breakfast was a long ways off, considering dinner was eaten at 4:00 p.m. sharp.

My mother wasn't stressed out at meal times. She planned her meals for the day and that would be it; she didn't concern herself one way or another whether we wanted what she prepared. I saw firsthand that it worked for her, so why I didn't do the same is beyond me.

I should have stopped myself the very first time my daughter said, "I don't want that for dinner. Can I have something else?" I should have picked up on the key words here: I don't want, not I don't like. I wouldn't expect her to eat something she not fond of, potato scallop for example. We all have things that we find unappealing. For me, it would be anything that contained blue cheese. Yuck!

There's a wise woman harbouring inside of me but didn't I listen to her. On more than one occasion, I prepared my daughter something else because she didn't want what I was serving. On another night, she probably would have eaten it. If my legs were long enough, I should have kicked myself in the behind. What was I thinking?

The stress I put on myself was of my own doing. Of course, if it worked for her one time, why not try again and again. I justified my actions by being afraid that she was not getting enough to eat, especially on school days. I rationalized that she didn't always eat breakfast and ate very little for lunch, so when dinner time arrived I wanted to make sure she got something to eat. Logic told me that if she was hungry enough she would eat; but to ensure that she did, I cooked whatever she wanted. Not only is cooking two meals time consuming, but also expensive. Understandably, I would use more groceries and at times, end up with additional leftovers. Or worse yet, I would gain five or more pounds by trying not to waste food. I'd eat my meal, only to eat later what she didn't finish. I often wondered if other mothers were guilty of this.

While browsing in a Christian bookstore one day, I picked up a devotion booklet written for women. On one page was a very simple but profound caption that caught my attention. "Don't complain about what you allow." Yes, I thought, that is quite a statement and one that I wish was true in my life. However, I confess that on many occasions, I've done the exact opposite. I've complained to friends that I've had to cook two dinners. The truth of the matter was; I made the choice and unless I intended to do something about it, I should keep my frustrations to myself instead of complaining to others.

Yes, without a doubt, changes had to be made in this area. Reality told me that there was plenty of healthy food in my house. My worrying that my daughter would go hungry if she chose not eat what I prepared was absolutely ridiculous on my part. It was time to be firm and to stick with my decision; I would no longer ask her what she wanted for dinner.

I must admit it was easier that I thought possible. She came home from school and asked, "What are we having for dinner?"

"Spaghetti," I replied.

She turned up her nose and said, "I really don't want spaghetti. Can I have something else?"

In that moment, I thought of my mother. I braced myself and said, "We are having spaghetti, take it or leave it." I must have used the correct tone, no mistake; she knew I was dead serious. To my surprise, she grabbed a plate and asked, "Are we having garlic bread too?"

I smiled and replied, "Yes, and there's salad on the table."

It felt so good to make a decision and stick with it. I no longer felt guilty if my daughter chose not to eat what I prepared. It took a while but the wisdom of my mother's "take it or leave it" attitude when preparing meals, finally rubbed off on me. I hope my children learn it earlier in life than I did, and it should be interesting to see how my youngest daughter handles this dilemma when she eventually becomes a parent herself.

*Anne-Marie Hood is a member of the Professional Writers' Association of Canada. She does book reviews for Brunswick News with over thirty published to date. Her writing credits also include: Pets Quarterly, Faith and Friends and Nimbus Publishing's* Christmas in the Maritimes *(2006) and* A Maritime Christmas *(2008) anthologies.*

# Sexworking and Motherhood
## Rajendar Menen

*A story of maternal devotion against overwhelming odds
From India*

A pleasant fall-out of my street beat is the continuous flow of heroic stories from those who have every reason to pull the plug on life. The tales of bravado are countless and it is difficult to pick on one. But, as I write this, on a wet Mumbai afternoon, my mind wanders to a journey made several years ago to a tiny brothel smack in the bowels of the city's flesh district. I was one of a team chronicling the life of sex workers in South-Asia for a book titled *Fallen Angels*. It was raining heavily when I entered the tiny brothel. The flesh district was a churn of human and vehicular traffic. Sanity had left the precincts long ago, and one had to be crazy to be there.

For those far removed from the urgency of poverty and the recourse to prostitution for a livelihood, I will digress a bit to explain the context. In developing economies with burgeoning populations and scarce or underutilised resources with gender, social, economic and cultural inequity snarling at life, the girl child is left with little choice. Without education and money, or any form of support, marriage becomes her only escape from complete destitution. It also safeguards her from everyday wiles and bonds her to some form of respectability and acceptance. If marriage doesn't happen, for some reason, or if it doesn't work out, she is condemned to join the parched fissures of the badlands. She may then starve to death. There is huge migration to urban centres for employment and red-light areas are in profusion. There is also freelance sex work. The well oiled and multi-tiered engine of sex work ensures that supply is kept alive. This is the easiest form of livelihood for those without any support systems. Hundreds of thousands of women in India find employment in prostitution. They get a life.

What I am about to narrate took place in Kamathipura, the legendary red-light area of Mumbai.

I started chatting with one of the women in a decrepit brothel rotting away like the ambience that supported it. She said she was eighteen, and then added that she really didn't know how old she was. She looked younger. We continued chatting and then I asked Lata (let's call her that) why she was here. Was she kidnapped or gangraped and then sold to the brothel like so many of the other women there? She just laughed and said no, nothing like that. She was also tricked into coming here and was paid for, but she had no alternative and so it worked out well for her. But now, she said, she had a huge responsibility and a definite goal in life. A goal, what was that? Did I miss something here? Give me a minutes, she said, and exited the room. She returned with a little gurgling bundle. Her joy and life. Her daughter.

"I am working for her," she continued with some excitement. "I will educate her and give her a good life." How old is she? "Seven months. A customer's child. I knew I was pregnant and didn't want to abort. I told him about it too." She had named the child Jyoti; the flame that can never be extinguished. All the girls in the brothel, some fifteen of them, and even the madam, take turns looking after Jyoti. She is the light of the brothel and they just can't stop pampering her. They pool in resources and have also opened a bank account for Jyoti. All of them want her to study and get a good job. The father of the child is also excited and comes regularly to see her. He is married with his own family, but is keen that Jyoti misses out on nothing. It may be pertinent to add here that most sex workers look forward to motherhood. If they love the customer, they will insist on it. They have been brutalised and abused from childhood and all vows of affection in their lives have been commercial transactions. They have been sold and re-sold, used and dumped like floor mops. As mothers, they hope to enjoy the fragrance of pure, unadulterated sharing. Circumstances may change when the child grows up, or when the harshness of reality raps the dream, but until then there is hope, love and some joy.

Jyoti is dressed in soft, pink muslin. There is a loving overdose of talcum powder on her cheeks and a large black dot on her forehead, slightly off centre and above the right eye, to ward off the evil eye. She has thin silver anklets on her ankles and a talisman for good fortune tied around her left upper arm. Her soft, silky hair is washed, oiled and combed and tied with a red ribbon. The moment she even threatens to cry, the girls make a play for her. If only she knew how much she lights up the lives of a motley bunch of girls living off the tenuous promise of young flesh! Lata breastfeeds her whenever she is free of a customer.

What about customers; don't you entertain them anymore? "Of course, I do," admits Lata. "I need to. I need to earn as much as I can now (she charges about three dollars a session; sometimes there are tips, and food and accommodation are free which makes it an excellent deal compared to back home; she is also lucky to work in one of the better brothels). The other girls look after Jyoti when I am busy and so there is no problem. Even her father understands my situation. He doesn't tell me what to do or what not to do. He also gives me money for her."

She then tells me that she plans to shift Jyoti to a missionary school with residential facilities when she is a bit older. "I don't want her to know what I am doing. I also don't want her to see the stream of customers. Actually, I don't want her to live in this area and have anything to do with it. Let her grow up strong and independent and unscarred. I have talked to the Sisters who run the mission and they have agreed. They know what I do and understand my situation. If I make enough money, I will leave this profession and do something else. Jyoti should never know the truth."

What sort of job do you want her to do? "Anything that can feed her. Anything that can allow her to make life choices. She should never be in the situation I was in. If she has education, she will always find some work. Look at my life. I have never been to school. There was no money even for food. Jyoti should never have to go through what I am going through. I just want her to live with self-respect and dignity." Where do you plan to go? "I don't know. Anywhere. How long can I live like this anyway? No man will come to me when I am older. So I have to work something out. I don't know the details but God will look after me. Finally, it's my *karma*, and I will face it."

Lata's story is a photocopy of the countless hard luck tales that blaze the land. Born to grotesque poverty and to misfortune that sharpened its edge very early in her life, she finally found redemption in a city brothel while still in her teens. Any other person in her circumstances would have lashed out at life and, probably, opted out. When young dreams are shattered, there is little reason to live. But Lata is fashioning a responsible citizen now, and the goal and the resolve to see it through only make her beautiful eyes and smile glow brighter. She has accepted her circumstances, rails at no one, is free from rancour and regret, insists on safe sex, and saves most of what she earns to secure her child's future. Her determination is tangible. We kept in touch for a while until the vicissitudes of life took us on separate journeys. Jyoti was growing up well and Lata was planning to leave the city and set out on her own.

But on days like this, when the wind howls in my ears and torrential rain lashes the megalopolis, my thoughts wander to a tiny, ramshackle brothel leaking in the corners, and the young dreams of a young mother poised to surmount tireless odds. Where would they be now?

I have been on the street beat for over two decades. Apart from enjoying what I do, I keep counting my blessings. The beat has changed my life from the inside. Any guesses, why?

*Rajendar Menen is an award winning journalist who has been published in several countries. He has launched and edited journals and authored books on healing, and on HIV/AIDS and prostitution in South-Asia. His latest book is titled Karma Sutra: Essays from the Margin. He lives in Mumbai, India.*

---

# Through the Stomach
## Sheri Ryan

*Showing love with well-prepared meals*

My week has been hectic, as usual. Putting in extra time at work, seemingly endless, not-so-fun-filled hours of homework with my less than cooperative 10 year-old, chauffeuring my teenager back and forth to her job, the husband, the dog, the phone, the bills; it's overwhelming. I have just picked up my youngest and now we must rush to the bank, the post office, and the drug store and then, I must figure out what I can feed her that she can wolf down before we have to run back out the door to soccer practice. Oh yeah, and it has to have some nutrition too.

I rush through my errands and finally end up at home. I jump out of the car and fly through the doorway and into the house. I drop everything on the table and direct my daughter to quickly run up stairs and change for practice. I take a moment to catch my breath and gather my thoughts to figure out what I can make that is quick. I open up the refrigerator door and scour the shelves. Deep down I know that there is nothing of the fast-food variety to be found in my kitchen. I don't even think we have cereal. And then I see it; a little note on top of the stove that is my salvation for the day. Mom has tried a new recipe and blessed us with a delicious, nutritious, warm and comforting, ready-to-eat meal. I open up the oven door and am greeted with not only a tantalizing aroma but also, in her own special way, a warm and loving hug from my mother.

My mom has been through a lot in her life. She grew up in an abusive home and married an abusive man. When that abuse started to happen to me, she left my father and proceeded to raise a young child on her own. She was not college educated and therefore had to work extra hard to make ends meet. I didn't always appreciate her cooking when I was a kid; after all, most kids have a tendency to be on the picky side and I was, perhaps, a bit pickier than most.

However, as I got a little older, I started to be able to appreciate the magic my mother could make every day in the kitchen. I think some of her best dishes came about when there was practically nothing left to eat but a little bit of leftovers and some basic staples she found in the cabinet. But what I also took notice of was my mother's heart and how she used her cooking to reach out to others in their time of need. If someone was sick, she would make them soup. If someone suffered the loss of a loved one, she would make a wonderful casserole that would comfort both heart and stomach. If there were a party, she would bake the most delicious cake, and, just for no reason at all, (other than to simply put a smile on someone's face), a warm and flavorful, pear, banana or zucchini bread or perhaps a batch of cookies. All were of exceptional restaurant quality. If you have ever been the recipient of this sort of priceless gift, then you know how blessed you truly were.

I look back fondly on the times my mother spent with me teaching me how to make magic just like her. We were like oil and water in our relationship most of the time, but as she showed me the small but important things that would make or break a recipe, all of our differences were put aside. I liked that she would stand back and let me do things on my own and the confidence and security that it built in me. Her gentle guidance allowed me to be the independent spirit I needed to be, but also reassured me that she was there if I needed her. Not much has changed over the years.

I have daughters of my own now and I am trying to teach them as my mom has taught me. Sometimes I have to take a moment and remember to let them measure and stir on their own just as my mother did. I teach them the importance of following a recipe but also encourage them to create their own. My mother spends time with them in her own kitchen patiently tutoring them so that they can one day feed their family as well as anyone else who can benefit from a lovingly cooked meal. It seems like such a small thing, making a dinner or a dessert but in reality it is so much more.

Thanksgiving is just around the corner. For many years I would pack up the kids and drive to my mom's house. Now I am the one to prepare the feast. It is a lot of work but I don't mind. I know that at the end of the day, there will be many happy hearts and tummies in my home. We usually try to find people who are alone or going through rough times and invite them over for Thanksgiving. It is a very special thing to be able to cure loneliness, pain and despair with a well basted turkey, apple stuffing, buttery mashed potatoes and a homemade pumpkin pie; even if only for the day.

Think back in your life to some of your most special gatherings. No doubt most of them included around a well-prepared meal. I really enjoy seeing the happy and satisfied look on everyone's face after they have been well fed. I get a warm feeling in my heart when I surprise a sick or hurting soul with a tray full of love. I look forward to the excited clapping and shouts of glee when I announce that a particularly favorite dish will be prepared that day, and I owe all those moments, to my Mom.

**Sheri Ryan** *is married and the mother of three daughters. She is employed as an administrative assistant and also does freelance copywriting and editing. Her first short story, "The Greeting" was published in 2008 in "The Ultimate Dog Lover" (HCI Books).*

---

# Linda Jean Says. . .
## Nicole A. Tatum

*Protecting oneself in relationships*

I remember seeing my mother sitting in the green recliner, weeping. I was about 5 years old. We were so connected, that if she cried, I cried. Of course, that made her crying worse. I cried because I didn't know what'd happened to her to make her sad. I cried because I was 5 and couldn't do anything. She stopped covering her wet face and looked at me. That's when I saw the black eye. I think it was at that point that I knew my job was to be her protector. She didn't have to tell me who'd done this to her. *Messed up my pretty mommy's face.* I already knew and was mad. Mad at him for doing this. Mad at her for not protecting herself. Mad at myself because I wasn't around to save her from this madness.

For days and weeks, I was afraid for our lives. I was unsure if he'd return and do us harm but I had plans for him. Would I have the courage to call the police or fight? That big kitchen knife was within my eyesight, day in and day out. The black eye had faded just like that "man" did. He was never seen or heard from again.

I watched my mother, Linda Jean grow spiritually and emotionally. I was proud of her for I was convinced that after our experience, she would never love or give again. It would be me and her forever. Wherever she went, her head was held high. She smiled again. She laughed harder. There was triumph in her eyes. I think good fortune followed her everywhere she went. A new man entered our lives, a good man. No more sorrow. No more black eyes.

She taught me to be strong, to be independent but not so where you could never ask for help when it's needed. I learned when one has bad moments, to turn to family and friends because they love you. It is unnecessary to handle things alone. Linda Jean said to pray to your higher power and have faith in yourself, always believe in yourself. She said I should always have my own and prepare for the future. This meant have my own place to live – my name on the lease or our names on the lease, not his name on the lease only. If the relationship didn't work out, he could kick me out. Made complete sense to me. Financially, have savings. Life throws so many obstacles that can set us back – loss of employment, death, loss of property, and so on. Be prepared.

I held her gems close to my heart, regarding them to the best of my abilities. My early twenties found me putting them to the test. I was in a relationship with my son's father whom I thought was the "be all, end all." My heart never felt for another. Believe me when I tell you, I've tried. We came around full circle, in constant gravitation.

He was a boy of misfortune and bad luck. Too many bad choices and decisions. Drugs. Lack of self love or esteem. Not exactly a victim of circumstance but I believe that he often took short cuts to get what he wanted and never thought about those he hurt during his pursuits. To him, life was a game. It was void of responsibility, work or sacrifice. My upbringing forced me to find some good within him and try to help him, change his way of thinking. This was a thankless job but I had faith in myself. I was doing a good deed.

Before I knew it, I was lover, banker, teacher, cook and maid. I felt myself sinking. I was unhappy. I felt used and taken advantage of. I allowed myself to become immersed into my pet project that I lost myself. When I saw no changes or improvements, I completely blamed myself. Surely, this whole thing was me or there was something wrong with me. Now I was stuck with this guy. Somewhere deep, I still loved him but knew I had to leave. This was not what being in a relationship is about. Wasn't it about give and take and not take-take? I was living with him. No, my name was not on the lease. I was a woman in love. I had to go, but remember, I was independent. Go where? Going back home represented failure, however, when one is in need, you turn to family and friends. I had no choice, I had to return home and leave this situation. Financially, I was not prepared to find a place of my own. I could not hire movers to transport my belongings. Another strike. What happened to the things my mother taught me? Everything was forgotten and ignored. What saved me is the very last thing Linda Jean said. Praying and having faith. I had to change my way of thinking. I had to learn to love myself. It was most difficult to believe that I had wasted time on a lost cause. You cannot help those who do not want to help themselves. He was that sort of case. If I stayed with him, I would sink to no return. I would have harmed him, possibly landing myself in jail. I recall pretending to have taken too many Tylenol or something, laying myself on the bathroom floor to get a reaction out of him, to see if he really loved me. I was carrying his child. He didn't panic. He didn't cry out in concern or offer to call 911. He left me on that floor. I cried. As I lay there, I thought to myself: *what the hell am I doing? Why am I doing this? When did I lose myself? Would my loved ones condone this behavior? For a guy who doesn't give a damn about me? Get up and stay up, Nicole! This is crazy!*

I got up, walked into the bedroom and did more thinking and planning. I had issues back at home but not so badly that I would not be received with opened arms. I still had my job. I wanted my things to move with me but decided to move them a little at a time. When I returned home, I was always asked if I was OK, if I was depressed. I left the father of our unborn child. We were a couple, seen together all of the time. Now we weren't a couple. I wasn't depressed and very much OK with this. I had been unhappy for so long. I began to focus more on myself and the baby. I felt myself creeping out of that hole I once sank in. I was blossoming, renewed, fresh. I was more than OK but very angry. I didn't listen to anyone, not even my gut instinct. I was angry for getting caught up and losing myself. But I knew I would be just fine. This was an obstacle I could overcome. This was my black eye. Although I was not physically abused, I was scarred mentally and emotionally. My mother saw this and talked to me to uplift my spirits and sense of hope. She told me I would be OK and I would get through this. She reminded me about those who loved me and supported my actions. I was hard working, determined, goal oriented and about to be a new mother.

I talked before about my things. My things are important to me but they are things. Materials can easily be replaced. My mom taught me that. Not to harp on things – for they come and go. She wanted me to learn to grow in a positive light. To be kind and forgiving. To love ME. I cannot love another if I do not first love myself. I should work hard and in time, I'd get new things. In time, I made careful choices. I knew the difference between true friends and acquaintances. I knew that if a person paid attention to me, he wasn't automatically my "man." Mom showed me to put my child's needs first and my wants last but don't be a martyr – I can treat myself to something once in a while.

Time has passed. I've gotten a handle on my spiritual and emotional needs. I have moved on. I love myself! I love my son! I am in a loving relationship with a good man which Linda Jean says I deserve. Neither of us foresees sorrow and black eyes but glee and twinkles in my eyes.

Thank you Linda Jean for all you have taught me. I promise to hold them dear and true. These guides have shaped me into the woman I am and care to be.

---

## come home
**gayle portnow**

come home before dark,
mom said when I was allowed to stay out alone.
come home early,
she said when I went on a date.
come home soon,
when I moved to my own apartment.
come home with him,
when I had a boyfriend.
come home for thanksgiving,
when I was engaged.

come home more often,
when I was married.
come home with the baby,
when we had one.
come home with the children,
when we had two and then three,
and mom and dad moved to Florida.

soon I was saying to my daughters,
come home before dark.

*Gayle Portnow was born in Brooklyn, New York, and now lives in Camden, Maine, where she is often rapt in fog, a favorite subject of her poetry. She still returns to her apartment in Manhattan, but spends more time writing and enjoying life near the harbor in Maine. She makes poems and photographs of atmospheric conditions, and writes stories about random curiosities, including growing up in Brooklyn.*

*She's been published in the anthologies:* Secrets, The Other Side of Sorrow, Friends *and the forthcoming* Wisdom of Our Mothers. *Her work has appeared in* Puckerbrush Review, Off the Coast, The Free Press, The Easthampton Star, Wind Magazine, *and* Wolf Moon Press Journal.

---

# A Contribution of Confidence
## Serena Spinello

I've never had a healthy relationship with my mirror.
I've tried avoiding it, covering it and removing it all together.
My reflection startled me, as if it was that of a stranger.

Slowly I'd saunter over to speculum and canvass my reflection.
Face to face with cruelest adversary.
My vicious opponent was me.

I'd scrutinize every mark on my skin;
appraising blemishes of defeat, lines of incapability and marks of
deficiency.

It became a ritual –
I'd wake up, clamber over to the mirror and begin my daily assessment.
I had each mark, scar and blemish memorized.
These alleged defects followed me everywhere.

One morning, my mom came down as I was performing my ritual.
Tears surfaced and began hastily leaping from my eyes.
This made me feel even worse –
Did my own saline want to escape me too?
I couldn't bear to look anymore
so I put up wrapping paper to conceal my reflection.
Defeat oozed from my pores.

My mom stood there and watched silently.
When there was no glass left to cover,
she took my hand and positioned me in front of the veiled mirror.
Slowly, she began to rip the wrapping off.
I was waiting for my feet to take off but they stayed;
firmly placed in a vulnerable position.

She'd look at me after she removed each sheet.
I knew what was coming and I shook my head in protest.
There, beside me on the floor was the mirrors veil that I erected.
She looked at the glass, then again at me.
She stepped closer to the mirror and surprisingly I followed.
She pushed my hair aside, exposing my eyes.
There I was.

Face to face with the enemy.
Her slender fingers caressed my face as she began to speak.
I don't know if she was addressing my aesthetics or me.
It was probably both.

"These alleged marks; you're ashamed of, the scars you're embarrassed by, the blotches that you fear..."
She had my attention now, though I wandered why she was facilitating my self defeating ways.

"They are trophies. I remember this one especially well, your strength your braveness...and this one (she snickered) this one is my favorite. It's evidence of your character. I never thought anyone could handle the cards that you were dealt. And the way you manage your disabilities, with humor and solace...these marks, these marks are... remarkable!"

She laughed again, "I sneak peaks at you all the time, partly out of concern for your health, but mostly and by that I mean almost always, I look at you and don't want to turn away. You are stunning on both the inside and out. Your drive, the compassion and solicitude you have towards others is inspiring. Look in the mirror and look hard. You are staring at evidence of your endurance; you're gazing at someone who beat the odds."

She took her hands from my face and placed them on her own.
Looking into the mirror she began to cry.
"I am so lucky," she said.
How many people do you know that have a hero for as a daughter?"

*Serena Spinello is 27 years old and lives in New York. Her recent poems have been published in the* Literary House Review 2008, Rogue Poetry Review, The Houston Literary Review, Conceit Magazine, 63 Channels, Sien en Werden, The Centrifugal Eye, Clockwise Cat, Mississippi Crow, Perspectives Magazine, The Flask Review, Contemporary Rhyme, *and* The Verse Marauder. *Her first chapbook,* Arousing Argot, *is available from Scars Publications. She dedicates much of her work to her mother Theresa, who continues to be both her inspiration and her muse.*

# Chapter 2

# THE JOY OF LIVING:

## Teaching children to appreciate their world

# A Shepherd Hears the Angels' Song
## Diane Kolb

*Angels' hair can be any color at all.*

## 1953

Twenty pairs of Buster Browns swung back and forth on the large wooden chairs in the Sunday school room. Miss April, the pageant director, fluttered about handing out piles of typewritten pages to various parent helpers. This was the moment everyone one had been waiting for. The parts for the Christmas pageant were to be announced.

I held my breath as Miss April walked with measured steps down the row of children. Maybe this would be the year I would get to be an angel. I could just see myself in the shimmering, blue, junior choir robe with the white tissue paper wings spread out behind me like a great white bird. The hanger twisted to fit like a halo and covered with aluminum foil would sit on top of my Dutch boy hair cut sparkling in the candlelight. At age seven I had been in the Sunday school Christmas pageant four years running. I had played every part except an angel. I even made an appearance one year as a sheep when there were too many children and not enough parts to go around.

I folded my hands together so tightly my knuckles turned white. The flowered dress stopped in front of my chair. "Short, dark hair," Miss April said to herself. "Diane, you will make a fine shepherd!" She said sweetly looking down at me. Then she smiled, patted my head, and moved on to the next child. I couldn't believe it. I was relegated to the burlap brigade again; scratchy bathrobe, kitchen towel head scarf, and wooden walking stick! I was stuck with all the boys again! Hot tears were already welling up in my eyes and I kept my head down and bit my lip so no one would see my disappointment. When all the parts were assigned I raised my head and snuck a peek down the row of children. Every little girl with pretty, long, blond hair was already in the costume box sizing up their blue robes and trying on halos.

All the shepherds were led to a corner and given our ragbag outfits. The boys had a lot of fun at my expense joking about me being "one of the fellas." I wanted to crawl under my chair and disappear. I was always taught never to argue with a grown-up and to do what I was told without comment so I spoke to no one and followed the director's staging. (Even though after several years in the same part I had become an expert at being "sore afraid.")

When the rehearsal was finally over, the sun made long shadows on the pavement and I had to hurry to be home before dark. I grabbed the dreaded sackcloth costume and stuffed it in a brown bag and ran for the door. The air was sharp and cold on my face as I raced up the side driveway my face still flaming after facing such a humiliation. One of my mittens was among the missing so I curled my fingers around the brown bag to keep them warm as I hurried down the two blocks to my house.

How would I ever tell my mother? She wanted me to be an angel so much because she knew how much I wanted it. Next year I would be too old for the pageant. I would be in the Junior Class which was in charge of passing out the programs. This was my last year to finally be the angel I dreamed about. I walked quietly up the porch steps and sat down on the top step under the living room window. I just sat there for what seemed like an eternity. The street lights came on before I had the courage to go in. I took a deep breath and crept into the house.

It was only a week until Christmas Eve and the night of the Sunday School Pageant. The holiday decorations in our house were all in place. The only things still nestled in the Christmas trunk were the cardboard fireplace painted to look like red bricks, and the tree ornaments. These would be put up with great ceremony on Christmas Eve just as they had been every year as long as I could remember.

The warm, dry air wrapped around my shivering body like a blanket. I could smell the aroma of sauerkraut and pork coming from the kitchen and my mouth watered. I didn't realize how hungry I was. There were freshly baked Christmas cookies cooling on newspaper on the dining room table. Everything was just perfect – except for me.

I thought I could escape unseen but my mother was too clever for me. She must have seen me from the kitchen out of the corner of her eye and came out to greet me wiping her hands on the towel draped over her shoulder. When I saw her bright smile and outstretched arms the tears came out of nowhere and I collapsed in my mother's arms.

"What is it, Sweetheart? What's the matter?" she asked. Without looking directly at her I explained what had happened between short breaths. "I'm a shepherd again, Mom!" I said through burning tears. "When do I get to be an angel? It's not fair! It's just not fair! Just because I don't have yellow hair! Didn't God make any angels with brown hair?"

"Of course He did!" she said gathering me into her lap. "Angels come in all shapes and sizes, and their hair can be any color at all. They're all around us, watching over us, protecting us. And every once in a while on Christmas Eve if you listen very carefully, you can hear them singing!" she said.

"Aw, that's just a story," I said running my finger across my dripping nose.

"Hmm, very possibly. But a good one!" she said with a wink. Mom reached into her pocket and pulled out a faded flowered handkerchief and wiped my face with it. "There!" she said. "Dry your eyes. The most important thing you can do now is be the best shepherd you can be. After all, the pageant has lots of children in it all trying to do their best to make it a success. What do you say? Want to give it a try?"

I smiled and hugged my mother. She could always turn a difficult situation into something wonderful. The disappointment melted away and I decided to make my final performance the best I could do ...for my mother.

The days dragged on until Christmas Eve. Finally it arrived. It was gray and frosty outside and there was talk around the breakfast table of a white Christmas. That added an air of excitement to our day! Snow was definitely in the air.

The cardboard fireplace was carefully unfolded and assembled in the living room. My dad gave each of us one of his black socks to hang on the fireplace with a thumbtack. The tree was brought in from the back yard where it sat for several days quite frozen. We all helped get it in the tree stand and fill the bottom with warm water.

Mom announced it was time to get ready for the Christmas Pageant. My costume was pressed and ready for me on a wire hanger. I washed my face and combed short hair. Mom let me wear my Sunday dress, even though it wasn't Sunday. She said tonight was a special night and deserved a special dress. Mom's eyes glistened as she hugged me and helped me on with my heavy winter coat. It was only 4 o'clock but the sky was already dark and gray. I had to go early. The rest of the family would come later. With my costume over my arm I walked up the hill to the church.

The cast was all assembled and lined up in order of our appearance in the play. The narrator went on stage first and the audience got still. The story of the first Christmas was read from the Bible and presented like a tableau. Christmas carols were sung here and there during the presentation. When the reader got to the part about the shepherds, I proudly took my place and did my best to look "sore afraid."

The boys had left their burlap robes crumpled in the brown bags all week. Mine was the only one pressed and neat. My mother told me I would stand out in the group and she would be very proud of me. I never took my eyes off her. When the pageant was over there were refreshments for all and even a visit from Santa Claus. Each of us got a small box of hard candy with a candy cane on top. It was the first gift of Christmas. As we left the church for our short walk home, the snow began to fall. Snow on Christmas Eve! What could be more wonderful!

After dinner we decorated the tree with our paper stars, hung the stockings, and got ourselves ready for bed. Our house was old. There were no outside storm windows to keep out the winter wind. Upstairs it was warm and steamy from each of us taking our bath one after another.

As I lay there in my small bed with my baby sister asleep in the crib on the opposite side of the room, I thought of how this Christmas was almost perfect. Mom helped me be the best shepherd. I knew my parents were proud of me. The snow was already falling and had coated everything with a blanket of white. It was the best Christmas ever and it no longer mattered to me that I never got to be an angel.

From my window I could see the lights at the top of the Fireproof Storage building if I stooped way down. They made an orange glow on the floor. I liked to sneak out of bed at night, raise the faded shade, sit in that spotlight and pretend I was on a stage. It was late and the house was quiet. Then it happened. I heard voices outside. Music. I thought at first I had imagined it. It seemed to be coming from far away. Could it be? Were the angels really singing?

I tip-toed over to the window. If I opened it, the blast of cold air would certainly wake the baby. So I scratched the ice off of a small area and pressed my ear to the window. The sound I heard was the most beautiful singing I've ever heard in my life. Not just voices but trumpets and other instruments. I stayed there listening as along as my now frozen ear could stand it.

I remembered what my mother told me about hearing the angels sing on Christmas Eve if you listened very hard. She was right again! The angels were singing for me! It was the best Christmas present I ever got or ever will get again. I never told a soul what I heard that night. It was my own treasure. Many years later I learned what I really heard that night.

It was when our pre-Revolutionary War era church building was being renovated and I had to write an article for the church newsletter.

The tower used to house bells, but they were sold during the civil war to buy medicine for the soldiers. After that, the only music that ever came from the tower was from speakers that were put up there during World War II. At Christmas and Easter the custodian would put on records of choirs singing hymns and it would broadcast from the speakers in the tower to the neighborhood. It is a reasonable explanation, but takes nothing away from the memory of a little girl who truly believes, even after all these years, that her mother somehow arranged to have the angels sing just for her that snowy Christmas Eve.

*Diane Kolb is a Philadelphia native who began her writing career as a children's librarian and storyteller. She received her master's degree in Library and Information Science from Drexel University and served as a children's librarian in both the public and elementary school libraries. Her middle grade novel,* My Father is a Clown *(Publish America), was nominated for the 2003 Christopher Award. Her short stories have been included in* Haunted Experiences *(Atriad Press), and* Whose Panties are

These? More Misadventures from Funny Women on the Road *as well as* Reminisce Magazine *and* Cat Fancy Magazine.

---

# Cattails
## Lily Alex

*Don't let the love of tidiness stifle the joy of discovery.*

My brother Mark is a scientist. He has liked discovering things since childhood. One day, when we were kids, he called me to his room. I saw him sitting on the couch, and a strange pile of fluff, like cotton balls, was next to him. I thought he had ripped open a pillow.

"Wanna see a trick?" Mark giggled, and showed to me a small brown tube. I looked closer. It was a bit of cattail. My brother started pinching out the flowers. I gasped with delight and surprise; those small pieces became fluff.

"Let me try!" I grabbed the next cattail. I could not understand how it was possible; how inside that small thing such big bulk could hide. We pinched and pinched, and piles of fluff grew. When we finished one we would take the next flower. We tried to find out if all the cattails were the same.

This new game captured us. Our dog Bertha came to us. The dog smelled the fluff, and started sneezing. Then Bertha tried to bite the fluff. Her mouth was stuffed with the cattail flowers, and from time to time the dog shook its head. Bertha choked, barked and growled. We laughed at Bertha and at each other.

Mark still pinched cattails, and I grabbed some fluff and threw them at my brother. We started a snow-fight. Well, it looked like a snow-fight. For us the funniest part was that it was autumn and not winter. The sunshine lit up our room, it was hot here and we were enjoying the game.

Suddenly someone opened the door, and the draught blew the fluffs up. "Snow storm!" we exclaimed together.

"Kids..." we heard, and turned toward the sound. Our mother was standing in the doorway, and looked around with horror. "What on Earth is going on here?"

"Mom, look!" Mark rushed to our mother. He still was pinching the cattails. Mom watched, shocked, for a while, then went to the couch sat on it and laughed hysterically. "I thought it was real snow," she explained, "I thought I had lost my mind." And she hugged us.

\* \* \*

This happened almost twenty years ago. Why did I recall this event now? When I went into the living room, my daughter ran to me, and showed a small cassette from my answering machine. She had unrolled the entire tape. "Look, how inside that small thing such big bulk could be hidden!" she exclaimed, still taking the tape out. I realized that all recorded messages were gone, but it was not important to me. I took my daughter into my arms, and told her this story.

\* \* \*

My dear mother! Thank you for the fact that you did not scold us that day. My brother did not lose his love for exploring. I understood the feelings of my daughter. In that hot autumn day, Mark and I both got a wonderful lesson in patience and love.

*Lily Alex is the author of two published novels:* Lost on Earth: Fateful Love *and* The Russians Are Coming! *She was born in 1969, Moscow, Russia. She started to read when she was four. Reading is still her passion. She prefers classical romantic literature, modern fantasy tales, and stories about animals. She's married and has a daughter.*

# Feed Your Soul
## Selene Castrovilla

*"My mother did more than give me life; she taught me how to live it."*

My mother taught me to feed my soul. To merely exist was to be nonexistent. Only by living through one's senses was one truly alive.

There were many feasts to choose from. The garden was one. Remember the saying, "Stop and smell the roses?" We did. The sweet fragrances combined with nature's radiant display of colors struck a harmonious chord within me. A stroll in the garden always led to a day of serenity and happiness.

The beach was another. How fortunate we were to be able to amble along the shore, the sand sifting between our toes. Our senses inhaled the salty exuberant waves that surged toward us, the chatty seagulls swooping through the air, the bright sky heralding the heavens above and the sun shining its rays of light down upon us. We collected seashells, driftwood and memories.

Mom showed me how to discover unknown frontiers without leaving my bedroom. Books were the banquet at which I met new people and journeyed to exciting places – a smorgasbord of magical settings and stories. I loved to unravel mysteries. After a hard day, I visited with the Hardy Boys or Nancy Drew...and later with Hercule Poirot or Sherlock Holmes. Books taught me to question the world around, and to know that there was something more than what was right in front of me. Barriers were broken – my imagination soared right through them! Literature fueled and filled my thirst for knowledge, and my hunger to write emerged. Without books I wouldn't be who I am today.

Even today, a trip to the bookstore or library is nirvana. All those words put together laboriously, all the effort exerted, yet appearing effortless to the reader. The written word is nothing short of miraculous. It is what ties us together, we humans.

Every time I discover a new title I silently thank my mother, for with that little snack my soul swells even larger.

Music was another delicious repast. From my birth my mother would sing arias to me, and play classical music. Melody filled my mind with joy, and kept me company on the day's adventures. There are studies that show the benefits of music to babies. My mother was way ahead of them.

Later we went to chamber music concerts and Broadway shows. Through this diverse sampling, I compiled a treasure chest of melodies I open even today. "Oh What A Beautiful Morning," "'Til There Was You," "Happy Talk"...these songs play in my head without warning, stirring me into concert at a moment's notice, much to the amusement of my sons.

My teenage years brought different kinds of melody to my house. I doubt my mother would call them melodious at all. But she didn't complain as I blasted the Police, the Go-Gos and Adam Ant on my stereo. Music is a key element to coming of age, and she realized that soon enough (or perhaps not soon enough, but eventually) my tastes would change. Now I appreciate all facets of music, and I try to keep an open mind when my six-year old son plays 'N Sync and Backstreet Boys. Indeed, although this is "plastic" music to me, I revel in his joy, and we often dance together to the strains of "It's Gonna Be Me."

Culture was another important source of nourishment. We spent countless hours visiting museums. The Museum of Natural History, with its massive marble halls filled with Indians, Africans and other amazing cultures. I loved to marvel at the animals and sea creatures more than anything else. I would entertain my mother with stories I fantasized about them.

And the Metropolitan Museum of Art, where I began my love affair with Claude Monet. I never tired of his dreamy impressionism, his amazing portrayals of nature. So peaceful, yet displaying a yearning for more. His paintings exhibited everything I loved and wanted out of life.

My own art was a buffet for the senses. Painting, clay, collage...there was no limit to what one could consume! I had an easel in my room, and not a day went by when some masterpiece wasn't completed. Bless her heart, my mother displayed them all! Experimenting with color, molding shapes from dull lumps of clay, piecing odds and ends together into stunning visual statements...these activities broadened my vision and taught me to care for life's details. Art taught me patience and the value of hard work. The fruits of my labor were always rewarding!

I remember entering a drawing contest for Father's Day. I depicted my dad lounging in bed with my cat and called it "Daddy Relaxing." It won first prize and was on display for all the world to see! I learned about pride that day. It was the feeling that resulted from the culmination of my commitment to accomplish my project. All this from a sketch pad and some pastels!

Still another contest involved decorating my bicycle for Easter. Mom lugged my pink four-wheeler on the subway and we traveled to a park in Brooklyn to partake in this challenge. I labored and labored (it seemed like forever at the time but undoubtedly was more like an hour), and Mom resisted the temptation to offer suggestions. She let me create my vision on my own, complete with flowers hanging, crepe paper draped ceremoniously all over and strings flung indelicately. Guess what? I won again!

These little victories in life spurred me on to greater challenges. If I hadn't partaken in them, how would I have the nerve to move forward now?

Each day is a challenge. A challenge to use it wisely. To live through my senses and not watch it drift idly by. My mind is up to the chase thanks to the lessons my mother taught me.

My mother did more than give me life, she taught me how to live it.

*Selene Castrovilla is the award-winning author of* BY THE SWORD *(an International Reading Association Notable Book) and* UPON SECRECY *– both American History, published by* Calkins Creek Books/Boyds Mill Press, *and the contemporary novel* SAVED BY THE MUSIC, *published by WestSide Books. She holds an M.F.A. in creative writing from New School University, and a B.A. in English from New York University. She lives on Long Island with her two sons.*

# The Gift
## Lucy L. Painter

*"As long as there is this much beauty in the world,*
*you will be OK"*

I do not remember gifts I received on my fifth or sixth birthday, or any birthday since and have long forgotten most Christmas presents. In the many years since my fifth and sixth birthdays, I have traveled throughout the United States and Europe and lived in many different cities, each strange and intimidating at first. I have celebrated and survived 40 years of marriage, reared two strong-willed children, and received many presents from friends, family and co-workers. But one summer evening when I was 10, my mother gave me a gift which I still cherish today.

We had all finished supper, and my brothers headed to their ham radios for another night of electronic static. To escape the heat in the kitchen, Mom and I unlatched the screen door and sat on the back porch steps in the evening breeze. Although the sun was just beginning to set, the backyard lay in shadow cast by the Blue Ridge Mountains behind our house, the darkness dotted with hundreds of fireflies. The sky radiated purples, oranges, deep pinks behind wisps of white horsetail clouds, but cast no light on us. Its glory was its own. Small, harried wrens darted in front of the dying sun as they sought their roosts for the night; the only sounds their chirps echoed by those of the crickets. The purples grew darker and bolder until the ragged, mountainous horizon was a black silhouette against a solid dark amethyst sky. Then, as it always does in the mountains, darkness dropped suddenly, bringing with it a serene silence.

Mom and I had not spoken for the ten or so minutes we watched the sun die, nor had we moved. Then she put her arm around my shoulder, chilly now in the darkness, and gave me my gift: "As long as there is this much beauty in the world, you will be OK. You only need to look for it. Remember that."

Just those words, nothing more.

In the 50 years since that summer evening, I have remembered. It may be a glorious sunset over a Florida key, a Vermont hillside in October, or the mist rising from a Scottish heath in early morning, but it is still my mother's gift. No matter what state, city, or small town I call home at the time, God's beauty and the peace it brings are there somewhere. It will be OK, if I just look.

*After retirement from years of teaching high school,* **Lucy Painter** *began to put on paper the stories her parents and grandparents told, stories of immigration to the United States from Scotland and about the personal lives of her ancestors. She intends to collect these stories for her daughter Emily in hopes she will continue them. Lucy lives with her husband Charlie and their two cats and two dogs in Mount Pleasant, South Carolina and in Sarasota, Florida.*

---

# Confessions of a Bibliomaniac
## Mark Scheel

*Mother passes on a love of books.*

My mother was a bibliomaniac. The earliest memories I have are of books, books, books staring down from all over the farmhouse. Dad tried, but he couldn't keep up building shelves. And so the books accumulated in corners, up the stair steps, even under the bed. Mother collected everything from Homer to Margaret Mitchell. But the special thing was, from the time I could first recognize words, she read to me. And when my early creative efforts began manifesting themselves – mostly in the realm of pencil sketches – she praised me.

I wasn't an easy child. Heaven knows, I frequently needed pushing. To accept the office of 4-H club reporter. To attend a high school that offered classes in art. To participate in honors English. For that matter, to even commence a college education. Nevertheless, Mother never gave up. And lucky for me, most of the time she could be just as stubborn as I was.

Later on, when I began seriously trying to write, she was a helpful critic and my most loyal fan. That's why I do have one great regret – that I failed to find the key to publishing a book before my mother died. She loved them so.

*Mark Scheel was born and raised on a farm in rural, east-central Kansas. After graduating from the University of Kansas in 1967, he served overseas with the American National Red Cross in Vietnam, Thailand, Germany and England. He later took graduate studies and taught at Emporia State University. Thereafter he was an information specialist with the Johnson County Library in Shawnee Mission, Kansas. His stories, articles and poems have appeared in numerous magazines, and his most recent book,* A Backward View: Stories & Poems, *won the J. Donald Coffin Memorial Book Award from the Kansas Authors Club.*

---

# Make It Beautiful
## Ryma Shohami

*Adding beauty to all one does*

My husband often comes home and trips over a piece of furniture that was not there when he left that morning. His inevitable response is to first choke back a colorful turn of phrase and to then complain exasperatedly, "Are you at it again?"

What I'm "at again" is beautifying my home, a never-ending project that periodically causes him to stub a toe. I point out that it could be worse; I could be replacing all the furniture rather than rearranging it.

"Well, are you just about done?" he asks wryly, accepting my logic.

"It's never done," I tease. "The fun is in keeping it going."

"Tell that to my toe," he counters.

I no longer attempt to explain my compulsion to keep adding finishing touches to all the nooks and crannies of my home. When I was younger I attributed it to PMS; better than murdering someone, I figured. These days I blame menopause, another convenient catch-all excuse. The truth is it's my mother looking over my shoulder and urging me to "make it beautiful."

My mother's philosophy was that beauty was as vital to the soul as food and water were for the body, and that all you needed for a life infused with beauty was a modicum of imagination.

She was talented and artistic, and every event, from a meal to an outing was an opportunity to add grace and adornment to our lives. Her simple touches transformed the ordinary into the unique.

We were not financially viable enough to live lavishly; in fact, we were poor when I was young, but my mother didn't let a lack of money stifle her passion for making life as lovely as possible. "Beauty is not about money," she intoned frequently.

My mother mastered every type of needlework. Seeing one of her stunningly embroidered tablecloths, no one could guess that it covered nothing more than several pieces of wood nailed together. And because she loved fresh bouquets on her table, my mother planted sunflowers.

In later years, she produced quite a portfolio of needlepoint while watching "her shows." I could gauge how awful life was for her favorite soap opera heroes by noting the tempo at which she completed each canvas. Two pictures per week spelled heartache and doom for Caroline or Spence; three per week, and Kimberly was probably out lining up a new part. My mother's needlepoint still adorns the walls of her children's and grandchildren's homes.

Long before it became trendy to mix flowers and stripes, she would have my seamstress grandmother create colorful confections for me to wear, using leftover bits of fabric. "You'll be the prettiest girl at the party," she would whisper conspiratorially as she fancied up my thin plain braids by plaiting in red velvet ribbons.

Rings and necklaces were not part of the family budget. Knowing we could not afford a heart locket "just like Rena's," my mother convinced me that there was better jewelry to covet. One day, she attached a sprig of luscious summer cherries to my new dress, just above my heart.

"Isn't that beautiful!" she exclaimed.

I concurred heartily, and checked myself in every mirror I passed. I also could not resist nibbling on the fruit while we strolled on the promenade with her friends. By the end of the walk, all that remained of my ruby pin was a cherry juice stain.

Snacks provided my mother with another opportunity to shine in the artistic domain. She never merely plunked cookies on a plate when my brother and I came home from school. Prepared cakes and pastries were expensive, so she created fruit sculptures for us. Every day I rushed home to see what production awaited me.

Once, she partially peeled an orange for each of us, leaving the bottom pole intact and creating a little "saucer" with it. She carefully separated the segments and opened the orange as far as the remaining peel allowed. Next, she filled the openings with mint leaves and a daisy. She then placed the orange globes on a crystal platter and surrounded them with lilacs from our tree. While my brother whipped through his orange in five minutes, paying not the slightest attention to the magnificent presentation, it broke my heart to dismantle mine. Snack time dragged on until supper.

Using her wonderful drawing talent and my box of crayons, my mother covered the wall over my bed with a collage of birds. Robins, nightingales, and bluebirds all vied for attention with stately peacocks. I lay in bed week-end mornings, entranced by the exquisite colors of the feathers. Years later, while wandering through the gardens of an English castle, I rounded a corner and stumbled onto my peacocks. I'd have given anything just then for my mother to see those shimmering creatures.

I was always dimly aware that my mother sang like an angel. She sang while baking and hummed while crocheting doilies. She was our background music. As I grew older, I discovered that she had actually given up a promising singing career to devote herself to her family, which included following my father to a foreign country.

"Are you ever sorry that you gave up singing?" I once asked her.

She blinked and furrowed her eyebrows.

"I'm not sorry about anything I've ever done," she responded firmly.

I was sure she was in denial, but one day, seeing the glow on her face as she sang at a birthday party, I suddenly understood that it was not the career but the singing that she valued. Singing filled her with joy, and performing at a family gathering was no less important than performing in a theatre. Singing was another way of making life more beautiful; as far as she was concerned, she had never abandoned her career.

I learned many things from my mother, some through conversation and observation, but most by osmosis. I learned that arranging cut vegetables was no less creative than arranging a bouquet of cut flowers.

I learned that even though a husband might not notice every detail of a design scheme for the living room, if you put your heart into it, he knows, without knowing why, that he enjoys being there.

I learned that a tablecloth makes a meal more festive, and that life is too short to squander a single opportunity for festivity.

I learned how important that extra little bit is.

Sometimes my daughters become impatient with my insistence on having everything just so. I'm sure they secretly think I'm a lunatic for matching the color of the platter to the color of the food. Their favorite mantra is, "Who's even going to notice that?"

But once I saw my older one casually adjust a figurine as she passed the console in the entry hall. And another time I watched my younger one arrange and rearrange the art books after dusting the coffee table. That's when I knew that my mother was sitting on their shoulders too.

Now whenever they complain about having to "waste their time with trivialities," I console myself with the sure knowledge that one day, just before serving a fruit salad, they will feel a tug. They will return to the kitchen, without knowing why, and they will add that extra little something to the bowl. Just to make it beautiful.

*Ryma Shohami is a Canadian freelance technical writer/editor and, recently, a newbie creative writer. She lives in Israel with her husband, two beautiful daughters, two dogs and a neurotic cat. Many years ago she freelanced as a book reviewer for* The Montreal Gazette *and for the Canadian Library Association. Her new blog site* Write It Down! *will soon feature links to her published stories. Visit at http://rymashohami.wordpress.com for her musings on life. She has two web sites under construction, one devoted to technical writing and editing, and the other to muffins. She dreams of visiting Hawaii and swimming with dolphins.*

---

# A Love of Annuals
## Deborah Straw

*Humility and simplicity matter.*

This summer, I can't get enough dirt under my fingernails. I'm gardening more than usual. I especially love flowers and, as they go on sale, keep buying more and more. I've run out of space, but that doesn't seem to stop me. This year, I'm also doing some sort of color plotting. My back patch, in full sun, is all pink, white and purple annuals, for example – ageratum, petunias, begonias, asters. Then the other day, I ran across some irresistible orange portulacas and, of course, bought them. I put two in the side patch but had to put the other four in the back, as that was truly the only space left. I just can't get enough color. Our summer is so short, why not take full advantage of the season?

Seeing flowers always brings me joy. These days, that's important – especially as we all hurry, hurry, hurry, as if we'll miss something. I love to stand and gaze at flowers.

When I tell people about my flower gardening activities, they ask, "Oh, perennials?" "Well, no, annuals," I respond. End of conversation. They seem to think that's nowhere near as interesting. It's true annuals are usually smaller, not as showy (with the wonderful exception of sunflowers) and, as a rule, less expensive. More humble. They're not flashy. They are also more work (except for not having to take them in for the winter), which I enjoy, and you can choose new varieties or color palettes each year.

My mother taught me to love annuals. At 82, she still has a small plot which always does better than mine. I don't think she ever planted perennials. She's so good at keeping up with her patch of earth, picking the weeds, arranging the flowers in a cohesive configuration, and getting them to spread. She picks them more than I do; she always has several bouquets in her home.

Because I want to acquire as much of her wisdom as possible, I asked her this year, "So how close should I plant them?" and she said, "Oh, I don't know. Not too close." That's frustratingly like her recipe advice: Oh, a pinch of that, a dash of that. No exact measurements. (My flowers are now spaced closer than hers are.)

What is constant each year in both my garden and hers are pansies. They are my favorite flowers, especially in shades of blue. Their little faces lift my spirits, always make me smile. And every year, it seems they come in more color combinations, but the solid color varieties are my favorites. In the back yard, I have light yellow and bright orange, and on the side of the house, six variations of blues and purples. I bought them before they were too leggy, and keep up with deheading. I want them to last. They may not smell as good as petunias, which I also admire, but I'm a sucker for pansies.

My mother always has liked humble bird species, as well. Sparrows, chickadees, red polls, the small friendly ones, not just the big spectacular ones like pileated woodpeckers or great blue herons. My parents, both raised on a farm, have always been observers of nature. They are thrilled to see a new, exotic species, but are equally happy to see their old friends, the chickadees or sparrows, come back to their feeders.

Back to annuals. Why are other flower gardeners often so snobby about them? It's as though those of us who prefer them aren't serious gardeners. Don't they see annuals' beauty, their dependability, their hardiness? Each year in the many greenhouses I visit, their colors seem to multiply. Each year, there are a few new varieties to try. I also enjoy rescuing those on sale, as I did last week with a six-pack flat of begonias. Only three or four small ones were left, and they cost a dollar. I could find room in my gardens, of course. It's sort of like taking in stray cats or hurt birds. (Which my parents did, too.)

My mother always was the flower gardener, and my dad the vegetable, especially the tomato, man. Although he died three springs ago, Mom keeps one tomato in her flower patch. It's not the same as those he patiently started indoors in April on top of their refrigerator, but the memory lingers.

Every time I visit Mom, we exclaim about how her annual patch is doing, and note any new growth or volunteers. Some do come back, like the cheerful Johnny jump ups, quite by surprise. In the last couple of years, Mom has taken to adding small animal figurines to her flower garden, and so have I. She has two tiny rabbits and a small squirrel. I have a larger plastic squirrel, which is almost too kitschy. If it were my husband's flower garden, it wouldn't be there. But as it's primarily my domain (he's the herb guy), the squirrel stands sentry over the pansies and portulacas. (My husband's garden has a flamingo, so he's not one to talk!)

I inherited a deep love of all nature from both my parents, but as I think more about it, the love of small, humble annuals is a unique thing Mom and I continue to share. It's not just about flowers, of course, but also about a vision of life, about priorities. Humility and simplicity matter to both of us. I've never been attracted to showy people, to castles and chandeliers, to large patterns and gaudy colors. I prefer small houses, furnished discreetly and comfortably, not grandly.

Give me the small, the humble, any day. That belief system has inspired much of my life. By example and by joyous enthusiasm, my mother has taught me well. In the summer, our fingernails are often dirty.

***Deborah Straw*** *is a writer and college educator who lives in northern Vermont with her husband, a mixed-breed dog and two Maine coon cats. Her first book,* Natural Wonders of the Florida Keys, *was published in August 1999 by Country Roads Press/NTC Contemporary Publishing. Her second is* The Healthy Pet Manual, A Guide to the Prevention and Treatment of Cancer (2005, second edition*). Widely published as a journalist, book reviewer and essayist, she has written for many magazines, and her work has been included in several anthologies. Besides inheriting the love of annuals from her mom, Phyllis Straw, she also acquired a fine appreciation for food of all kinds.*

# My Mom's Playbook
## Sarah Wagner

*She taught me to play instead of to fight.*

It was never committed to paper but my mom had the greatest playbook for life. There were the occasional Hail Mary plays but most times, she could dance her way right through any problem that threatened to sack her. It wasn't by force or by speed but her way was just as good. A simple, overlooked method, Mom's play was just that. Play. Take joy in the simple things, live for the moment and paint your dark clouds neon purple.

All my favorite childhood memories are those joyful moments when she made green lemonade from what life gave her. I remember running around the house attacking each other with shaving cream and water guns when she was working too much and not often home. We played 'I Spy' in the grocery store when the lines were too long and slow. We made snow angels and painted them bright colors when I was upset that there was still snow on the ground on my birthday.

Christmas presents were great but the ones I remember best are the ones she made me and the ones we made together for other people. One year we turned the butter green and minty when we made peppermint taffy. Another year we had to play Cinderella and scrub the floor clean of red cat prints when the cat tried to help us paint Santa Clauses.

I know there were occasions when we argued, all families do, but those moments have no place in my internal scrapbook. The only arguments that stand out weren't real. Which of us was cuter. Who could come up with the most ridiculous insults. Who could make the better silly face and who could resist laughing the longest.

When we got stressed, frustrated, or angry, we played. It was better than letting everything get to us. We dug a pond in the back yard when work was being cruel and school wasn't much better. We named all the fish after movie stars and the turtles were Bogie and Bacall. It became our favorite place to sit and talk and watch the fish be fish.

She taught me to play instead of fight. To hold the joy close and redecorate the hurt. Because of that, the hard times, and there were some dark ones, are softened in my memory. They're all still there, making up part of my foundation, but they're nothing more than that, sturdy blocks to build on and paint crazy colors.

*Sarah Wagner lives in West Virginia with her husband and two young sons. Her work has appeared in* The Front Porch, Celebrations: Love Notes to Mothers, *and* Cup of Comfort for Cat Lovers. *You can find her online at www.sarahwagner.domynoes.net.*

---

# Creek Crossing
## Mark Scheel
(in the voice of my late sister, Marianna Leigh)

Mother –
how unseemly
you appear; I'll
think of you
this way ... Gray hair
escaping
out from under
Dad's old tattered hat,
stick in hand
to pole each step,
while eddies whirl
about your feet, spin
and swirl as out
you go – wading
in the creek.

Sunshine spilling
down like honey,
willow branches greenly

sway. Were ever
a mother and daughter
so delinquent?
Forsaking dishes
in the sink and
leaving Father
at the plow: to
steal away
to shady banks
and splash.

Tell me once again
how Uncle John,
with fishing line and
school clothes on,
split out his seat –
there, in the mud –
chasing down
a perch
that slipped the hook.
Mother – why
must those old days
all recede, like
this creek
in a dry summer?

The shadow
of the opposite bank
enfolds you. The veins
branch down your meager arms
like twigs
in winter time.
More wrinkles cluster
greedily round your smile
than yesterday ... (I hadn't
seen these things
before).

The pastel sky
admits but one
small cloud – tiny,
just there,
beyond the timber line;
impassive, yes,
and white
as the doctor's smock,
this morning,
at the clinic, when
the stern voice
shaped
that quiet word:
cancer.

---

## Quilting Remembrance
**Virginia Fortner**

Mom steps out of worn slippers,
corns and bunions pressing into carpet,
hands me a great pile of Dad's shirts,
lifeless now, thoroughly used.

Today we'll quilt remembrance,
this farmer's wife and daughter,
calling forth a new design
from remnants of life when Dad was with us.


Mom smoothes a sleeve, pieces stories together.
I hold my breath and listen.

Memory brightens faded colors
as our fingers smooth cloth, touch the past –
denim for milking on chilly nights,
cool chambray for shucking corn,
blazing sunbursts on square-dance cotton,
bold roses on a cowboy yoke
bordered with bias piping,
steer's head embroidered on a pocket
still smelling of peppermints.

Focused now, we move beyond disappointments, disagreements.
Growing pains faced and understood.
With prayerful hands, we pick up scissors,
cut exact squares, careful points

for Texas star, drunkard's path,
log cabin, chicken tracks,
double wedding ring, bow tie,
broken arrow, nine patch.
So many patterns, a sampler of one man's life.

We sew
a riot of red, gold, turquoise,
balanced by blue, occasional black blocks pieced together,
set inside a white crisscross boundary.

We quilt
circles on blue squares,
unending swirls along white borders.
Hope patterns eternal life in tiny stitches.

I concentrate, try to match Mom's perfect march of thread,
repeat the mantra, "Good quilting's the same topside or underneath."
I rip out stitches, rethread my needle.

Learning Mom' perfection, I add wrinkles, beauty, hope
to one day warm my daughter's memories

# Chapter 3

# VIRTUES:

## Courage, honesty, hard work, and creativity

# Moon for Momma
## Amanda Hyslop

*"There is a part inside, you must keep to yourself. That is your spirit, and your own free will!"*

One summer, late in the afternoon, Daddy came home drunk. He was yelling up and down the stairs, leaving a string of curses in the air. The heat and the alcohol had been comin' on ever since the beginning of July. However, the steam had been rising off of my Momma and Daddy's backs for years on end. On that specific summer day, when the teapot whistled as Daddy slammed the kitchen door; Momma took it as a knowing sign. Her train was taking off. She packed up her babies, and headed for the lakes of Arkansas.

My Granddaddy was fisherman up there by those lakes. Grandma, she was a churchgoer. My Momma, on the other hand was their Southern Belle. We would visit their home maybe once, twice a year. Only for a short time though. When I saw all the luggage in the car, I knew there would be something particularly different about this visit.

"Momma, is everything all right?" I asked.

Closing her eyes and taking a deep breath. "Everything is just fine honey. Your Mother needs some breathing room from this place. She's got to clear the clouds in her head. Go get your sister. We need to be leaving soon."

As the night was thinning down, Baby Brie and I held each other in the back seat of the car. The moonshine was glowing into the window, pressing up against Momma's face. She must have thought we had fallen asleep, because I saw tears in her eyes. She never cried in front of us. Her babies needed to see a sweet Southern light pour from her, not anything sad or wet.

Everything was nice and still for a bit up in Arkansas. Forgetting my troubles, melting into the sun, I played, drank lemonade, and ate cookies. However, on the tenth night of our stay, while Baby Brie and I lay in bed, we overheard Momma yelling at Daddy over the phone.

"We're not coming back till you clean up Haden. I've said this before. You've self medicated your pain with alcohol, and you take it out on us. The kids deserve better. I deserve better."

Baby Brie started bawling when she heard Momma's anger. I choked on my tears, and held her close to my heart. Momma came into the bedroom and saw our nursery scene. By the look on her face, I swore I thought she was going to break. Of course she didn't. Momma never did.

"Girls, come with me," she said gathering us up out of bed. "It's time we go down to the water."

Grandma and Grandaddy's lake is holy water. It heals the heart and cleanses the spirit. There is a Southern Comfort down at those docks that I will always take with me in my home of praise. Every time we were up visiting we would go down in our pajamas, tickle our toes, tell stories, and listen to the crickets. It was the same ritual that night. Except this time, I knew Momma needed to talk, and I was ready to listen.

"Girls, its time for your Momma to teach you some lessons. My mother never told me anything about men. In fact she never told me much about anything. I feel like it is my duty to prepare you for the mishaps of life. Sister Mandy you sit here on my left, Baby Brie on my right."

Like a blanket, she wrapped her arms around both of us. "Your ears need to be by my side. This is a serious Momma talking."

Squeezing us real tight, she began, "Men are controlling," she said narrowing her eyes. "They are possessive, and only want you to live for them. You are your own woman, and don't let anybody tell you different. There are rules on how to treat a lady. The first one mandates respect. Now, if a man treats you unfriendly, you just go ahead and walk away from that trouble. You don't need that, trust me. Ain't nobody ever gonna tell you what to think or feel, what to say, or what to do. Stay true to yourself! Deep down in our hearts, we women know what is good and right. Don't ever question yourself on that."

She swallowed in another breath, "Girls, there will be time when you fall in love, and want to give yourself completely. That's fine and all if you have chosen the right man. But there is a part inside, you must keep to yourself. That is your spirit, and your own free will! It is our secret to never being destroyed. Now, if you ever find yourself lost and confused, get down on your knees and pray. You say 'Spirit, Come to me. I need you.'"

Looking up at the moon, Momma softly repeated, "I need you."

Baby Brie and I lowered our heads. It was tough for us to hear Momma say those words. She quickly noticed our solemnity. Kissing us on the forehead, she gingerly said, "Then you pick yourself up off the floor, and eat some peach ice cream!"

Laughing, "Okay enough about that. Your Momma's done for the evening. You girls want to sing a song?"

"Oh yes, Momma, I want to sing a song," I desperately pleaded.

"Sister Mandy wants to sing a song. Does Baby Brie?"

"Yes Momma, I do too. I want to sing," Baby Brie shyly added.

"We'll sing 'Harvest Moon.' You ready?" We nodded our heads and opened our lips. "Shine on, shine on harvest moon, up in the sky. I ain't had no love since January, February, June or July. Nighttime is the right time to sit around and swoon. So shine on, shine on Harvest Moon. For me and my gals." Momma kicked the water in our faces. We giggled.

I bit my lips and asked Momma a hard question. "Momma," I said, "Does the moon get lonely being up there all by itself?"

"Yes, Sister Mandy, the moon does get awfully lonely." With a graceful pause she continued, "But she has the stars in the sky to keep her company. Do you want to make the moon happy?" Momma asked.

"I do Momma."

"I wanna make the moon happy too, Momma." Baby Brie whispered.

"All right then, you have to follow my lead. Stand up, turn around. On the count of three. One," Momma slowly said, "Two," she gained a little bit more pace, "Three," she screamed. "Moon the Moon girls, Moon the Moon."

With tremendous excitement, Baby Brie and I tore down our undies and stuck our little fannies up into the sky. "Shake your tailfaithers,"

Momma hollered. Baby Brie and I bent our knees, twisted our hips, and let the moon glow like an egg yolk on our derrières. I knew right then and there that moon was smiling down us, and Momma was smiling back.

---

# Never Too Late
## Julie Curwin

*A mother fulfills her lifelong dream of a college education.*

The one room school house that served the children of Cedar Camp, New Brunswick, was just down the hill from my grandmother Millie's place. It had eight grades, one teacher and a pot-bellied woodstove for warmth in the winter. My mother, Marjorie, remembers it as a magical place – the place where she developed her lifelong love affair with books and learning. Marjorie was the top student at the Cedar Camp School throughout her years there. The teacher told her she had great potential and encouraged her to continue with her education. But there was no money for higher education in Cedar Camp. The nearest high school was several miles away, in the town of Sussex, and there were no free school buses in those days. "Book learning" was for those who didn't have to worry about where their next meal was coming from.

Things might have turned out differently for Millie and her children, but in 1937 my grandfather, Fred Brighton, died of typhoid fever. He was twenty-nine. On the same day that she buried her husband, Millie had a miscarriage, losing what would have been the couple's sixth child. Mom was the second youngest of Fred and Millie's five remaining children, just three years old when this tragedy struck. Her only memory of her father is of a simple pine casket being carried through the kitchen and out the door of the old farmhouse by men in somber steel-gray suits. She had never seen adults cry before. Her mother was too sick to comfort her.

My grandmother soldiered on, physically weakened, grieving, and desperately poor. She had no choice. In those days, if you couldn't provide for your children they were taken away from you and placed in orphanages. The family grew whatever food they could on their small farm and wore hand-me-down clothing from relatives and neighbors. In the spring, when fresh food was scarce, there would often be nothing left to eat but potatoes. Millie did the best she could to vary the menu: Potato pancakes for breakfast, mashed potatoes for lunch, baked potatoes for dinner. Potato famine was one tragedy, at least, that was never visited upon Cedar Camp.

Millie eventually regained her wicked sense of humor and tried to make things fun for her kids. At Christmastime, they each got an orange in their stocking and the family had a goose for dinner. They crowded around the old radio and listened to Bing Crosby singing White Christmas – something they didn't have to dream about in Cedar Camp. There were no expensive toys, no crowded malls, but Marjorie remembers these as joyous times. Poverty didn't seem like such a burden as long as she had her family around her and her beloved schoolhouse.

These times came to an end all too soon, however. When she completed the eighth grade, the schoolhouse had nothing left to offer her and Marjorie did what her brothers and older sister had already done. She moved to the city and found work. It didn't seem to bother the rest of them, who were quite happy to leave behind the drudgery of school work and the isolation of Cedar Camp. For Marjorie, though, it left a tiny ache in her heart, the vague emptiness of an unfulfilled dream. Not that she was one to sit around and mope about it. She took a job at the local Eaton's department store. She made friends. She joined a church group. A few years later she met my dad and they were married shortly after her twentieth birthday. Mom got her hairdresser's certificate and opened her own beauty shop. In 1959 my sister was born and six years after that, I joined the family.

By 1979, Mom was a success by anyone's standard: an accomplished businesswoman, a loving wife, a proud mother. Life was good, but she still had that tiny ache in her heart, that gnawing feeling of things left undone. She began studying for a high school equivalency exam. Later that year she took the test and passed it easily. Then she did something really bold: She signed up for a university course – Philosophy 1000, via the Extension Department of Mount Allison University. She was terrified. She was fifteen years older than her professor. She still had a full-time job and a family.

I remember coming home one evening and seeing Mom at the kitchen table, books and papers spread out around her, face contorted with concentration. She was writing her first essay, a one thousand word piece about Socrates and the Socratic Method. She looked discouraged.

"I only went to grade eight," she said, "what do I know about the Socratic Method?"

But she persevered and ended up making one of the highest marks in the class. The scene at the kitchen table became a familiar one over the next few years. Classical Mythology, World Religions, Shakespeare, Modern Philosophy – one by one, year after year, she tackled these subjects and more.

Her friends didn't understand. "You're too old," they said. "I don't know where you find the energy."

"You'll never get a job out of it – why would you put yourself through all this hard work?"

But Mom wasn't doing it to make money or to impress people. She loved learning for the sake of learning – and she was good at it. Eventually, after she had enough credits, she got a letter informing her that she had made the Dean's List.

Life went on. Mom and Dad celebrated their 30th and then their 40th wedding anniversary. My sister got married, had three sons and became an elementary school teacher. I finished medical school and married one of my classmates. The grandchildren got older. My sister's oldest boy, Adam, started high school. His grandma tutored him in some of his subjects. And she kept studying.

Finally, in May of 2001, twenty-two years after she started her unlikely journey, my mother graduated from Mount Allison with a Bachelor of Arts degree. She was sixty-six years old. Her grandson, Adam, graduated from college the same month. He was twenty-two. They had their grad photos taken together.

I'm a psychiatrist now and I often find myself in the position of being a "life coach" for people who have not yet found the strength or the courage to tackle their dreams. "I'm too old," they say, "I'm not talented enough. What if I fail?"

I tell them about a middle-aged woman I knew with a grade eight education whose dream it was to get her university degree. How it took her twenty-two years to get there and how she was sixty-six years old when she walked across that stage at Convocation Hall with her head held high, surrounded by twenty-two year olds. How it's never too late.

*Julie Curwin writes:*

*I am a psychiatrist and part-time writer in Cape Breton, Nova Scotia, Canada. My fiction and creative non-fiction has appeared in various publications, including the Canadian Medical Association Journal, The Medical Post, The Undercurrents Anthology, and on the web at www.coffeehousefiction.com. In November of 2008, my short story "World Backwards" was selected as the overall winner of the Commonwealth Short Story Competition (www.cba.org.uk).*

---

# A Moment for Truth
## Laura Aviella Davis

*A mother stands up to abuse.*

"Kids, come in here. I have to tell you something." My mother's voice sounded serious. She sat in the back of the apartment, in the cold stillness of the bathroom. We gathered near her, waiting to hear. "You know that Daddy and I fight a lot. We are going to do something about it."

Some evenings, my mother would dial through a list of phone numbers, asking quietly, "Is Tommy there?" until finally she would hear someone say yes, and then she'd ask "…Is he drinking again?" I would hear banging when my father stumbled in to the apartment, long after I'd gone to bed. My stomach would clench as I'd hear him yell, and then I'd hear a smack, and then I would hear her cry. The police sometimes arrived at the door, but my father keep the chain lock pulled across the doorway.

"Yeah, everything is fine in here, Officer," he would mumble through the cracked opening. He was a drunk, and it was a wonder that police didn't faint from his breath.

"Okay then, sir, have a good night," and the cop would turn around and leave. Just leave my mother leaning against the wall, tears pouring down her cheeks, as three tiny faces peaked out from the behind the bedroom door, silent and scared.

That was just wrong.

I saw the world in strict terms of right and wrong. I was her eldest, and had just finished third grade. I used to fume when my third grade teacher used to hit Harold, a hyper student, on the head with her rolled up newspaper to settle him down. That seemed so wrong to me that when she died one weekend, I believed God had intervened to stop a mean teacher. It was my naïve but strong faith that wrong should be stopped. That my father could continue with his meanness brought confusion to my young mind.

Leaning towards us while sitting on the edge of the bathtub, my mother spoke: "Your father and I are going to get something called a divorce. It's not your fault," she gushed, seeming to gulp down air. "We just can't get along and before it gets worse, we are going to try to live separately. It's not your fault." Tears rolled down her face, and the three of us crowded around her as she sat on the top of the closed toilet seat, rocking. We clung to her, and we loved her.

"Divorce? What's that?" my brother asked. It was 1967, and divorce was not yet common.

"It means that Mommy and Daddy won't live together anymore, so we won't fight all the time."

"Where will we live?" I asked, looking at her and then my brother and sister.

"Well," my mother said slowly, and I would become familiar with that particular tone, used when she needed to hesitate. "Well, I will still be your Mommy, and Daddy will still be your daddy, but since we aren't going to live together, you are going to have to live with just one of us."

"Who?!" my little sister exclaimed, her eyes as big as egg yolks.

"You kids will live with your father. And a new mother, even though I will always still be Your Mother, she will be living there and helping your father take care of you three, like a mother."

"Who is she?!" my brother demanded to know.

"You will meet her. This Sunday. When Your Father moves his things to her house." My mother lifted the damp towel off the counter and refolded it, straightening the edges as if that could straighten out a bigger mess. My head swirled; there seemed no logic in this.

"Sunday we are moving?!" I asked.

"No, not that fast. We will wait until they settle in, and I pack up this apartment. Your toys will go with you and some of the furniture will go with me," she explained.

"Where?" my sister asked, "Where will you be going?"

"Well," I heard her hesitate again, "Well, I am going to have a new apartment in New York City and try to find a job so I can get you kids back to live with me when I have some money. You will come visit me every weekend. Every single weekend." And then she began to sob. We huddled closer again, and hugged her, without any more questions.

I know she was scared, with three young children and nowhere to go but onward. Never again would our family be the same. There were years ahead of us filled with confusion and struggles through emotional and financial hardships. But for that moment in the bathroom, I saw my mother through loving eyes – she was brave, in a fresh and fragile way. I respected my mother for finding her courage, and for her determination not to be beaten any more. By her action, my mother showed me a truth that guided me well into my adulthood:  A good husband is a man who is strong enough not to hit someone he loves.

## Tale of Tails
### Mary Dempsey

*A lesson in honesty and tall-tale telling*

The smell of Mr. Ashenbach's feed store is something that will remain with me until the end of my days. The air was permeated with heavy farm smells of hay, grass seed, bulbs, and insect sprays. The old wood floors that creaked beneath my small feet had been worn over the years by the mud-filled boots of local farmers. Mr. Ashenbach seemed to have a bit of everything in that old feed store but best of all were the huge barrels filled to over-flowing with sunflower seeds, bulbs and mysterious combinations of feed for chickens and wild birds. My mom would tell Mr. Ashenbach what she needed and the old man with wooden scoop in hand, would dig into one of the barrels, fill a brown paper sack and shuffle off to the hanging scale to be sure mom got JUST what she ordered.

There was one barrel that held a special fascination for me. I spent most of my time reaching into it and running my hands through its contents. Inside were thousands of small dog biscuits just waiting to be carried home to some unsuspecting, lucky pup. I hung over that barrel telling any customer who would listen all about MY dog!

Some days my dog was a big playful red Irish setter. Folks marveled that I could be in such command of this exuberant animal. Occasionally I was mistress of the most adorable blind toy poodle who slept in my bed and was groomed by me every day. Usually I saved this story for ladies with white hair who would ooh and aah and say what a good caretaker I must be. The story that really kept the attention of my Saturday morning audience was that of my dog, Dolf, the black German shepherd who chased cats, scared mailmen and frightened the neighbors but didn't scare **me** one bit.

Of course there was no dog in my life but that didn't stop me from standing sentry over that barrel of dog biscuits, telling my tales and dreaming my dreams.

I suppose Mr. Ashenbach had overheard my dog stories and I suspect I may have shared a variety of stories with the same customer but to me it was all real if only for a few minutes on a Saturday morning.

On one hot July morning, I was stopped in my tracks by a sign in Mr. Ashenbach's feed store window reading, "Free Puppies to Good Homes." I squeezed my mom's hand hoping she had taken notice of the bright red sign. Mr. Ashenbach met us with his usual kindly greeting as though it was just an ordinary day. I hung back looking and listening for a cage-full of yapping puppies but was met with a strange silence. On my way to the biscuit barrel I stumbled upon a small box. Inside was one dozing puppy curled into a ball. Startled by Mr. Ashenbach's voice, I turned to see him coming toward me.

"Cute puppy," I said.

"Yes," answered Mr. Ashenbach. "That's the last little girl. No one ever wants the runt of the litter."

"Oh, that's not true! I'd take her in a minute! I'd name her Abigail, teacher her to walk on a leash, let her sleep in my bed, brush her every day." All my plans came rushing out.

"Oh," said Mr. Ashenbach, "I don't think your family could handle one more dog. That Irish setter and German shepherd must be eating your mom out of house and home and then of course you need to spend so much time caring for that blind poodle. Oh no. If I were to give that puppy to you I would be in the doghouse with your mom. Mr. Ashenbach chuckled and wandered off.

Here I was, caught in a bold faced lie. My chances of having my dream come true were dashed due to my tall-tale telling. Upon overhearing our conversation, my mom asked me what Mr. Ashenbach was talking about. With hanging head, I confessed that I had been sharing tall tales with customers in the feed store. Mom asked me what my plans were for telling tall tales in the future as she picked up Abigail and gave her a scratch under her chin.

It wasn't until Abigail was an entrenched member of the family that I discovered there never was a litter of pups in the feed store but just one pup mom had chosen from the pound. Mr. Ashenbach and mom had conspired to teach me a lesson in honesty. It didn't stop me from creating tales but it sure made me think twice before I shared them with my public!

*Mary Dempsey is a former New Jersey early childhood teacher. Following her teaching career, she was co-owner of an independent bookshop in Clinton, New Jersey. She has had short stories published in several magazines and local newspapers. Mary is now retired and resides with her husband in Bluffton, South Carolina.*

---

# Cerebral Chaos
### James W. Lewis

*A "punishment" unleashes a boy's special talent*

"No!" my mother yelled. "You can't go outside! You're on restriction for a week!"

I swear my blood boiled upon hearing the horrid word "restriction." You can't ban an eleven-year-old boy from his BMX bike and buddies, especially during the summer!

But I had disobeyed my mother. She told me to be home at two; I didn't come home until seven that evening.

I stomped toward my bedroom, but before reaching the doorway, a hard grip around my elbow curtailed forward progress.

"Don't walk away from me!" My mother pointed at the couch. "Sit down!"

I folded my arms across my chest, my forehead furrowed. I turned to the couch and slammed my bottom on the cushion.

"Oh, okay," my mother said, nodding. "Since you think you can ruin the couch *I* paid for, you can't sit there. Get up!"

Oh, so now we were playing musical chairs. I rolled my eyes and stood up.

Mom grabbed my wrist. We walked through the kitchen into the dining room area. "Sit down."

I pulled out a chair from the dining table, plopped down, and fixated on the wall. Hated pushing my spine against the chair's curved iron backside, but I ignored the slight discomfort and leaned back. And my defiance wouldn't have been complete without my folded arms and pouty lips.

My mother took a pen and pad of paper from a kitchen drawer. "I have an assignment for you."

*Assignment?* I thought. *School is over!*

She dropped the pad and pen in front of me. "You must be a genius," my mother said, grinning. "Something in that hard-headed noggin of yours convinced you it was a good idea to come home so late."

I gazed at her, head tilted. She had something up her sleeve.

"So," she continued, "since you have such a creative mind, let's see you prove it. I want you to write a story every night of your punishment, starting tonight."

I twisted my face as if a raw odor had stunned me. I stared at the paper, then looked up at her.

"Write about what?" I asked.

"Anything you want. You have an hour, and I'll read it when you're done." She walked into the kitchen. "I'll warm up your dinner, so get goin'."

Talk about ball and chain. Bad enough I had to stay in the house; now my mother wanted to torture me. No TV, no ATARI, no handheld video games. Just me, the dining room table, a pen and a blank pad of paper.

I grabbed the pen. With a scowl, I transferred my anger through my thin fingers – and wrote. Didn't care about plot or structure; I wanted my revenge on paper.

My hand didn't stop. I wrote myself as the main character and hero; my mother became the villain and enemy to kids of the world. Of course, I defeated the "evil" villain with supersonic weapons.

I ate as I wrote and finished an hour later. When my mother read my story, she asked why I wrote about bad things happening to her. I didn't respond, just shrugged. My eyes fixated on the wall again, bottom lip sticking out.

To my surprise, my mother loved the story and couldn't wait to read another one the next night. I sucked in my bottom lip to keep from smiling. Dang it, I was still mad! She couldn't see me smile!

But I felt good inside. I'd written a story – something I'd never done before – and my mother praised my effort.

The next night, I banged out another story. Mom was still a villain, but this time I used my mental powers to make her an ally.

As my Mom's eyes scanned the pages of my story, she chuckled once or twice. Again, she praised my art of storytelling. She kissed my forehead, and I felt my hard resolve against her fading.

The third night, I wrote a little earlier than usual. An idea had been bouncing in my head and I itched to create another "masterpiece."

My fingers whipped across the page and within minutes, I had created a story about a kid taking his own life. I'd seen a TV special on teenage suicide once, and I always wished I had the power to prevent such tragedy.

A look of sadness draped my mother's face. After she read my story, she hugged me and said she loved me. I didn't ask how she felt about the story. Her glassy eyes said it all.

Sleep didn't come easy that night. Characters crystallized and swam in my head, much like in my dreams. I saw their faces; heard their voices; knew their likes and dislikes – everything.

And they wanted out.

Luckily, I had brought the pen and paper with me. With so much tug-of-war in my mind, I had plenty of ideas to create more stories for my mother. I wrote a story for myself this time.

The next few days, the stories kept coming. I looked forward to my mother's comments, but I didn't have to wait on the hour my mother had allotted for writing. I had plenty of time to write in my room. And with so much "cerebral chaos," I could create any adventure I wanted. Being stuck in the house couldn't limit my mind.

That same cerebral chaos stayed with me even after my mother lifted the outdoors ban. It carried on through my teenage years and lives with me today as a man. The people in my head still hold me captive sometimes – until I release them. Only this time, I use a laptop vice pen and pad to set them free.

I never told my mother why I was so late that day twenty years ago. In the downtown library, anyone could lose track of time in the wondrous world of Encyclopedia Brown, Charlie Brown and Snoopy, and choose-your-fate adventure books.

I still immerse myself in books, and sometimes, my mother buys me books for special occasions. But I also create my own novel-length manuscripts. And although I haven't published a novel yet, the thrill of seeing my name in print doesn't drive me. Cerebral chaos does – thanks to my mother's "assignments."

---

# So You Want to Hear God
## Caryl McAdoo

*A simple, fool-proof, Bible-based way to get an answer from the Lord*

Something had to change. I refused to live a minute longer in the muck and mire my life had become, so I made a decision. Determined, I buckled up, sniffled away the sobs, then phoned my mother.

"Mama? I'm going to the chapel to pray and I'm not coming out until I hear from God! If you want to bring me some bread or water in the next few days, that'd be great. I'll appreciate it." She could most likely still hear I'd been weeping.

"Oh, Caryl." Well aware of the fights with my husband and the pressure of our paving company's financial woes, she empathized fully with her dearly loved firstborn. I could hear it in her voice. "I'm sorry. Are you sure that's what the Lord wants you to do?" She was probably thinking of our four children and how they would manage without me, but it was my sanity I needed to be most concerned with, and her question was that old proverbial straw!

"No, Mother! Of course, I'm not sure!" Without a doubt she had to hold the receiver away from her ear and could still hear at arm's length. I battled a bad temper since forever, a paternal generational curse. "Aren't you listening to me? Did you hear a word I said? I can't hear anything from God. I've been praying and praying and praying and I hear NOTHING!"

I slammed down the phone and went for my purse and the car keys. Before I got to the door, the phone rang. I've never been one not to answer a ringing phone. It seemed rude.

"Hello?" I tried to sound as sweet as I could.

"Caryl? Honey, I thought I might share with you what the Lord showed me to do through His Word when I really needed to hear from Him. Would you like to hear it?"

"Sure, Mama." I dropped my purse to the floor where I stood and stared at the ceiling. What she told me that day has impacted my life in a wonderful way. A simple, fool-proof, Bible-based way to get an answer from the Lord.

"Okay. All those voices in your head come from three sources only. The first is yourself, it's you mind speaking, reasoning with your spirit man. You're probably most familiar with it. Second is the Voice of God through His Holy Spirit, teaching, guiding, comforting. That's the voice that always encourages you to do what's right and show love to everyone. You're always so good at that, Caryl. Everyone says so. Thirdly, you hear from the devil or his powers and principalities. Some people call them demons and they're not so wrong.

"So the first thing you want to do when you really want to hear from God is to pray. Repent of any known or unknown sin. Go boldly into God's throne room and right up to the steps because you are sinless now, covered by Jesus' blood. Say something like, 'Father, I really need an answer to my question today. But according to Your Word, I do not want to lean to my own understanding or ability to reason. I only want to hear Your wisdom, so in Jesus' name, I lay my flesh down before You and ask that You silence it. I do not trust in anyone but You and I only want to hear Your Voice."

Well, so far so good. That sounded logical and certainly easy enough. "What then?"

"Keep in mind this is all by faith. You have to believe that God will silence your inner voice."

"I will, Mama. Then what?"

"Next, we need to address the demonic forces that would lie and lead you astray from God's will and plan for your life."

"Yes, yes. How, Mama?"

"God's word says that whatever we bind on earth will be bound in Heaven and whatever we loose on earth will be loosed in Heaven. Believing that Truth, you need to bind Satan and any of his powers, principalities, and minions from speaking to you. Say something like, 'In Jesus' name and by His power, it is written that I have the authority to bind and loose, so right now, I bind Satan and any of his emissaries from speaking to me so that my ears will only be open to the Words of my God. You all are bound and cannot speak to me when I ask the Lord my question.' Then again, by faith, believe it is done according to the Word."

"I can do that. Then what?"

"That's all."

"That's all?"

"Absolutely. Ask your question and know that the next voice you hear is God's."

"But that sounds so easy."

"Things don't have to be so complicated and hard as often try to make them. Works every time I've done it. The father of lies tells us everything is too hard and won't work. Resist the devil and he will flee. That's what the Bible says."

"Well, okay then. I'll try it. Still, you might want to check on me. I may need that bread and water if it doesn't work for me as good as it works for you."

"Remember, it all depends on your faith. You believe the Word is true, I know that."

"Yes, I do. If it is in the Word, it's settled. Okay, Mama. Thank you. I'll let you know. Bye."

I went on to the chapel, the old sanctuary used decades ago before the newer and grander one. It was always available for the members to go and have a place to pray, protected by a keyless lock, a pad you pressed the right number code into. It was quiet and peaceful there. I could hear my breathing. I tiptoed to the front and knelt.

First I repented of not honoring my husband and all the other things I could think of including screaming at Mama when she was only trying to help. I asked Him to forgive me of anything I had forgotten. Most the time I asked Him to let me know if there were any I'd forgotten, but I wasn't trusting that I'd hear from Him yet, and He had been so silent in the days and weeks previous. That's exactly what brought me there in the first place.

So I did all that Mama had told me to do. Faith had not been a problem in so long I couldn't remember because God so proved Himself over and over again in my life, and I knew that I knew He was able and His Word was true. When I got to the end of binding the devil and his cohorts, the strangest sensation I ever encountered came over me.

It was as though someone had turned off the TV in my head. You know, like at night and the TV's blaring even though everyone else in the house is asleep. And when you turn it off, it's so extra silent? That's how it was. My mind was empty, no thoughts, no talking up there. Just dead quiet. Weird! I mean, the weirdest.

I proceeded to ask my question. "Lord, what do you want me to do?"

As clear as a bell's ding-a-ling, I heard, "Give the company to Ron." I repeated the answer as a question back to Him, then He told me again. "Yes, give the company to Ron."

"Well, okay then! That's easy! Thank you, Lord."

The mind-speak returned immediately. 'Wow, that was easy,' my flesh said to me. "Sure was," I answered aloud. "Praise the Lord. You are good, God, all the time!"

I phoned Ron first and asked him to meet me for lunch, then called Mama. I told her how awesome the experience had been and what the Lord instructed me to do. Her response was so disappointing.

"Oh, Caryl! Are you sure?"

"Mother!"

"Well, sweetheart, you're the one with the business sense. You're the one who started the company and did over a million dollars your third year! It's only gone downhill since Ron came into the business. Are you still at the church?"

"Yes."

"Would you at least, please, see if Henry is there and talk to him?" She was on a first name basis with our pastor.

"I guess so, Mother, but I know I heard from God. I'll go see if Bother Henry's here."

Well, I did go talk to him and he advised me not to give the company to Ron. We both had already been in and counseled with Brother Henry, agreeing ahead of time to abide by his judgment. Ron never thought in a million years that the pastor would have put me in authority over my husband from eight to five! To tell the truth, it surprised me, too, even though I can be pretty persuasive.

I got in the car and drove out of the parking lot in tears. As I rounded the corner to meet Ron at the restaurant, I thought, I'll try it again. Make sure. So I did, and the same blank, quiet brain thing happened. I asked the same question and heard the exact same words. "But Lord," I contended through my sobs. "Mama doesn't think I should and Brother Henry doesn't think I should!"

"ARE YOU GOING TO GO WITH MAN'S REASONING AND TRUST IN YOUR MOTHER AND YOUR PASTOR, OR ARE YOU GOING TO GO WITH YOUR HEART AND BE OBEDIENT TO MY WORD? WILL YOU TRUST ME?"

The answer to that was very easy. I did trust Him above all else. "Yes, Lord. I'm going to trust You and be obedient." It was settled in my spirit and that peace that passes understanding came over me. I sang on the way to meet my high school sweetheart.

I told him the story I've just told you. He said he thought I had summoned him to lunch to fire him. That paving company had seen wonderful successes, but it was the boom and bust '80s. We worked so hard putting out twice as many proposals. It was during the time Ron and I had committed to early morning prayer and went to the church building every morning six days a week from six until seven to pray. Longhorn Paving was covered in prayer. I had told the Lord, if the door had to close, we knew whose hand was on the knob.

We only wanted His perfect will, and so we believe that's just what happened. It's funny to think that was twenty years ago. It's so true how time flies, especially the older you get! But Mama's wisdom offered that day, her Godly advice to a hurting daughter has helped me so many times since that I can't even count. I continue to hear God's Voice and do my best to walk in obedience to it. Mama went home to be with her Lord, our God, in August of 1997. While on this side of eternity, I miss her every day, but look forward to being reunited then to never being parted again.

# A Mom is a Mom
## Hugh Neeld

*Teaching compassion in the most trying of times*

In 1942, shortly after America's entry into World War II, my mother started work as head librarian at the Army's Quartermaster Depot in Fort Worth, Texas, where we lived. My dad, too old for the draft, worked in the main post office. I was thirteen, my brother ten.

The play of boys our age at that time was mostly war-related. All the news and adult conversation we heard was about the war. Movies with John Wayne, Robert Mitchum and other top screen stars glorified it. The names of all our generals and admirals were known: MacArthur, Patton, Nimitz, Halsey, Eisenhower, Bradley – their pictures were on book covers and writing tablets in every classroom in America, and they were accorded the same adulation as today's sports heroes.

Among my contemporaries, the overriding concern was that the war would be over before we were old enough to go. All junior and senior high schools offered R.O.T.C. It wasn't compulsory, but most boys belonged. We wore uniforms, drilled with dummy rifles and had "war games," using small, flour-filled paper sacks as "hand grenades." Our training was even supervised by a real U.S. Army Sergeant. I used to boast at the dinner table about what I was going to do to those "krauts" and "japs" when I got old enough.

It was during this time that my mother did something which taught me a lesson in understanding and compassion. A large number of German prisoners of war were interned at the depot and used for labor. A young soldier was assigned to the library, and under mother's supervision, did filing and other jobs. He could speak English and talked to her a great deal about his family back home. Many times at dinner, usually following one of my boasting sessions, she would repeat her conversations with the soldier.

Once a week she would stuff her lunch box full of cookies or candy and slip them to the soldier. I remember questioning her one time about showing kindness to the "enemy." I've never forgotten her response.

"Imagine yourself in his place, Hugh Earl," she said. "I do. And I imagine myself in his mother's place, too."

Had it not been for this incident, how long (if ever) would it have taken me to start thinking of individuals first as people like myself? I'm not sure. I do know however, that although war may be hell, a mom is a mom. Thank God.

***Hugh Neeld*** *is a native Texan, born in Fort Worth in 1929. Educated in public school and Texas Christian University, he served in the U.S. Navy from 1945 to 1948 and retired from a forty-five year career in radio and TV in 1994.*

*Today, he and his wife, Cris, live on a golf course in Jacksonville. He is the author of* The Curmudgeon Report, *a collection of newspaper columns he wrote for East Texas papers starting in 2000, and dozens of articles and short stories for various publications.*

---

# Knit One, Purl Two
## Lisa K. Winkler

*Life lessons from knitting*

"Barbara, put the god damn knitting away and read the map!" We'd hear my father's familiar refrain more than once growing up. We'd been driving for hours and my father suddenly realized we were lost. And of course, it was my mother's fault because instead of reading the map and watching the road, she was knitting. But when she finished a garment, usually something for one of us four, he'd be the first to praise her handiwork. We might have gotten lost those countless time regardless; I'm not convinced it was entirely the knitting's fault. But the knitting, one of the many handicrafts my mother does, serves as an example of her ability to keep her hands busy while still keeping an eye on the road.

For my mother knitting is much more than a handicraft; it's part of living. By teaching me how to knit, she taught me how to live. What she exemplifies in knitting – patience, perseverance, and pride – transfers to daily living.

"Preparation is everything," she insists. I make a swatch to check the gauge, the formula that determines if the yarn is the correct weight for the needle and the needle the right size for the yarn. I wind skeins into manageable balls, hearing my mother remind me that if I don't do this the yarn will knot into unyielding masses that I'd waste. Though I'm always eager to begin, I remember that she made sure I was ready. I read over a pattern and circle the size I'm making, so as not to read it quickly and make mistakes.

When I'd get frustrated that a project was taking too long to finish or I felt bored and wanted to start something new; she'd make me keep at it. "Don't be a quitter," she'd say, "Finish what you start." She'd mention the money spent on yarn and the hours I'd already done. "What are you going to do with a half finished sweater?" she'd ask, urging me to complete the second half.

"If you're not happy with it today, you won't be happy with it tomorrow," she said. She'd make me undo and rework rows and rows to fix a mistake or rescue a dropped stitch. And she refused to do it for me. "What do you learn, if I do it?" She is a perfectionist and wanted me to be one too, at least when it came to knitting. Stripes and patterns had to match up, so a sweater wouldn't look "like you slapped it together in a hurry."

For her, no knitting project is too difficult or too large. She welcomes every challenge knitting presents. She encourages me to try new patterns and stitches. Knitting, like life, should include risk-taking. "You don't learn anything if you do the same thing again and again," she says. While she's happy to buy new yarn, she always looks for ways to utilize scraps. Like leftovers from a meal, unused yarn presents a challenge – what can I make with this? What colors and textures would work together to create a new garment? So like her, I don't throw anything out – you never know when it can come in handy.

For her, no needle size is too small or large, no yarn too unyielding, and no project unimportant to ignore attention to details. She spends as much time blocking and finishing a project as she does knitting; proudly sewing in a "Handmade by Barbara" label in each item.

From my early forays in knitting at age 7 to my knitting as an adult, I continue to seek my mother's advice about my projects. She lovingly shares her talents – she taught my left-handed best friend to knit, helped design a suitable pattern when the mothers in my toddler's playgroup wanted to knit matching sweaters for our three year olds, and now, fingers gnarled with arthritis, teaches her granddaughters to knit.

From entrelac to fair isle, from intricate lace to complicated cables, she's crafted jackets, skirts, baby outfits and blankets, countless sweaters, hats and mittens and socks. I still wear a pair of royal blue cashmere cabled socks she knit for me years ago. I could never understand why anyone would make socks – why spend time on something that's going to be hidden by pants and covered by shoes? For my mother, it's knowing "I'm keeping your feet warm that matters, not what others see."

When my father retired after 35 years as a poultry farmer, he began traveling the world, volunteering as an agricultural consultant throughout Africa and Eastern Europe. My mother, who'd worked beside him on our farm while raising four children, accompanies him. And like any journey, whether a short drive to the next town or a long plane ride to Kazakhstan, she brings her knitting. When they return and regale us with their adventures, more often than not, they share stories of how her knitting helped breach the vast differences between cultures and languages and created trust between them and the people they're sent to assist. Strangers approach her and admire her handiwork, or the hand knit garment she's wearing, and pull out their own. She describes the many conversations, often wordless, she has with villagers that compare stitches and patterns, methods and tools, materials and textures.

Like my mother, I carry knitting wherever I go – you never know when you can get a few stitches or even an entire line done. It makes waiting to board airplanes or in doctors' offices more bearable, watching children's sporting events less stressful, and even listening to concerts more enjoyable, knowing my hands are busy. My husband and children wear my sweaters, proudly displaying the "Handmade by Lisa" labels. I know I have too many sweaters – and I can't pass a yarn store without stopping in and buying another project.

Unlike my mother, I do several projects at once – easy items I can do without paying too much attention; and more difficult ones for when I want to really concentrate. I've learned to design patterns – my daughter wanted a 1950's style cardigan like the boys wore in the movie "Hairspray"; and I've learned to take risks – with internet ordering, I can figure out what weight yarns would work for a garment. I've learned patience. I rip and redo again and again. If I want my family to wear what I've made, I want it to look right. I throw nothing out, especially hand-knit sweaters. I've recycled some by taking them apart and reusing the yarn, carrying the old garment with me as I wear the new. My daughter found a magenta lace top my mother had made for me years ago buried in my dresser. She's claimed it for her own; wearing it layered over tank tops and adorned with accessories I'd never thought of putting together. Though she's learned to knit, she's not obsessed. Not yet.

*Lisa K. Winkler, an avid knitter, lives and writes from New Jersey. A former newspaper reporter in Connecticut, she's been free lancing and also taught middle school Language Arts. She continues to write and teach. Her children's story, "Amanda at Bat" was published by Fandangle.com. Contact info: lisakwink(at)aol.com.*

---

# Mama Said
## Eve Cogdell

Child, don't you go letting these little boys fill your head with nonsense
You go and get yourself some edumacation
So's you can learn to be a secretary or a nurse or a teacher
Or whatever position your little heart desires

Study yourself to be somebody
So's you can stand up to the nobody's in this world
Make something outta yourself
So nobody can tear you down
'Cause life's trials, they be acoming
They be acoming sooner than you think
Don't let nobody tell you different
When they try to turn your head
You just hold yourself together
And walk in the opposite direction

Chile, ain't nobody got no sympathy
For you in this life
Its everybody for his or herself
So don't go chasing after them little boys
Who don't mean you no good
Don't you get yourself knocked up now
Not without a man to take care o' you
No!  You go get yourself an edumacation
So you can be ready

So you can be the right woman
For that good man
That got hisself an edumacation, too
Then y'all can get hitched
And have a house fulla youngins' if you want to
Now you run along
Go on to that schoolhouse
And make your Mama proud

***Evelyn (Eve) Cogdell*** *writes: I am a Chicago author/writer/poet, with a few published books and several published articles and poems to my credit.  My writings cover a variety of topics such as romance, religion, nature, characterizations, and adventure, as well as other issues of life. Two of my books include "Cashmere & Silk," a novel, and "Matters of the Heart," a short story collection.  Both books are available from me* *at Green Apple Publications; please contact me at evecogdell(at)sbcglobal.net for more information.*

---

## Mama Matters
### Gwen Russell Green

Mississippi Mama, New Albany Mother
Standing vision forward
Establishing
Building families
crafting men and women
Who would contribute
Who would build
Who would stand
Granite immovable
Purposeful people

Mississippi Mama, New Albany mother
Would will their way north
Seeking education
Opportunity
Mothers would teach
Lessons
Make achievement
Accomplishment
Attainment
Demanded
Expected

Mississippi Mama, New Albany mother
Would savor solidarity of
bloodlines
men who managed to stay
to provide, to polish

prideful progeny

Mississippi Mama, New Albany mother
Made miracles manifest
With melt in your mouth meals
Created symphonies with prayers and praise
United in God choice
Climbed on learning as life ladders

Mississippi Mama, New Albany mother
Gave family building focus
Made motherhood matter
In my soul

---

# For All You Didn't Do
## Carole Davis

Many times I've thanked you,
for all you've done for me…
but somehow it doesn't seem like it's enough.
I'd like to also say thank you,
for all the things you didn't do.

Thank you for not treating me differently
just because I was a child,
but as a person with thoughts and feelings
that were worthwhile regardless of age.

Thank you for not letting me make
so many unwise mistakes,
and for not saying "I told you so"
when I did make them.

Thank you for not severely sheltering me,
for had you done so,
I would have been shocked

to see what the real world is like.

Thank you for being careful
not to embarrass me in front of my friends,
especially when I was a teenager,
and for not being an irresponsible parent.

Thank you for never giving racism
asylum in our home,
and for not valuing people less
because they are unlike ourselves.

Thank you for never giving up on
your marriage or our family,
and in particular for not losing faith in me,
when I had no faith in myself.

Thank you for not complaining when any of us needed you,
even when you were too tired or sick to be needed,
and for the times we weren't very loveable,
that you didn't stop loving us.

For all these times and so many more,
I thank you Mom… for all you didn't do.

*Carole Davis's publishing credits include writings in* The Whimsic Alley Book of Spells, the Language of Leadership, Pawsitively Awesome Pet Poems, The innocence of Children, Best Modern Voices, Volume 1: A Poetry Anthology, *in greeting cards from www.boomerwomenspeak.com.*

Chapter 4

# EMOTIONAL SKILLS:

## Building inner strength

# Don't Dance til the Music Starts
## Sr. Josie Palmeri, MPF

*'The valiant only taste of death but once.'*

The wig was ugly! Flo thought she was helping mother by bringing the brown "furry critter" as a get-well gift.

"It's best to have a wig before you lose your hair" Flo said. "Later you'll be too sick from the chemo to go shopping for it."

Mom looks at the fake hair her cousin was holding and said sweetly, "Florence, let's not dance until the music starts." Flo insisted, so mother took the wig to be polite, and hung it on the wooden peg of her bedroom mirror, where it hung unused.

Instead of "cross that bridge when you come to it," my mother liked to say, "Don't dance 'til the music starts." She began to wave her arms around like a wild woman, and said, "See? If you dance without music playing you look crazy, right?" We laughed until tears fell, and laughed even more as we took turns trying on the wig.

And mother was right! One of those people who do *not* go bald from chemo, she never needed a wig. It hung there to remind us not to worry in advance over things that may never happen.

We had many visitors that last year of mother's life who enjoyed hearing about the wig and "don't dance 'til the music starts."

My convent gave me a leave of absence to care for mother that year. Although terminally ill, she was joyful and positive. Neighbors and relatives loved to visit. The coffee pot was always perking, and the table set with our blue willow-ware dishes. Since she was a good listener and disliked repeating gossip, visitors told mother their problems and asked her advice.

Near our home was a high school, where I sometimes worked as a substitute teacher, a job I enjoyed. One day I had my first run-in with a troublesome teen. "I dread going back tomorrow, Mom" I told her. "The principal said everyone finds that boy hard to handle."

"Honey, maybe he'll be good tomorrow," she offered. "They might not even *give* you his class. Enjoy *today*. Dance only when the music starts."

The next day I scanned my sub assignment. Rats! I *did* have the trouble-maker's class. Not until last period, but I let it cloud my otherwise pleasant day.

When zero hour arrived, I learned the problem child was absent! And as good luck had it, his teacher never missed another day, so I never had his class again. A wasted worry!

Visitors kept streaming to see mother. The rug literally wore out and we re-carpeted the entire first floor with a handsome dark green called "Mallard." Company relaxed in mother's calm presence and she enjoyed them.

Mary Theresa, who taught at the same school with me, dropped by one day with roses, intending to stay just a minute. She had never met my mother, but wanted to pay her respects. "You look tired," Mom said. "I'm feeling down," admitted Mary Theresa, "I miss my dad who just died."

"Tell me about him," invited mother. And the young teacher sat near the sickbed, pouring out a heart full of emotions to a captive audience. Mother was delighted with the beautiful, blue-eyed visitor, with her waist-length blonde hair, and Mary Theresa was comforted by Mother's undivided attention. She stayed for supper: pasta primavera made with crushed garlic cloves sautéed in olive oil, and tossed with parmesan cheese. I looked up occasionally from my stove to glance at the sick woman and the young girl in the next room, completely absorbed in each other's company. Years later, Mary Theresa would remind me that it had been one of her most memorable evenings.

Each day of chemotherapy, mother went to the hospital all dressed up in a different outfit. There was the red dress, the gold suit, the teal blue, the leather jacket with black slacks and heels. When neighbors asked where she was going, she'd call out, "For a beauty treatment!"

Once mom overheard me tell a neighbor about the awful nausea following chemo. "Honey, don't give details," she said. "People have their own troubles. They're trying to be kind. When they ask how I am, just say, 'Coming along, thank you!' "

We remembered a joke my dad had told years ago:

> Don't tell folks about your indigestion.
> "How are you?" is a *greeting* – not a question.

Mom liked to quote from the poem, "Optimism," by Ella Wheeler Wilcox:

> You cannot charm, or interest, or please
> By harping on that minor chord – disease!
> Say you are well, say all is well with you,
> And God will hear your words – and make them true!

"Don't you dread chemo?" a friend once asked.

Her answer: "I don't think about it until I get there. Dance when the music starts. Remember what Shakespeare said: 'The coward dies a thousand deaths. The valiant only taste of death but once.' "

To distract ourselves during chemo, Mother and I told the silly "elephant jokes" of the sixties. We had our own little dialogue:

> Q: How can you tell if an elephant is following you?
> A: By the smell of peanuts on his breath.
> Q: How can you tell if an elephant is in your fridge?
> A: By his footprint in the butter.
> Q: Why do elephants paint their toenails red?
> A: So you can't see them when they're hiding in cherry trees.

Our routine brought comic relief not only to us, but also to the nurse, especially when Mom gave the right answer to the wrong question.

On Good Friday, a rookie nurse stabbed Mother's bruised little arm three times before finding a "good spot" on the vein. I began a joke. Leaning back in her chair, Mom whispered, "No elephant jokes. It's

Good Friday. Three nails pierced Our Lord." No whining. Just her simple belief in the redemptive value of suffering when united with Christ's.

A friend once asked, "Why did this happen to a good person like you? This isn't fair!"

"Yes it *is!*" Mom protested. "I got away with sickness for 80 years – never in a hospital! *That* wasn't fair. Before this, I looked like 60. Now I look 80. Well, I *am* 80, so it's fair. Little children get cancer, but I got away with it too long. Anyway, look what happened – I got my daughter back. I gave her to God when she became a nun, and now He sent her back to take care of me."

Her friend worried, "What if the convent orders your daughter to return next year?" Mom shrugged, "I might be on another planet *this* year. Anyway, let's not dance 'til the music starts."

Thanks to my godchild Faye, a nurse, who stayed at our house many nights to help me, Mother never had to go to a nursing home. If a death could be called "beautiful," hers was. I had just cleaned the house to perfection, since friends were coming to visit. A new amber light bulb in the parlor lamp cast a golden glow on the room. A storm watch was predicted, so our friends called to postpone their visit.

It was just Mother and I. I watched her sit with closed eyes in her recliner chair, dressed in pink pajamas, bathed and smelling of rose lotion. Knowing she was too weak to talk, I thought she might like to hear something from the book I was reading. I read psalms and other lovely prayers. "This is so peaceful, Mommy," I said. "Here we are in our own living room. The house is clean and beautiful, bathed in golden light. It's dark and snowing out, but warm and toasty here." She emitted a slow, peaceful sigh...and was gone. It was a moment I will always treasure.

Once I had worried about being alone in the house when Mother died. But now I was happy that no one was with me, to talk or cry or break the beauty of the moment. It had come, and I was at peace. A sense of loss pervaded me, yes, and tears would come later, but right now I was at peace. She and I had often talked about eternity and the joy of the afterlife. Why had I ever worried about being afraid? Don't dance...until the music starts.

Mother is gone nine years now, but I still hear her gentle, reassuring voice. "Honey, enjoy the present moment. What you fear may never happen. And if it *does,* God will be with you. Dance...when the music starts."

*Sister Josephine Palmeri, MPF, has been teaching Spanish and Speech to teenagers for 47 years and still has a "purple passion" for school. Her first book about her Dad,* TALES from the BARBER SHOP, 100 Jokes of Tony Palmeri, Barber and Joygiver, *and its sequel,* MORE TALES from the BARBER SHOP and PITTSTON, *can be had for $16.95 each from Sister Josephine Palmeri, 455 Western Avenue, Morristown, New Jersey, 07960. Proceeds go to the nuns' Third World mission countries and their infirmary for the elderly. Both books are refreshing, especially if you're from a small town where everybody knows your name.*

---

# "So What?" Staying Valid
## K. K. Wilder

*A specific question opens the door to alternatives and – ultimately – contentment.*

Sundays, for church, my strawberry blonde hair was in long curls, my favorite style. My pastel green dress with the delicate ruffles and black patent leather shoes that shone like starlight made me feel like a special 5-year-old-girl.

"Oh, what a pity. Such a pretty little girl, too," I heard people say as they passed me on the street. The stage whispers referred to my severely turned-in leg. But instead of concentrating on the word "pity," I must have decided somewhere along the way to simply hear the word "pretty."

It would be many years before I understood what a difference that choice made in my life, and how I happened to make it in the first place.

When I was 15, after undergoing removal of cartilage damaged in an enthusiastic volleyball ball game, the doctors were finally able to explain why I often favored one of my legs so much. "You have osteoarthritis and chondromalacia," the surgeon told me, using the medical terms for degenerative joint disease and softening of the bone. "Extremely rare in anyone your age. We don't know what causes it and we have no cure." Then, quietly, "You'll be in a wheelchair before you're 30."

Along with issuing the gloomy prognosis, the doctor put an immediate end to my volleyball as well as most other sports. "No more skating or skiing," he said. "Stop the basketball. And positively no more majorettes." Most, I could live without, but twirling batons and doing acrobats with my friends in the majorette section of the high school marching band—well, that was a blow too big to take. As soon as we got home, I raced to my bedroom and began to sob in the way only a 15-year-old can.

In a few minutes, my mother came in. "What's wrong?" she asked, sitting on the edge of the bed.

"I ca-can't be a majorette any more," I stammered, still crying.

"So what?"

The tears abruptly stopped, replaced by the all-too-usual anger at my mom's response to my life dramas. "'So what?' What do you mean 'so what!'" I blurted out angrily. "Don't you understand? I can't be a majorette!"

"So you can't be a majorette. So what?"

"You just don't give a darn!" I accused her. "You don't care that I can't do anything any more. You don't even get it. Leave me alone!"

"Okay," she said, heading toward the door. "But that'll be the day when you can't do anything," she said. "And when you're ready to talk about it, let me know." She went back downstairs. Probably out to her precious garden, I thought to myself. It's all she's concerned with anyway.

In truth, I loved the family garden, too, but wasn't able to help out much in it that summer. I do remember crawling along on the ground, though, my leg in a cast from hip to toe, weeding the edges of the strawberry patch. It was hard work, but I felt the pride of accomplishment when that patch took on the cared-for, tidy appearance resulting from my efforts. And I knew that later, when we all shared in one of my mom's scrumptious strawberry shortcakes, I'd be glad I helped.

"I have another job for you," my mother said one sunny morning. Her arms were overflowing with huge bouquets of fragrant, gaily colored sweet peas. "I'm going to set you up a stand out front of the house so you can sell these."

Sweet peas were not only my birth flower, but also one of my favorites in my mother's many park-like beds. It was pure enjoyment to see the pleasure in my customers' eyes when they approached from their cars. "Ohhhh," one woman murmured, "sweet peas! I haven't seen these since my mother used to grow them." Many mentioned the flowers' perfection and expressed enthusiasm when they learned of the small asking price. Before long, I had sold them all, again pleased with my day's work and achievements. Later that evening, my mother and I laughed easily, sharing our strange brand of humor. "Those people probably stopped to buy the flowers just because of seeing me, the poor young girl with crutches and cast, sitting by the side of the road," I joked.

She laughed. But then added, "They have no idea of what you can accomplish, dear, even with that thing on your leg."

"But...but I still can't be a majorette when school starts in September," I told her, finally ready to continue the conversation we'd started weeks before. "I can't accomplish that, can I."

My mother looked at me blankly and was silent for a moment.

"What?!" I blurted, the lighthearted moment quickly disappearing.

"Well, what is it you'll miss so much about being a majorette?" she wanted to know.

I sighed from frustration. It seemed self-explanatory as far as I was concerned, but she'd asked the stupid question, so I'd give her an answer. "Marching with the band," I explained, as if to a child. "Being on the bus. Going to the games. Being part of the whole thing."

"Being part of the whole thing?"

"Yes. Now I'll only be able to watch from the sidelines."

"Not true," she said. "By the time school starts, you'll be walking again. Take up an instrument. Join the band. Then you can still go with them without having to do your high-stepping struts and acrobatics."

It was my turn to be quiet. While I was thinking about what she'd said, she got up and was off again, back to one of her many projects. My mother, the perpetual motion machine.

When the second surgery came, this one on the other leg, I was in my third year of college. Laid up in another full length cast, this time for six months, I had to leave school; the doctor said it would be a year before I could return. My days in bed were long. My mother, running a small restaurant at the time, left lunch where I could reach it on one side of the bed. On the other side, covered discretely with one of her hand-embroidered towels, she put my bedpan. "Call if you need me," she said. "The front door is unlocked in case any of your friends come to visit." And off she'd go. I played my flute, a constant enjoyment and accomplishment in my life by this time, and read voraciously. I made phone calls, did a lot of thinking. I wrote.

Once able to get around on crutches, I took a part-time job nearby in a real estate and insurance agency, dreaming of leaving my small, mill hometown and heading for Boston where I could explore my freedom as a young woman of the exciting '60s. Meanwhile, my mother accepted part of my modest weekly paycheck to contribute toward my room and board. I never questioned this practice, even under the circumstances. By now, I was long used to being productive under any circumstances.

Noontimes, I'd hop faster and faster on my crutches along Main Street to my mother's restaurant where I'd flirt with some of the customers, play the jukebox, and eat pizza from our town's first pizza oven. Daily, the storekeepers greeted me all along the half mile walk. "Slow down!" the man in the flower shop yelled. "You'll get a speeding ticket!" Mother looked up as I raced in the restaurant door every noon. "Break your record time yet?" she asked as she continued working.

Eventually, I left the home, moved on to Boston, and married. Age 30 came and went, and, rather than being in the wheelchair as my surgeons had predicted, I danced until the band folded up at the local night spots, never drove anywhere I could walk, and–like my mom–was a perpetual motion machine. Life was punctuated with occasional bouts of arthritis and its side-effects, but whatever disability I had did not define who I was.

I was in my 40s, on a lunchtime shopping trip, when a co-worker and I were climbing a flight of stairs.

Watching me, she began laughing. "Hey! Stop it!" she said.

"Stop what?" I asked.

"Stop walking like that, like Frankenstein!"

"Oh," I said, continuing on without a break. "This is just how I do stairs. I guess you never saw taken them before. Some joint problems."

She looked at me, incredulous. "How come I didn't know that, after all this time working together?"

"Guess it just didn't come up," I answered.

It wasn't that I ever tried to hide such things. It was exactly as I'd said: It just never came up.

Not until my 50s, after suffering many of the same disappointments and occurrences everyone eventually encounters in life, did my ability to choose how I responded to challenges became even more important. Now divorced, a writer and college writing teacher, I was also serving as the night manager in a retirement home, a place of gentility and beauty, where my quarters were part of my salary. Gradually, my osteoarthritis became erosive, going further into my bones, making it more and more difficult to maneuver the stairs of the old Georgian mansion. Further, I began to develop heart/lung problems, leaving me exhausted and weak. Eventually, I had to use oxygen 24 hours a day and was nearly crawling up and down the stairs. The time had come. I had to leave my beloved ladies and home. And, unless I wanted to leave my community, I had no where to go.

For seven months, while I waited for space to open up in a building for disabled and elderly people, I found rooms where I could take along my noisy oxygen equipment and try to get well. I no longer had the stamina to teach college courses. At 55, a full 25 years after predicted, I finally needed a wheelchair. Instead, I acquired an electric scooter, like an electric wheelchair except longer in the base – and racier. Definitely racier.

Today, I only have to use oxygen when I sleep. Whenever able, I attend therapy and arthritis swims at my local Y. In spite of discovering diabetes a few years back, I have an active, productive life and consider my health far improved from when it took such a perilous dip with the heart problems. Approaching 60, I am a person with a loving group of friends who experiences great joys in many areas. I still write, edit, and coach amateur and professional writers. For years now, I've had a column called "Disabilities Happens," all about living with disabilities. Notice the word is "living," not "surviving." And only within the past few years have I started to realize the part my mother played, and is still playing at age 85 (and going strong), in my continuing outlook and ability to stay valid.

My realization started one day during a telephone conversation with her: "Sometimes I really feel like a boring wimp," I complained.

"What?" she said, her voice rising several decibels over the phone. "You've always been so strong, dear. And I've never seen anyone so creative in dealing with whatever life hands you."

It was my turn. "What?" I said, as astounded as the 15-year-old girl who couldn't believe her mother could be so clueless. "You think so? It's always been you who is the strong one," I told her. "I'm a wimp," I repeated.

"Wimp?" she asked. "Do wimps keep going, even when it doesn't seem there's anywhere else left to go? Do wimps make up their minds to make a life out of whatever they can?"

I was quiet, uncomfortable with her accolades.

She continued. "And what about the way you're so creative? The car carrier you helped design for your scooter. The way you have your apartment set up so you can get around from place to place without using a wheelchair. The 'K. K.'s Care Group' you developed among your friends to help out in times of need." She paused. "And, honey, I can still remember you running, literally running on your crutches. Do wimps run full tilt on their crutches, just to see if they can beat their own best time?"

After this conversation, I began to question how I got the way I am. Looking back, I see clearly how I began to learn to make the choice to be valid, an authentic person, not an invalid who felt powerless and out of control because of physical challenges. I've realized one of the most valuable, life-long gifts my mother has given me, although to this day she doesn't take credit, was this: From childhood on, she never treated me as an invalid, never acted as if anything should hold me back, and encouraged me to do whatever I was able to do, even if it meant being physically uncomfortable at times. When I complained that I looked different, she constantly told me that anyone worth my time would see the beauty inside. If surgery or illness prohibited my participating in one thing, she told me to find another.

My occasional use of canes, crutches, and braces became just tools to me, to accomplish whatever I had set out to do. "Teach me to do these modern dances they're doing in Boston these days," my mother would often say when I'd visit home as a young woman. And we'd boogie down to the latest rock and roll records, whether I happened to be on or off those "tools" at the time. I might have looked a bit awkward dancing around with a crutch, but I still danced. Even now, I "dance" with my upper body while sitting in my chair. Just as importantly, when I was a teenager first setting off to scout the trails at Acadia National Park with my pals, then a young single woman living in Beantown's turbulent '60s, then a middle-age woman setting out on my electric scooter for an excursion to unfamiliar territory, I've always much more often heard "Have fun!" from my mother than "Be careful." And not once have I ever heard, "Don't do that; you're not able."

Now, hopefully, I pass the reminder that we all have choices on to my readers. Whatever life hands us, we get a choice on how we respond. By living my own life as a valid person, by remaining who I am in spite of whatever happens around me or to my body, I invite others to do the same. I want them to remember that they are never invalid unless they decide to be. There are always choices in our reactions to life; there are always alternatives to create and find. We need not be "invalids."

Today, inside me, that little 15-year-old majorette I once was still remembers the first "So what?" uttered by her mom. Today, "So what?" seems to me a wonderfully succinct and challenging philosophy to embrace.

My mother didn't teach me a specific answer to living. She taught me a specific question, one that has made all the difference in my world, opening the door to decisions, alternatives, choices, and – ultimately – contentment.

# Water's Edge
## Dee Ann E. L. Horvath

*When things pull you down, relax, you will be released and you will be free.*

I was very young, barely five years old, when I learned that my whole life could be totally changed in a few agonizing moments. It all started out so innocently on a hot summer afternoon. My mother had worked very hard to create a safe environment for my sister and me on our lake front property in Wisconsin. She weeded and raked the whole beach area around the pier and chained off a safe area for us to swim. My sister and I being five and four years old, our lake was a wonderland to our senses. Snails, mussels, fish and turtles were our consideration as we explored their world and the area we were allowed.

We noticed a man fishing close by in a boat and looked forward to fishing with our father when he came home. We would have a nice dinner and then get dressed for fishing on the pier. Dad had so many neat gadgets for night fishing, bobbers that lit up when the fish nibbled and time to be with us. That was the best part. We were very patient because it was so much fun to spend special time with Daddy. So my sister Lori and I played for hours in the sanctuary my mother had created for us looking forward to evening time with father.

The warm winds picked up. Being children, we never paid attention to our inner tube that had blown over the chain and gone into the forbidden zone, a vastly weeded area with a spring in the middle that was cold as Alaska. My mother, being our savior, made it her quest to get the tube back. She dove in but the heat of the day and the cold spring caught her off guard. Mommy was a good swimmer but her thrashing caused the weeds to wrap around her legs and pull her down. Lori and I watched as we saw our mother drowning, pleading for the fisherman to help her. He froze and seemed to watch the drama unfold unable to emend the situation. Lori and I stood on the water's edge and beheld the worst disaster in our life. Our mother was our effervescence that propelled us to grow and we were watching her die, slowly. I always felt stronger than my years and she yelled out don't Dee Ann.

Then something special happened. She suddenly relaxed and all the weeds let go and she lay floating on the water. Mother made her way back to the sea wall and although tired she remembered something someone had told her a long time ago. When things pull you down take a deep breath and relax, all of a sudden you will be released and you will be free.

My mother is gone from this earth but never from my mind. She taught me so many things but most of all she taught me how to float. At times when things overcome me I remember what she told me: Relax, don't panic, breathe and you will see another beautiful day and you know what, it works. Life's lessons can be hard and they can hurt but in truth they can also be sweet, rewarding and enlightening like my day at the water's edge.

*Dee Ann E. L. Horvath writes: I was born in Chicago, Illinois in 1955. Married to my high school sweet heart for over 33 years and we have three wonderful daughters together. To me every person is a novel waiting to be read. Some are better reading than others are but there is always something to be learned. Recently I have found writing poetry and short stories to be my passion. You can reach me at Ambereye3(at)aol.com or http://hometown.aol.com/ambereye3 to find out where to read more of my writings.*

---

# The What-If's
## Sally Jadlow

*Apply your "what if's" to positive possibilities.*

I came home from school with a heavy heart. I dragged into the kitchen, dropped my books on the floor, and slumped into a chair.

"What's wrong, honey? You look like you've got the weight of the world on your shoulders."

It was 1956. I was about to be fourteen. To this point, my life had been relatively simple. Mom made a point to shield me from much of the unpleasantness of the world. Daddy spent WWII in Germany. When he came home, she shut the door on the world and like Scarlet O'Hara, she would "think about that tomorrow." When I was nine, I was barely aware of "The Korean Conflict." We had a TV, but didn't watch it much. When the news came on, Mom usually switched it off.

All of her shielding couldn't keep the world out the day President Khrushchev, leader of Russia, spoke before the UN. Everyone at school was abuzz about it. Did he really take his shoe off and bang it on the podium and say "We will bury you!"

How could a leader of a country talk like that? Why did he hate us so much?

Mom set some cookies before me with a glass of milk.

"Wanna talk about it?"

I ignored the snack and stared at the floor. My swirling thoughts had trouble forming themselves into words. Finally, I spoke.

"Mom, do you believe what Khrushchev spoke at the UN yesterday?"

"What did you hear he said?"

"He said the Russians would bury us. What have we ever done to them? Why does he hate us? My friend, Susan, said her folks are going to build a bomb shelter. What if the Russians do bomb us?"

Mother sat very quiet for a long time. She took my hands in hers and looked into my eyes.

"My dear, 'if' is the biggest little word in the English language. Most folks worry their lives away on what never happens. Apply your "what if's" to positive possibilities rather than the negative."

As I look back on that conversation over fifty years ago, I'm grateful for her wisdom delivered to me on that day. I don't turn off the news, but I do pray over what I see and invite God's mercy and grace into the situations played out before me. I know whatever happens goes through His loving hand first and therein lies absolute security.

*Sally Jadlow is author of* The Late Sooner, *available at* http://AWOCbooks.com *or* www.SallyJadlow.com. *Her blog is at*

http://thelatesooner.blogspot.com. *See the review at* The Daily
Oklahoman http://www.newsok.com/article/2989064/

---

# By a Star
### Jayne Moraski

*"We live by a star, not by a tree."*

It was a full moon, plenty of light to see the path through the
Mojave. I crept from the house and walked my bike to the top of the hill.
I was headed to the other side of the Air Force base de jour. My heart
was surprisingly calm – no racing other than the exertion of peddling.
My thoughts wandered. New kid in school again, but I didn't really care.
I had my horse and he never judged, never made me feel stupid for not
knowing the inside jokes.

The night was clear and cloudless. I pulled the halter from the tack
room and clasped it on Pretzel. His speckled white coat glowed in the
moonlight. He nuzzled me hoping for an apple to munch. Of course I had
brought him one. We walked toward the big corral as co-conspirators.
No need to make a sound. I led him all the way to the far edge of the
corral. Then I sprang onto his bare back and let out a yawp. His hoofs
flew as fast as that little pony could run. The wind stung my face a bit on
that cold desert night, and I felt like I was flying. He jumped to a stop at
the fence and snorted bright puffs of air. I let go of the lead to tell him we
were done with the run. I lay down on his back, looking up at the wide
open sky. I took in a deep breath. The connection to the earth, the stars
and my horse – this was all I needed. Wants are many, needs are few.

My Mom's favorite saying was "We live by a star, not by a tree,"
referring to our nomadic family life that never let us put down roots. That
night I knew just what Mom meant.

*Copyright Jayne Moraski 2008*

*Jayne Moraski lives in North Florida, and works as the director of homeless services for the local government for her day job. She writes children's picture books and does landscape acrylic art for her hopefully-someday-job. Her mother believed introducing girls to horses was the best way to keep them from boys. So she knew exactly what she was doing when Mom bought her 10-year-old a beautiful speckled pony.*

*"By A Star" is the true story of one night when Jayne was a 10-year old at a new Air Force base. Jayne can be reached at j_moraski@hotmail.com.*

---

## Mamma Said, "Why Should You Forgive?"
**Althea Gael Coupé**

"You've been trampled in the ground, till only your fractured
shadow stumbles weakly round; seeking some tiny fragment of
your heartbeat's broken sound. Life's love is bound; tossed
in a dark and dank surround; beneath a brutal burial mound.

So why forgive?
 To truly live!
This choice is for your gain!
Don't you deserve a better deal? Emotions free from pain?

So retrieve the worth you owe yourself; unshackle every chain,
Set yourself free; you have ability; a great life to maintain,
Why choose to stay a voluntary captive of sorrow, or of blame?
Raise up a new standard yourself, believe in your own campaign;
Take back control; move ahead; and then full life retain.
Don't succumb to harsh defines, or let wild dictates reign,
Nor long for lost apologies - you may forever wait in vain,
We often need to give ourselves what others can't contain,
Your heart will be revived; old barriers will not remain.
Turn the key to your own success; you will ease much strain,

Though few there be that learn the value of this wise domain.
Grant yourself this priceless gift, great reward will follow you,
Our Father also said: 'Forgive, they know not what they do'."

*Althea Gael Coupé (née Everton) is 55 and lives in Grahamstown, South Africa. She is a Secretary in the Physics and Electronics Department, Rhodes University. She is mother to three married children, and became a proud grandmother in 2007. Her devoted parents are recently both deceased. Her Christian walk is grounded in God's provision of so loving the world that He gave his only Son that we might find His forgiveness, as evidenced in the conclusive line of this forgiveness poem.*

---

# My momma told me
## Loraine Lawson

There's meanness in this world, baby girl,
You can't begin to understand.
But that's not the way I raised you
So no matter what they do
Hold your head up proud.

There's cheatin' in this world.
They'll lie to you just to be doing it.
But don't let them get the best of you.
Do like I do and like I said:
You hold your head up proud.

And when you need a good cry,
You come on home first, child.
Cause it's a rough, tough world out there.
And you remember what your momma said.
If they hurt you, smile

# Chapter 5

# RELATIONSHIP SKILLS:

## Getting along with others

# The Blue Danube
## Myrna McKee

*Fighting prejudice and ostracism*

The pressure started to build in the last semester of my senior year in high school. I didn't know what college I was going to attend or even if my grades would be good enough to go. Not knowing I had dyslexia, a learning disability, I struggled with some relatively easy subjects, which made no sense at all. Learning from experience, I realized that if I tried harder and studied longer, I could do better.

The girl who sat next to me in homeroom, Ann was a whiz, a straight A+. We began to work together on our homework during study period and lunch. She had so much patience. Soon the results started to show as I pulled up my marks in both math and chemistry.

Ann is black, I am Jewish, and this took place in Worcester, Massachusetts in early 1954, where we lived in a very restrictive society. Jews kept with Jews. If you had non-Jewish friends you were suspect, but if you dared to date a non-Jewish boy, no Jewish boy would go out with you, for your reputation would be ruined.

Another perfect example of the fine line of prejudice in our society was Salisbury Street. It is on the West Side of Worcester where all of the City's wealthiest families live. The street is also a dividing line where respective ethnic cultures live in big opulent homes. On the East Side of the street, Protestants owned homes, while on the West Side lived mostly Jews mixed with a few Italian Catholics. Everyone kept to his own side of the street.

I am talking about bright, educated, rich people who were so prejudiced. By today's standards this behavior is silly, but then, that was the way it was.

You can just imagine how the white Jewish population (the establishment) viewed Blacks. Worcester is a big city, but because of the social restrictions, we all lived in a very small community. Everybody's business was common knowledge. The Jewish women who controlled where and with whom the teenagers socialized were the wives of the leaders of the city's businesses and the Temple Emanuel (our synagogue). The ladies thought they could dictate the rules in our small society. They just didn't know my mama. But I am getting ahead of myself.

It all started one afternoon as I came home from school carrying my load of schoolbooks. Mama was waiting for me at the door with a very strange expression on her face. "What's the matter?" I asked. "Myrna, come into the kitchen and sit down," she replied. "I want to talk to you."

Mystified and trying hard to remember if I had done anything wrong, I followed her. As we were seated, Mama began to speak. "I received a phone call today from Mrs. Rubin, who thinks she is in control of the teenagers. The gist of the conversation was, you are associating with a Black girl. You spend your time studying, but still the ladies feel you are making a big mistake. Mrs. Rubin told me, you are to break off the relationship at once or you will be sent to Coventry. I explained that I won't tell my daughter what to do, but I told her I'd give you her message."

My instinctive response was, "Mama, tell her 'NOT NO, BUT HECK NO!' " I couldn't believe my ears! How dare the ladies threaten me? For Coventry was a threat. The dictionary defines 'being sent to Coventry' as a state of banishment or exclusion from society.

That meant total ostracism. None of my girl friends would be allowed to telephone me. Not one of the young people in our group would speak to me on the street or at school. I wouldn't have any casual dates, there would be no invitation to the pajama parties, no one to shop with and no date for the Senior Prom.

Mama understood Coventry a lot better than I did. She had seen it in practice once before, many years ago. However, she told me, it was my decision.

I was in mental turmoil. The last five months of the senior year of high school were supposed to be full of festivity. As a class, we had been together since the first grade. Next year we would all go off to college and our separate ways. Numerous parties, celebrations, barbecues, swimming trips, sleepovers, and of course, the Senior Prom had been planned. The more I thought of what I would miss, versus someone telling me who my friends could be, the angrier I got. I thought of the consequence of being totally ignored.

You see, there was always a large group of students, friends, and family at our home. Mama made everyone feel welcome, especially my school friends. I have to admit I was afraid. Before going to bed that night I talked to Mama and told her I had made my decision. Carefully I explained to her, "This is not a black or white issue to me. It's one of my personal freedoms of choice. That right is part of my heritage. So I'll just ignore the whole situation and keep on studying with Ann."

Mama replied, "Somehow I knew you would make that choice. It's not going to be easy. But I promise I'll make it better." She reached out and hugged me and said, "I love you, honey."

Well, the word got out, and talk about a change. The phone calls stopped. No one came to visit. My best friends said a cool "Hello" when we met. Casual friends averted their eyes, and of course no one asked me out for a date. At first I was hurt and then I got angry. I even contemplated giving in, but some how I knew if I did, I'd never stand up for anything in life. I made the conscious decision not to become more or less friendly with Ann, as I felt I could handle the pressure. We still studied together as much as possible and I never told Ann what was going on.

Mama watched and worried, as I became more solemn and depressed. She could see the toll that the exclusion from society was taking on me. Mama got angry, for she saw first hand how hard Coventry was to bear.

After a particularly bad week, she smiled at me as I came in from school and said, "Pack your clothes! We are going to the "Borscht Belt's" Concord Hotel for a long weekend."

The well-known "Borscht Belt" was about 90 miles north of New York City, in the Catskill Mountains. It was "THE" resort area of great popularity among the Jewish people. There were many hotels that catered to them with accommodations of luxurious rooms, fantastic food and great entertainment. Daddy, Mama, and I went, and the "Borscht Belt" was a blast. I even met a young Jewish man named Sonny from New York City. He was over six feet tall, a freshman at Columbia Law, had a mustache, and best of all, he owned his own custom-fitted tuxedo. We had such a good time that Sonny asked Mama to bring our family back in a month, when he would return.

Mama was ecstatic to see me smiling and laughing. She said, "Yes." Over the next three months our family traveled a lot. My parents took me to New York City where we would stay at the famous St. Moritz Hotel, shop on Fifth Avenue, go to see Broadway shows, eat fine food, and visit with Sonny and his family. But the best times were at the Concord Hotel, where there was a big ballroom with a live orchestra and dancing every night. Sonny loved to dance, especially to Straus's "Blue Danube." He did the waltz with a great deal of zest and flourish, and as his partner, so did I. We circled the room with big swoops, turns, and dips. It was pure theatrics.

At first I got dizzy, but soon I was used to the flow and rhythm of the music. Sonny was such a perfect partner, I became more sure of myself every time we danced. We got to be so good that when we started to waltz, other dancers would clear the floor to watch. Often they would applaud when we were finished. Then Sonny would twirl me around into a deep curtsy. It was fun.

At the end of each weekend, I began dreading more and more going back to Worcester and Coventry. I knew if I had a date for the Prom, I'd make it through.

So one night I asked Mama, "Can I invite Sonny to the Senior Prom? I know he will have to stay at our house, but I promise I'll help, so there won't be too much work for you."

Mama nodded, "Go ahead Myrna, and invite him." I did and he accepted.

The year was drawing to a close and final exams were given. Thanks to Ann's help, I was accepted at a good college, albeit, not the one Ann got to go to – Radcliffe – but I don't think I would have made a good Cliffy.

The only thing missing was the Senior Prom gown. Unbeknownst to me, Mama had the situation well under control. There was a classy department store in downtown Worcester called Richard Healy's. One of Mama's best friends, Lily, worked in the gown department. When she told Lily the story of me being sent to Coventry, Lily was furious at the unfairness of the small group of women who were in control. She told Mama, "Leave the gown to me. I'll choose the very best. I promise she will be the most beautifully dressed girl at the Prom."

One night the phone rang and I heard Mama say, "Yes, Lily, we will come at once." She turned to me and said, "Get your long one piece girdle. We are going shopping."

Now I knew we couldn't afford a gown from Healy's, so I was confused why we were going there.

We arrived at the store and took the elevator to the fourth floor where Lily was waiting. Lily hugged Mama and me and made us feel welcome. "Come." She pointed to the large central dressing room. "It's in here."

I thought, "What's this all about?" As I opened the door of the dressing room, there stood on a mannequin the most gorgeous evening gown I had ever seen. It was all white and strapless. The lace bodice was a vision, crusted with hundreds of tiny white seed pearls.

Lily told us, "The skirt is of fine silk net and cut in seven layers, so that as one whirled the net forms a tulip." There was even an extra length of material to make long opera-style gloves.

Before I could tell Mama we couldn't afford this dress, I heard her say, "Dear, get undressed and put on your girdle."

As she and Lily left me alone to change, I couldn't help myself. I went over and looked at the label. CHRISTIAN DIOR. The price tag originally said $400, marked down to $300, down to $200, and finally to $100. $100 was expensive but still within the very outer range.
With Mama and Lily's help, I tried on the gown. It fit like a glove. As I looked into the mirror I couldn't believe the reflection. I was beautiful, a vision in pearls and white, with long blond hair. I felt like a fairy Princess.

Mama and Lily were jumping up and down with excitement, hugging and kissing each other.

You see, when the gown first came in, Lily had called Mama to come have a look at it. Mama did and fell in love with the gown, but 47 years ago in 1954, $400 was a small fortune.

As Mama told the story, Lily was determined that I would look the best for the Prom. She hid the ball gown in the back of the closet in the alteration room. Each time there was a markdown, Lily would bring the gown out to be repriced, and then return it to the closet. When the buyer reduced it to its final $100, Lily made the call to Mama.

Minor adjustments were made, as well as, a pair of long white net gloves. Mama told me to write Sonny to let him know she would take care of the flowers. She ordered a circle of tiny white Zimbedium Orchids for placement in my hair. Then long white velvet streamers were attached to the back of the circle with a myriad of orchids affixed to the ribbons.

At last the day of the Prom arrived. Rose, Mama's hairdresser came to the house to fix my hair and apply my makeup. Rose created a real "Do." My long blond hair was piled on top of my head with orchids peeping out of all the curls. The velvet ribbons, full of tiny white orchids, cascaded down my back.

I was so excited I could barely sit still. Finally my hair and makeup were finished and I put on my gown, shoes and gloves. As I walked into the living room to show Daddy and Sonny, I overheard Daddy say, "That gown is so expensive I am going to have the dressmaker put in sleeves for her wedding."

He turned to the doorway and caught sight of me. Daddy stopped talking and looked, then a big smile crossed his face. He never said another word about the cost.

Mama got her camera and took lots of pictures of Sonny and me. Finally I said, "Mama, we've got to go or we'll be late." Sonny had come to Worcester by train, therefore he was going to get to drive my Dad's car.

Now, no one could find the keys. It kept getting later and later. At last Mama found the keys behind the pillow on our couch. So with a flurry of hugs and kisses we left, a half-hour late. We drove up to the auditorium where the dance was to be held and I could hear the music of the live band.

Sonny parked Daddy's car and we walked to the entrance of the hall. As we entered, there were three steps down to the ballroom floor. The big spotlights that focused on the bandstand swung around to face the steps and the band began to play the Blue Danube Waltz.

In the glare of the spotlights, Sonny held out his hands and said, "Shall we?"

In a daze, I stepped into his embrace and we began to waltz to the familiar melody. All the other couples in the room stopped dancing to watch.

As we waltzed, the velvet ribbons flew behind me, the silk net dress formed a tulip shape. We circled the room as one would in a real Viennese Ball. Oh, it was grand!

Then Sonny softly whispered, "I am going to swing you where the chaperons are. You go into a deep curtsy and bow your head."

And he did just that. As I dipped into the curtsy, the flowered ribbons covered my shoulders as a mantle. The only fear I had was getting up without falling flat on my tail.

When I looked up into the eyes of Mrs. Rubin, I drew on all my strength to rise with grace. I gave her my best smile. Her face was furious as I presented Sonny to her and the other Chaperons, making sure they all knew he was a first year law student at Columbia.

The Prom went on and I was the Belle. My dance card was full and I danced every dance. All my girlfriends chatted with me, making note of my gown, flowers, hair, and the fact that my date wasn't wearing a wrinkled rented tuxedo, but he did have a mustache. Two girls even said they'd call me tomorrow.

Later, one of my girlfriends told me that when we were dancing the waltz, it was a vision of white tulle, flying orchids, graceful dips, pure Hollywood.

Well, Coventry was over and I had won the right to have whom I wanted for a friend.

Later that night back at our house, as we hashed and rehashed the whole evening, Mama explained, "I wasn't going to let the women break your spirit." She told how she plotted the revenge with Lily's help and Sonny's cooperation. Mama even knew the bandleader George. She arranged for the spotlights and Blue Danube Waltz. Then she hid the keys to the car so we would be late enough to make an entrance.

I had survived Coventry and learned a good lesson that has stood the test of time. Thank you Mama.

G/D IS GOOD

*Myrna McKee is a transplanted Yankee who has lived in the south for 30 years. She is a nationally published journalist, syndicated columnist, and comedic storyteller; member and co-founder of new guild, Upstate Story Tellers 2009; co-founder of new guild Clemson Area Story Tellers (CAST) 2009; National Organization of Woman Writers; "Prime Time" Senior Advocate; Inspirational Speaker. Her columns include "A Slice of Life" and "How to Live life Lower on the Hog" in the* Seneca Journal, Clemson Messenger, *and* www.UpstateToday.com. *National Blog:* PainlessPennyPinching.com. *E-mail mmyrnamckee@bellsouth.net.*

---

# Parting Gifts
## Carolyn Piper

*A mother's final illness reveals a painful – yet healing – secret.*

I ducked as the wallet Mom had been holding sailed past my head. "Damn you, I told you not to come," she screamed. The soup I had made for her went flying one way, the tray it was on another, and from way deep down a little girl gave one last cry of "Mom!" and the role reversal came full circle.

It had been two months since my mother's diagnosis with Alzheimer's, and I knew as I watched the soup dribble slowly down the wall in bright red streaks, that the hope of keeping her independent for any length of time was futile. Turning to look at her, I saw terror etched in her eyes. "God help me, God help me. God help me. Don't let me last long. Please don't let me last long," she cried as she wrapped her arms around herself and began to rock back and forth. Stricken with panic though I was at that moment, wonder filled me, as I realized that for one of the first times in our life together I was hearing a simple emotional truth expressed from a woman who had always been an enigma to me.

Mom, you see, was never one for facing reality. She had always seen things as she wanted to see them, and fought hard to make them as she wanted them to be, especially when it came to her children. Our relationship, to put it mildly, had always been strained. In any bad relationship there is fault on both sides. I certainly was not the daughter she had hoped for, nor she the mother I wanted. She, socially conscious above all else, was concerned with niceties and appearance, while I, bookish and rebellious by nature, was, as a result of a childhood illness, hard of hearing from the age of three, which made me more than a bit socially inept, and for a panicky while, a scholastic failure in a family of achievers. The result had been 53 years of constant strife.

Appearances had always been of the greatest importance to Mom, who was a "proper" lady above all else, and kept a flowered hat and white gloves at the ready for every occasion. Her glare when one transgressed social rules could freeze you at thirty paces. I've never forgotten that glare. Forty years later when she leveled it on my firstborn son and I saw him shrink in fear, I was still powerless to move against it. Doing it "right" was paramount. Looking anything but respectable was unforgivable. There were, in her view, certain paths in life which one followed regardless of one's own desires or emotions, and the result was that the two of us circled warily around each other through the '50s, she disapproving, I sulking, clashing regularly, achieving at best an uneasy peace, and at worst open warfare.

Of course we all know what came after the 50s. The 60s hit with a bang. I went off to college, hormones in full swing, and things went from bad to worse. Society and social norms were in a state of flux, which must have terrified my mother. I neither thought, nor cared, about what she might be feeling about this new world. I simply left, going home as infrequently as possible, while enjoying the fruits of new freedom as frequently as possible. When I was home, pleasantries were not in great supply. My dress was wrong. My language was dreadful. My attitude toward my family, and in particular, her, was unforgivable. The men I dated were regularly judged as being odd, too old for me or disreputable. Once looking at me she blandly mentioned out of the blue "you are not nearly as attractive as you think you are." She then took a picture of me for her scrapbook. I have that picture still. It shows an attractive young woman, with eyes full of sadness.

At the time "let me out of here," was all I could think.

And out I went. When I checked in at all it was to tell her I was en route somewhere as far from home and hearth as I could get. I toured South America, traveling via thumb and planes held together with tape, and eventually left for an extended trip to Central America with an old friend of the male persuasion. Home again, I moved with him to another state, and only our eventual marriage kept the slow smoke that was coming from her ears from breaking into a full conflagration.

Married, I moved to yet another state and commenced a life as different from the social milieu I had been raised in as I could convince my husband to allow. Grunge was in, and, needless to say, flowered hats and white gloves were out. We bought an old maple sugar shack on 30 acres in Vermont and began to renovate. We purchased goats for milk, chopped wood for heat, grew our own vegetables, and raised pigs, sheep and chickens. And incidentally, my eventual, and, perhaps, only, saving grace in Mom's eyes, had two sons, whom she adored, but who were, like both her own children, scared to death of her. "Isn't it amazing" she once remarked to a neighbor of mine who made haste to repeat it to me "how great the kids are when you consider who their mother is?"

Sanity prevailed, I suspect, only because of the 600 miles that separated us. I saw her as infrequently as possible, lambasted myself for not making a total break, and ground my teeth audibly when we were together.

But, as the old saying goes, life is what happens when you are expecting other things. My father died, and mom decided, when my brother made it clear he wanted nothing to do with her, to move to a retirement village in a nearby town. I screamed. I cried. I described in excruciating detail the horrible cold winters we have in our state. I pointed out how far she would be from former friends, and when all else failed, became downright nasty in hopes of scaring her off.

Of course, she came anyway.

A year later I was staring at a soup-stained wall, and facing the fact that panicked beyond her ability to cope, she needed to be in assisted living in the nursing home, and, that like it or not, I was in the driver's seat, entwined in a situation I had never imagined myself being in.

The six months following that day were horrendous as mom developed ever-worsening anxiety on top of actual psychotic episodes.

Medical decisions had to be made. Financial decisions had to be made. Emotional decisions had to be made. The first two were easy – well, relatively easy, made easier by the help and support of some superb nurses and social workers. The last was more problematic. I had hated this woman. A minute in her presence was like an hour, and now, she was at my mercy. Literally. The choices were mine: I could ignore her and let any decision being made in her behalf simply happen. I could advocate for her financially and medically while ignoring the person within. I could, for heaven's sakes, being in possession of her holy of holies – the check book – rob her blind, for after years of pleading poverty, it was now revealed that mom was well off indeed. What I could not do, I found, was grieve or care deeply.

At first I chose the second of these choices, becoming a daily advocate for her care, keeping a wary eye out for the emotional blind siding I had learned to expect from her. It didn't happen.

Instead I found the saving grace of a gradual terminal illness.

For one thing, her condition mandated psychotropic medication – something she would have benefited from long ago. Antidepressants and anti-anxiety medication made a terrific, and positive, difference in her personality, Alzheimer's or no Alzheimer's. So, amazingly, did the Alzheimer's itself, for as recent memory faded, so too did the defenses she had built around herself, and for the first time in our lives we began to talk. When I visited her, we developed the habit of sitting in her room, safe among her cherished possessions, as she shared with me what she *could* remember – her past.

"Do you know," she asked me suddenly one day as we sat quietly together, "what it is like to grow up feeling hated?"

"Tell me mom," I answered.

And so she told me the story of a little girl who never felt loved a day in her life, who one day at the age of 10 went sleigh riding, "on a sled," she added, "with wooden runners. After one run I turned," she continued, "to see a friend pointing at me, and she suddenly yelled at me: 'Your mom isn't your mom.' I didn't know what was going on. All I could think of to do was to run home to see Mama."

Mom-Mom, as we grandchildren would later come to call her, was baking cookies when Mom burst in the door, and, with scarcely a pause, asked THE question. Turning to her, the woman Mom had called mother for all the time she could remember, calmly told her that it was nothing to concern herself about. "Your father's first wife died when you were born," she revealed for the first time as if she were talking about a change in the dinner menu rather than an emotional avalanche suddenly launched without warning, and "he and I got married when you were two. It wasn't a matter of loving you," she went on quite calmly as she put another batch of cookies in the oven, "you came with your father, and I had no choice but to take you on."

This to a ten-year-old child. This she repeated from that time on, again and again and again, as the child, compliant by nature tried and tried and tried in utter futility to gain love and acceptance. Sitting there listening to her tell me the tale, I recalled all the times I had seen her fawning over Mom-Mom, waiting on her, buying her special gifts, worrying about her. Desperate, I realized now, to shift reality in hopes of changing what was unchangeable.

Well, almost unchangeable. On her deathbed, Mom told me, Mom-Mom apologized to her and pleaded for forgiveness. Mom gave it.

I sat in awe of my mother when I heard that. Such forgiveness was quite beyond me. Looking at her, I realized how the past had frozen something in my mother. Unloved, she had no idea how to give love, and the cycle of deprivation had gone on for another generation. How could anyone do that to a child? I don't know. We all paid the price though. Mom spent her whole adult life trying to bend reality, endlessly, desperately, seeking the love she felt perpetually denied, driving, in her desperation, those who should have loved her most, away with her demands that they meet her emotional needs. I spent a life longing for a mother, finding solace in relationships with other older women – but never with my own mother. My children missed the legacy of love from a grandmother who was smart, caring, and had a crackerjack sense of humor.

We paid for it. We all paid for that absence of love, that willingness to wound with words and deed. For in the presence of wounding words and deeds, in the absence of the simple capacity of caring for each other, we wilt and die. We erect defenses around ourselves to protect from further hurt that we have come to see as inevitable. Her willingness to forgive such a thing, even as she still carried the scars, astonished me, and I realized that now, in the closing years of her life, I could do no less.

I realized the truth of the words of W.H. Auden that we must "love one another or die."

My mother no longer recognizes me – though when I visit her I see her face light up – as mine does – when I see her. But she does know I am someone very important to her – and I think, I hope, she knows that she is important to me. And when I leave her, I put my arms around her and give her a huge hug and can say, for the first time in my life, in all truth, and with the great vulnerability of the knowledge of her coming certain loss. "Mom, I love you."

I do. I do. I always did. I just didn't know it – until she and I took this last journey together and learned what love means in our lives.

---

# Laying a Foundation
## Vijayalakshmi Chary

*... common ground from which to begin conversations and build relationships.*

After an 18 hour flight from San Francisco to Singapore, my exhausted family checked into a room for transit passengers. Everyone claimed their bed and dropped off to a deep slumber. A few hours later, one by one, we awoke and showered.

My mother disappeared into the bathroom wearing wrinkled casual dark pants and a plain knit top. Fifteen minutes later she emerged draped in a blue-green sari. A bindi between her eyebrows, a black beaded necklace and golden earrings and bangles were the mark of a properly dressed married Indian woman. She was ready to meet our family in India.

"Amma has made her usual Singapore transformation!" I announced.

"Why don't you change at Thatha's house?" asked my younger sister.

"Because your grandparents feel like I'm still a part of their family when I arrive in a sari," explained Amma. "That's how I dressed when I lived in India. Besides, I see them once in four years. Why not make them happy?"

I was plagued with many questions. Didn't she want to be her own person? Shine in her own individuality? Not conform to society? Did she really want to give up her identity to make someone else happy?

Even when family visited us in California, my mother would dress in traditional attire and serve three traditional Indian meals. "Yes, it's more work. But we need to make our guests feel like they're at home," she would say.

On my sixteenth birthday, Amma threw me a party with family friends. I gushed at all the new clothes I received. During the following months, whenever we were invited to one of the guests' homes, Amma reminded me gently to wear the clothes they'd given. "They'll see that you appreciated their gift," she said. "It's a small gesture."

Amma was right.

But what about being who you really are? Wearing and eating what you want? Being true to yourself?

Even though it was not expressed, Amma's actions laid a foundation where both parties' customs and identities met. They had common ground from which to begin conversations and build relationships. From there, it was safe to express independent opinions and views.

Dressed in a sari and having established an initial rapport, Amma felt comfortable talking to her Indian cousins about her work as an accountant, pursuing higher education and later, her job as a CPA. Her female cousins were intrigued about her life in the US. None of them had dreamed of continuing their education. None of them had worked outside the home.

Years later, when I married, my husband was not particularly traditional. Our out-of-the country visitors however, were orthodox. My father-in-law began his prayers at 4 am. Not only was he a vegetarian, but he did not eat garlic, onions or 'new world' vegetables like cauliflower. He ate only home-cooked meals. For me, vegetarian cooking was simple but not without garlic and onions. I learned to cook new dishes and relishes. Without realizing it, I was laying a foundation for my relationship with my father-in-law. From here, I was able to go about my day to day activities without alienating him.

Was I doing what I wanted? Was I being true to myself? Yes. I wanted a secure base so that I could be free to be myself.

A few years later, my husband and I lugged two children to India. As we were in our transit hotel in Kuala Lumpur, I changed from my blue jeans and sweatshirt into a chudidhar and khameez, loose pants and long tunic. A bindi between my eyebrows, black beaded necklace around my neck, dangling golden earrings and bangles jingling on my wrist, I was ready to meet my family in India. I was ready to lay a foundation.

---

# Mom's "Flat as Walls" Advice
## Brooke Mullins

*A lesson in how to handle teasing*

At my mother's memorial service in June of last year, a group of us sat on the front porch of my mother's farmhouse to reminisce and talk about her influence on our lives.

My closest friend Sara, overcome with emotion, broke down and began to cry.

"Who will give me advice? No offence" she said gesturing to the five or six of us that surrounded her, "but none of you ever had the answers like Dale did." She then looked at me and said, "Brooke, I'm sorry, my loss is nothing compared to yours, how will you cope?"

I had no answer for her that day and to be honest, I still do not. I take every day one day at a time and try not to feel too sorry for myself although life has seen fit that I should be a young, motherless daughter. I stay strong, don't listen to the sad thoughts too often and constantly remind myself that I am still very fortunate because I had a beautiful, wonderful, funny and intelligent mother and although she is gone, her love for me will always go on. I believe that her words of wisdom will continue to guide me during the rest of my life and hopefully they will help lead me in the right directions.

There are so many insights, streams and pools of advice that I could share that I inherited from my mom. But what made my mother so amazing to the many people that fell in love with her was her great sense of humor, her creative mind and her ability to not take herself or life too seriously. She kept all of these attributes right to the end.

My favorite lesson learned from my mother makes me laugh even today because it embodies all of the qualities I like most about her. While she would probably cringe and say "I can't believe that you are telling this story, sharing this advice over all of the wonderful tidbits of knowledge I have bestowed upon you!" Secretly, I believe that my mother would be quite pleased with my selection. She was the type of beautiful woman that liked to be remembered not just for her beauty but also for her brains. For me, she is utterly unforgettable and I am certain that no matter what you think of her advice, you will not forget it and that gives me great joy.

The teenage years were as painful for me as they are for all adolescent girls. I dealt with all the worries and insecurities that all thirteen year-old girls do, and enjoyed the little bit of extra misery that is reserved solely for late bloomers.

My lack of breasts made me a daily target at school and I spent a lot of time trying to avoid the worst of the perpetrators, which wasn't very easy. Luckily for me, my best friend also lacked curves and so we were stronger as a pair and able to commiserate about being flat-chested together.

One day, when Sara and I had been hanging out at my house in the kitchen, we found ourselves whining to my mother, who was cooking, about the negative comments being said about our chests. My mother, always a stickler for details, wanted to hear some of the comments.

"You're so flat the walls are jealous," was always one of my favorites.

"You're so flat you confuse an iron." Ouch.

"Flatty Patty!" "Concave"! "Fried Eggs"! "Boobless Wonder"! We could have gone on, but I think my mother got the gist of it.

My mother, like any mother, nodded sympathetically and cringed in mock horror at all of the insults. But she also had some wisdom to share.

"Why don't you just stand up for yourselves?" she asked. "Stop allowing yourselves to be victimized by these immature boys."

Huh? We had never thought of standing up to the boys.

"How?" We of course wanted to know.

So my mother told us what to say to the boys the next time they insulted us. She explained that by teaching them what it feels like to be insulted over something that you have no control over and that others have no right in insulting you about, they would quite likely stop.

The next day was a school day. We made it through the morning with no significant comments made and then lunchtime came.

Halfway through lunch the teasing began. Sara began being teased by a boy, the worst of the boys actually.

"You're so flat the walls are jealous!" he said and all the boys laughed. They really had limited material.

Slinking up to my desk, where I was quietly working on some homework and praying not to be pulled in by the firing squad, Sara whispered, "Can I say it?"

We both knew what that meant. It was time to see my mother's powerful words in action. I gave her the affirmative nod and she turned about-face like a solder and strutted back to the boy and his friends.

Right hand on her hip she loudly said, "I don't see any big bulge in your pants!" and pointedly stared at his groin region.

There was absolute silence for about thirty seconds and then everyone started laughing, except the boy, who needed an additional few more seconds before he was able to halfheartedly join in the laughter. Victory was ours.

Nothing more was said that day or any other day, for that matter. During the ride home on the big yellow school bus that evening, the boy even apologized to Sara for insulting her. In the past, we had dreaded the bus ride, as it was commonly an occasion for an on-slaughter of insults. That day we rode home in peace and while there were to be more insults during future years, they were never about our breasts.

So that is my favorite bit of wisdom that I received from my mom. It probably wasn't the most life-changing advice I ever received from her, but it had an instant effect, during a time in my life when I really needed my mother's help and advice. My mother taught me to not allow myself to be victimized. I hope that those who read my mother's words will pass them on to the young girls in their own lives, who may one day need advice in this matter. There will always be boys who make girls feel badly about their bodies. In the future, if my daughter needs advice about how to handle teasing, I will definitely have an answer.

---

# A Second Hand Christmas
## Perry P. Perkins

*A shared Christmas, with rewards better than presents*

In the winter of 1975, my parents divorced. My mother had a chronic heart condition that made it impossible for her to work and the two of us couldn't quite make ends meet that first year on our own.

In previous years, Christmas had been a grand event in our home. Money had always been scarce, but my parents scrimped and saved for the holidays. My first memories are of bright lights, rich smells, and a pile of gifts with my name on them. That year, however, would be different. My mother received a meager social security check each month that almost, but not quite, covered the bare essentials, with nothing left for the luxuries of Christmas.

I remember that most of our meals consisted of potatoes and the big blocks of American cheese that the Government passed out at the Social Security office. My mother, alone for the first time in her life, found it difficult to put aside her own hurts and fears and participate in the holidays. I do remember that we had a small tree and brought a box of decorations down from the closet shelf, but there wasn't much joy in our home that year.

One thing that did worry my mother was that there was no money for gifts that year. She fretted over this for weeks but the funds just were not there for presents. One day, a neighbor told her about a local toy charity, an organization dedicated to providing donated presents for children in need. My mother applied for the program and visited their office, bringing home a small box of gifts, which she wrapped and hid under her bed.

The night before Christmas, we ate our baked potatoes and Mom read to me from a book of children's Christmas stories. Just before bedtime, there was a knock at the door and my mother answered to find a young woman who had just moved in next door to us. She was Hispanic, speaking very broken English, and had twin sons who were my own age. She was also divorced and was in as bad, or worse, financial straits as we were. She came to the door asking to borrow some flour and looked so exhausted that mother invited her in and made her a cup of tea. I was hustled off to bed, lest I still be up when Santa made his appearance, and they stayed up and talked awhile.

I remember my mother coming into my room and gently waking me up, then sitting on the side of my bed and asking me if I minded if we had company for Christmas. I said no, unused to have my opinion asked in such matters. Then she took my hand and asked if it would be all right with me if Santa gave some of my presents to the two little boys next door. I thought about this for a while, wondering why Santa couldn't bring them their own presents, but somehow my young brain sensed that it would make mother happy, and she hadn't seemed happy in a long while, so I hesitantly agreed. Mother kissed my forehead and I went back to sleep.

The next morning I awoke to the most wonderful smell wafting under my bedroom door. Hunger banished even the memory of Christmas from my mind and I ran from my room to the kitchen to find the source of that glorious aroma. I skidded to a stop as I rounded the corner into a strange dark faced woman standing at my mother's stove. She was rolling out tortillas and dropping them into a smoking pan, while a large pot bubbled noisily on the back burner.

I blinked once or twice in confusion, until my mother walked in, then remembered that we had company, and even more importantly, that today was Christmas! I spun on my heels and ran into the living room to look under the tree. Two little Mexican boys sat, looking uncertainly around them, on our couch. Several small wrapped packages lay beneath the tree.

Mom followed me in and began to pass out presents, there were just enough for one gift each. I gazed longingly at the brightly wrapped packages in these stranger's hands, knowing they should have been mine, clutching my solitary present tightly to my chest. I unwrapped the box to find a GI Joe action figure, the old fashioned kind with the moving knees and elbows, the kind that came with a little rifle and a little backpack and a string that you pulled to make them say cool army things. Except mine didn't have a rifle, or a backpack, and there was only a hole in the back where the string had once gone. I stood there in the middle of the living room, my lip trembling, clutching my broken toy.

I looked to see what the other boys had gotten, what gifts I had missed out on. One package revealed a cap pistol (without caps) and a worn plastic holster (I had a much nicer set in the toy box in my room), the second box revealed a plastic bag full of legos, in various shapes and sizes. I stood there and watched these two boys whooping and laughing like these were the only toys they had, turning their meager gifts over and over in awe, and suddenly I realized, that these WERE the only presents they had. Soon I would learn that these two, who would become my closest pals, each had exactly two shirts, two pairs of pants, and a worn sleeping bag that they shared on the floor of their room. As I watched my mother talking to this strange woman in our kitchen, tears running down their cheeks, I was suddenly happy that she had woken me up, that Santa had shared my presents with these boys, for how terrible would it have been to wake up with nothing under the tree, no presents to play with, no Santa at all?

The boys, Jay and Julio, followed me to my room, where I showed them, to their amazement, the wealth of my toy box. Soon we were playing like old friends, until called out for a breakfast of seasoned eggs and potatoes wrapped in fresh, warm tortillas. It was the best breakfast I could ever remember having. I'll never forget that morning, as I'll never forget my friends from Mexico who taught me that there is always something to be thankful for, often much more than we think.

*Christian novelist Perry P. Perkins was born and raised in Oregon. His writing includes* Just Past Oysterville, *and* Shoalwater Voices, *as well as dozens of articles in national magazines. Perry is a student of Jerry B. Jenkins Christian Writer's Guild and a frequent contributor to the*

Chicken Soup for the Soul *anthologies. Examples of his published work can be found online at www.perryperkinsbooks.com.*

---

# Bunk Bed Blunder
### Annmarie B. Tait

*"You didn't need any lecture from me. Your conscience took care of that."*

For a full twenty minutes I begged my older sister to trade bunks with me for one measly night. I just had to know the thrill of sleeping in the top bunk bed or die of disappointment. Life is just that dramatic when you're eight years old.

My sister, the self appointed secret president of the "Do-Gooders Club," was not so all fired up sure that this was such a great idea. After all, Mom was no stranger to my appetite for adventure, and more than once she warned me to say away from the top bunk.

Eventually she gave in to me on the pinky promise condition that I never, ever, as long as I draw breath, speak a word to Mom about our shenanigans. "Deal" I said, with a grin that stretched from one earlobe to the other.

After supper I attacked my homework with the speed of a gazelle and the dedication of a Rhodes Scholar. With that behind me, I ripped off my clothes, jumped into the tub, then into my "jammies," then into Daddy's comfy chair. That's where I waited, and waited, and **waited** for Ricky Nelson to sing "Travelin' Man" or some other hit which signaled the end of the "Ozzie and Harriet" show, and the start of my bedtime escapade. I bounded up the living room steps two at a time.

"You didn't forget, did you?"

"No." My sister said. "But, I still don't think it's a good idea."

"I don't care. You promised!" I shot back in a panic.

All evening I imagined the top bunk bed as a flying carpet upon which I could dash off to Disneyland, a cowboy ranch, the Circus or anywhere I wanted. I imagined it as a tree house, a hot air balloon like the one I'd seen in the "Wizard of Oz," and a magical flying unicorn.

One thing was for sure, I'd never get anywhere unless I got myself up into that top bunk with the lights out before my two oldest sisters came to bed, found me out, and blew the lid off my little caper.

Our bunk beds, purchased at the local Army Navy Surplus Store, were made of gray steel that Mom had painted white. They were not equipped with an adorable little ladder like the maple bunk beds I saw advertised in the Sears catalog. Launching to the top was strictly up to the strength and dexterity of the occupant.

To get me up there my sister stood bent over with her fingers laced together. I stepped into the cradle of her hands with one foot, grabbed the top bunk, and then hoisted myself up while she pushed me at the same time. It wasn't very graceful but it got me to my destination all the same. Hardly had I made to the land of OZ on my flying magical unicorn when wouldn't you know it? I fell fast asleep.

The real excitement didn't start until well after midnight when I woke up and realized a trip to the bathroom was in order. With a sleepy yawn I threw back the covers, swung my legs over the side, and stepped off into thin air plummeting to the floor with one loud thud. That sure woke me (and everybody else in the house) up in a hurry.

Mom and Daddy ran to our bedroom with breakneck speed. When they arrived, Daddy picked me up off the floor and my sister scooted over in the lower bunk. Then Daddy gently put me down next to her. I never complained, cried or said a single thing except, "I'm so sorry." My mother bent over and kissed me asking if I was all right. I answered, "Fine. I'm fine. I'm so sorry." She just whispered, "Go to sleep now." Mom never scolded me. She never so much as reminded me of her warning to stay away from the top bunk bed.

When the commotion settled down my sister asked me if I was really okay. "I'm not sure," I said. "My arm hurts a little. I'll probably be okay in the morning." She drifted off to sleep and I lay there filled with shame. My arm throbbed and I never closed my eyes the rest of the night.

As daybreak approached I saw my navy blue school uniform hanging on the hook where my mother left it for me with a freshly pressed uniform blouse. I knew I would never put it on that day. When I saw daylight I woke my sister and asked her to go get Mom for me.

My mother arrived and sat down on the bed next to me and the tears I had held in all night long now flowed freely. "I don't think I can move my arm," I said, between sniffles.

"Why didn't you tell me last night?" She said smoothing my long brown hair away from my eyes.

"Because… I'm so ashamed." By now I was sobbing.

Mom didn't drive and Daddy had long since left for work. So, after she dressed me we trudged three blocks to the bus stop. The bus was crowded with people going to work. She stood next to me with her arm around my shoulder to steady me as best she could as the bus rumbled down the street.

When we arrived in the Emergency Room I was whisked off to the X-Ray Department. As we waited together for the X-ray results she put her arm around me and assured me that everything would be okay. The ice pack the nurse gave me kept sliding off my arm but my mother held it in place and spoke softly to calm me down.

When all was said and done, my wrist was fractured. A plaster cast was applied from my knuckles clear up over my elbow. What a day!

On the way home from the hospital we got off the bus two stops early and went into the "Five and Ten" where there was a lunch counter. The butter pecan ice cream they served was top notch and we ordered two cones. Somewhere between licks I summoned the courage to ask why I didn't get in trouble for sleeping in the top bunk. Mom said, "You didn't need any lecture from me. Your conscience took care of that. What you needed was someone's hand to hold, someone's shoulder to cry on, and someone to buy you an ice cream cone when the whole thing was behind you."

We walked home from the "Five and Ten" store nice and slow so I could collect sympathy galore from anyone who spotted my arm in a plaster cast, resting in a brand new white cotton sling.

I remember that special day with my mom when it is on the tip of my tongue to say, "I told you so" to someone already suffering the consequences of a poor choice. I think twice and then suggest we go get an ice cream cone.

*Annmarie B. Tait resides in Conshohocken, PA with her husband Joe and Sammy the "Wonder Yorkie." In addition to writing stories about her large Irish Catholic family and the memories they made, Annmarie also enjoys singing and recording Irish and American Folk Songs. Annmarie has stories published in several* Chicken Soup for the Soul *volumes including:* Bride's Soul, Mother and Daughter's Soul, Father and Daughter's Soul, Celebrating Moms, Living the Catholic Faith, *and* Teens Talk Middle School *You may contact Annmarie at: irishbloom@aol.com.*

---

# An Education
## Laura Tamayo

*A grandmother's lesson in setting one's limits*

Across the street from my grandmother's house there was a family with two daughters and a white curly puff-of-a-dog named Mimoso. Despite the scar he accidentally left on my left hand, the dog was actually very sweet – unlike the younger of the two girls, and yet, she was the one I always played with.

Her name was Marcia and she was three years older than me. She had long black hair past her waist that I envied. My family kept my hair in a neat cut, no longer than shoulder length and in layers that made my curls look like choppy ocean waves. Cute, until Marcia pointed out that girls were supposed to have long hair.

Marcia was allowed to play outside as much as she wanted. I had to be watched over and couldn't go more than two houses over on either side of my house. Marcia could go in and out of everyone's house. I could lose all outdoor privileges if I even thought to try. Back then those protective measures simply felt like the unfairness of the universe.

Marcia made fun of me when I didn't know something, but always included me in her circle. Marcia half ignored me when we were at her house, but always invited me to come and play. I was often the butt of Marcia's jokes, but as long as I was with her, the other kids wanted to hang out with me.

My grandmother would often get upset at me for begging to be allowed to play with Marcia. The girl's self-centered, un-empathetic nature was on grandma's list of worst human traits. "She makes you cry and then two days later, knocks on the door and you want to go play with her. Where's your pride?"

I was eight. I was still trying to figure out what pride even meant. I was proud of my white-boot roller skates with yellow wheels and stoppers. What did that have to do with the neighbor? Plus, I was the new kid on the block living with grandparents in a sea of nuclear families, going to a different school than everyone else. My brother and sister (my natural playmates) were far. And the uncle that still lived at home was in college.

Wasn't it clear why I played with the eleven-year-old girl who knew the entire block?

"She likes me… and she's sorry. Aren't we supposed to forgive?" I half believed my little girl words, and half knew they were no more than a weak defense; I was eight, not dumb. But no way I was losing a neighbor playmate – my school friends and cousins lived too far. How else would I be included in tag or superhero pretend marathons?

And this I remember. Well, maybe not the exact words, but the exact meaning. My grandmother made two cups of chamomile tea and told me stories from her childhood, from her youth, from her adulthood. We sat at the kitchen table and had laughs sprinkled with serious moments of intense retelling. Grandma was a fabulous storyteller. She practically relived every moment as she told it. I was captivated, if confused at times.

She used mysterious words like dignity and respect. She spoke of boundaries and a person's right to be. When the stories wound down, she stood, placed both our cups in the sink and pulled me to her. I stood with my arms around her waist looking up at her smiling face. She always smelled so sweet and looked at me like she could see straight past my skin and bones, and into my heart. Brushing my hair out of my face, she spoke.

"Forgiveness isn't permission. People have no idea how to treat someone they don't know. They learn.

"From the way we dress, to the way we speak and the limits we set, our entire way of being is an education for everyone else. Dignity is being who you are, limits and all. And respect is understanding other people's dignity – their way of being. If it fits with yours, then play. If it doesn't, then maybe just wave from afar."

Best cup of tea of my life.

---

## Mother in Despair
### Dee Ann Horvath

Climbing out of my big bed
The house dark and dead
Making my way down winding stairs
Unafraid and having no cares
Drawn to the moonlight
And the shine of her hair
In awe of the sight of her sitting there
In front of the window
All alone in a big chair
She is beautiful but sad
So full of despair
The smoke from her cigarette
Causing a heavenly haze
A being not of this earth
An angel is what I think she's worth
She is my whole world
A single tear runs down her cheek
This is not the time for hide and seek
She turns and sees me standing there
I climb up with her in the wing-backed chair

Thinking mommy what are you doing here
So late at night and all alone?
But I was silent and shared her despair
My presence seeming to comfort her
Our love for each other so deep and pure
Something happened that night long ago
It has stayed with me through all the years
And now I know
That our moment together that we both shared
Has helped me get through all my tears
She is part of me now
And when I need to know how
I will climb back up into that wing-backed chair
Feel her warm body and smell her sweet hair
And together we will conquer despair

---

# My Mother Cyber-Dates
## Sharon Skinner

She is strong, able to appear emotionless,
Ready to move on, but my mother hurts.
Her heart crumbles even as she sits before the computer
sending email to a man she has never met.
She made a date with one last month,
called it a $CO_2$ date,
"no sparks," she says laughing into the phone.

In my youth, her strength seemed hard and
I never realized how deeply I cut her,
how much blood was shed from her heart,
a heart I thought was
puncture-proof.

Now, we share our painful moments,
commiserate over betrayals,
and thank one another for "being there."

The distance that once separated us
has become a geographical nuisance.
The once insurmountable differences,
a no-longer-hurdle we step over hand-in-hand,
like a cracked sidewalk we avoid in
superstitious reverence and fear.

And I, now a mother of step-children,
find that I have a hard strength to me,
a strength I use to cover up the pain of separation,
the distance I use as a shield
to allay the anxiety of departure and
the sadness of good-byes.

I have raised the banner of stern discipline
to slay the beast of closeness and
avoid reliving the feelings of an outsider
by remaining outside the sphere of emotion.

But when the cuts come, my heart will bleed,
my heart that has never been puncture-proof.
And I will call my mother, and we will share our pain,
commiserate over betrayals,
thank each other for "being there,"
and ultimately
laugh into the phone.

# Chapter 6

# PRACTICAL SKILLS:

## Handling the mundane necessities

# Mum's Legacy: A True Tale
## Lyn McConchie

*"Many a mickle makes a muckle."*

My father died when I was three and a half and my mother died a month after my ninth birthday. She left me money – which was promptly taken by my guardians. It had been intended to send me to university, they used it for other things and I left school at fifteen to get a job – after which they took all my money until I could legally flee their house.

Mum was a warm, loving woman of great charity and limited imagination and, while a good Baptist, she lived by a set of adages in her ordinary life. These were said over and over so that even after she died I never forgot them. The truth is that for years I thought them silly, trite, and banal. The sort of thing older women said but that had little or no relevance really. I was in my thirties before I started to see the very real sense in them.

I'd been crippled in an accident in 1977, retired from the 9-5 rat race, purchased a small farm, and was now writing. I was living on a small disability pension, didn't have a lot of money and I found that at times I was muttering one or another of mum's sayings. Often, I wanted to donate to local charities too, but couldn't afford it. But by that time her adage, "waste not, want not," was making sense from an ecological as well as a financial point of view. On that principal I started recycling many things from around the farm and from elsewhere.

Yes, I accept plastic bags for my groceries, but any that are plain, without marketing logos, go to our local arts and crafts shop for reuse. (The bubble-wrap I receive, that arrives wrapped around posted books, goes to the same destination.) The marked plastic shopping bags become containers for used kitty litter – and since in New Zealand such bags are treated to break down in a few months anyway, both bags and their contents when dumped down my farm's offal-hole, biodegrade quite nicely. Any surplus bags are donated to our local annual fair in November where the stalls can always use them.

Mum was particularly good in not wasting clothing. She was skilled with her needle and clothing could be made over from larger to smaller, using all the best bits of material. I'm hopeless at sewing, but I crochet quite well. I follow suit in that I buy, or am often given unwanted hand-knitted items which I unravel and crochet into five foot square rugs – or larger – which become gifts for friends, presents to overseas acquaintances who stay regularly with me, or donations to our local charities. (Two old folks' homes, our police station, fire brigade, and health clinic all appreciate my rugs.) And now and again one sells.

Mum's adage of "waste not, want not," covers the berry-fruit in my cat-park. (A 1,000 square foot enclosure in which, Thunder my Ocicat, can safely roam – while keeping the birds off the berry-fruit.) In planting those berry bushes I simply followed my mother's adage, that "there's nothing like a garden."

I'm crippled and can't spend too much time on my feet digging a proper vegetable garden or preserving fruit, but fruit on low bushes can be picked from a sitting position. The raspberries are then swapped with a friend who turns them into pots of raspberry jam and returns me one third of the pots. I have sufficient jam for the year – and the surplus goes to local charities and friends.

The red currant bushes bear solidly each summer and I pick as much as thirty to forty pounds each year. These go to our local Cancer Support group. They turn them into redcurrant jelly; some jars being sold on their annual stall and others given out at their Christmas party. I enjoy entering competitions too, and often win small items. The surplus items from that enterprise go into a box, which also goes to the Cancer Support Christmas party each early December. (That latter based on another saying of my mother's – that if you have good fortune "you spend a bit, save a bit, and give a bit away.)

Other vegetables appear from my own garden – in a way. I provide the land, the tools, and the seedlings or seeds. A young, local couple who have no land of their own do the planting, the weeding and watering, and the general care. We split the results – which provides my own vegetables, along with gifts to friends and more donations to charity.

Something that also applies well was mum's saying that "many a mickle makes a muckle." No, I have no idea what a mickle or a muckle are – and I suspect that she didn't either – but the sense of the adage is quite clear.

Save small items and in time they'll add up to something worth more. My version of that is to save "points" in a system that we have here covering a large number of chain stores, services, and trades-people. Once a year I consider my accumulation of points and find that I can "buy" items from that.

Saving the points costs me nothing; I'd shop at the stores anyway. All it takes is having the card in my purse and presenting it along with my payment. The items again tend to end up split between things I want, gifts for friends, and donations. All items free.

And finally, there was mum's greatest saying. One that has kept me out of trouble for most of my life – and the one time when, in my twenties I ignored it I found out why it's something to live by. She used to listen to gossip about those foolish enough to live beyond their means and shake her head.

"Ah, she would say, her face serious. " If you can't pay cash for it, you can't afford it!"

She didn't mean a house, she accepted that for a house you might have to go into debt. If she was still alive I think she might also accept that for many people, particularly those who live some distance from their employment, a car you own may be cheaper than public transport, even if you do share ownership of the car with a bank or finance company. But for everything else that you might want, the adage applied.

The real revelation of the truth in this saying came for me when I wanted a new television just after I bought my farm. My own television was old, and, I feared, on its last legs. It was as if my mother's voice spoke to me while I browsed down the line of new – and expensive – televisions in the shop. I'd spent all my cash on the farm, the livestock, moving in, and other essentials. I looked wistfully at the bright new items, hesitated, and asked how much the interest would be on a hire purchase and over what period.

I left and once at home I sat back to work out what a new TV would cost based on interest rates and how much I could afford each week or month. I was startled to discover that in effect I would be paying for two televisions. I wavered, reluctant to pay that much and, my mother's adage kept repeating itself. A month later our annual fair was on and while there I found a television amongst the bric-a-brac for sale. It was secondhand, but a decent size, in good condition, and only $50. I had that in cash so I bought it, and the previous owner who went past my place dropped it off for me.

I put a container on the mantelpiece and started putting small amounts of cash in that. I added some of the payments received for small pieces of writing, a dozen eggs sold now and again, (yes, I have free-range geese, hens and bantams,) and cash for the occasional crocheted rug that someone wanted to buy.

After two years when the secondhand TV was starting to look a little weary I checked the container and I had sufficient cash in that to buy a new television. Not only that, but in a way it was half-price since I wouldn't be paying all that interest. In fact it was cheaper still, since with cash in my hand I could bargain the price down about ten percent – and did.

The TV was delivered free, installed, plugged in and I sat and contemplated it. In my mind mum's voice echoed. For much of my life I'd thought that her adages were the narrow-minded parroting of convention. I was realizing that they could be that, yes, but they could also be the distilled wisdom of women down the ages. Sayings based on the hard-learned experience of women who had little money.

For the past twenty years I've taken mum's sayings to heart. My farm is freehold, I have no credit cards, I owe nothing to anyone, and using her other adages as a guide, I manage to give reasonable donations to charity and gifts to friends where I wish. However I watch sadly as successive generations do as I did earlier, and ignore wise advice as the babbling of the elderly.

Recently I wished to buy an item shown in a Television advertisement. I rang and was told that I needed a credit card. I pointed out that they could send me an invoice, I'd pay by check, and they could send me the item after that – and in fact under our laws, they had to. I could not be penalized because I don't use credit cards. The girl on the phone was exasperated.

"Don't you HAVE a credit card?"

"No, I don't believe in them."

"Why not?"

"Well, my mother used to say, 'if you can't pay cash you can't afford it.' "

"Oh," she said dismissively. "That's so old-fashioned. Well, we'll send an invoice."

I put the phone down. She's right, it IS old-fashioned. My mother was born in 1906. I was born in 1946. But increasingly in the current recession I see people having their cars repossessed because the hire-purchase interest went up. Furniture, refrigerators, washing machines, dishwashers, plasma TVs, DVD players, all being taken away again because they can't keep up the payments – amounts that the stores assured them would be unnoticeable and easily paid.

And I'm grateful for the real legacy that my mother left me. Not the cash that was so easily diverted to other paths, but the wisdom distilled from the hard-learned experience of the women in her generation and those gone before – trite or not. Use it up, make it do, waste not, want not, many a mickle makes a muckle, and if you can't pay cash you can't afford it.

I'm sorry for some of those younger ones who dig themselves deeper and deeper into debt buying brand new items they must have now, and end up by losing all they have without ever quite understanding how that happened to them. I live on a disability pension and they think I'm poor, I'm not, in fact, financially I live quite comfortably – and I have mum's legacy.

I owe nothing to anyone because all that I own or have is mine alone. So in the end I'm richer than they are in another way too – I live on my small farm without stress or the fear of missing a payment to someone, and nothing can be taken from me by angry creditors appearing on my doorstep. I inherited a great and lasting legacy. Thanks mum!

*Lyn McConchie started writing professionally twenty years ago. Since then she has seen some 250 of her short stories appear and sold twenty-four books in several genres – two of the latest appearing this year from Cyberwizard Productions* (South of Rio Chama *and* Summer of Dreaming), *one from Daverana Enterprises* (Vestiges of Flames), *and another from TOR* (The Questing Road) *in 2010. She owns and runs a small farm breeding black and coloured sheep, and sharing the 19th century farmhouse with Thunder, her Ocicat, and 7,000 books.*

---

# In Training
## Tara Masih

*Women should not be reliant on men.*

My mother didn't lecture or preach, she generally left that to my father. But that day, she had something to say. It was sometime in the 70s. The exact year, I can't remember. All I recall is that my mother finally had her own car to escape the house with when her husband was at work, but we still had black-and-white television and Geraldine Ferraro was still more than a few years away from being the Democratic nominee for vice president.

My mother called to me from the base of the stairs to the attic, which was my escape. I hid away from the daily rips and tears that my parents made in each other with their words. With a dull headache, I climbed down to see what she wanted.

"It's time I showed you how to wire a lamp."

She was holding one, a converted kerosene wall lamp she'd purchased at a yard sale. "Every woman should know how to wire a lamp. It's very easy."

I followed her down to our basement — not a place I liked to step into. It was moldy, dusty, cobwebby. The mice made nests in our ice skates and Christmas stockings every year. But my mother was in that mood; if you broke it, she could crumble. I stood with my arms folded, and watched.

"Women should not be reliant on men. What happens if your marriage breaks up? Or if your husband dies? That happened to Joan, you know. It's why she ended up dead herself. She couldn't make sense of the world anymore, so she just left it."

My mother's best friend. After her husband died, she developed breast cancer, went to bed and refused treatment. No one could convince her to live.

"Women know how to take simple household things and turn them into tools. See these manicure scissors? I'm cutting the cord just so . . . to expose the copper wire. See, who needs wire cutters? Now I wrap the wire around these two screws . . . and put the cap back on. You can buy all of this — the cord, the plug, the socket — at the hardware store. Don't be afraid to go in there. They may look at you a little funny, but you stand your ground. You have every right to be in there, and ask any questions you need to ask. I go to Mack's Hardware on Main Street — he's used to me now. . . . OK, see how you insert the other end into the plug? Then you just slip the cover over."

I am now kneeling beside her, watching her hands manipulate the wire and brown plastic. It's not a sight I'm used to being privy to — I have seen her hands work the soil, the suds, the covers, the hair, but not this. Not the materials of plumbers and electricians and inventors.

The bulb springs to life. I can't help but be impressed by this tiny technical birth.

"Now you know something many men don't even know. Isn't it easy? Remember that — women can do almost anything men can. In their own way, of course."

*Tara L. Masih has published fiction, poetry, and essays in numerous anthologies and literary magazines, and her essays have been read on NPR. Two limited edition illustrated chapbooks featuring her flash fiction have been published by The Feral Press (Oyster Bay, NY: 2006). Awards for her work include first place in* The Ledge Magazine's *fiction contest and a Pushcart Prize and Best of the Web nomination. She judges the intercultural essay prize for the annual Soul-Making Literary Contest, and is editor of* The Rose Metal Press Field Guide to Writing

Flash Fiction, *due out from Rose Metal Press in 2009.*
*www.taramasih.com*

---

## One Man's Trash is My Mother's Treasure
### Stephanie Holbrook

*Creative recycling of cast-offs*

"Here she comes. . .and she's carrying a Big Wheel," my brother said as he peered out the curtains of our living room window to observe my mother's latest treasure. "Oh God, not again. I wonder how many neighbors saw her this time?" I mumbled to myself.

In the beginning, my mother would take out under cover of night to look through the neighbor's trash. "I'm going for a walk," she'd say nonchalantly. My two brothers and I knew what she was up to, but pretended we didn't. "OK, see you later," we'd reply. Then we'd close the curtains and hang our heads in shame. "Mom's digging through trash again."

My mother has always been frugal. She's a coupon-clipping, free-gift-with-purchase, buy-one/get-one, but-it's-really-better-if-you-can-get-it-free-out-of-the-trash kind of mom. My brothers and I were always wondering what she might bring home next, a doll that wets and cries, a GI Joe, a coonskin Daniel Boone cap, a refrigerator, a cuckoo clock? We never knew exactly where these things came from and we never asked. We wished to remain innocent as to which neighbor was last plundered – that way we wouldn't have to avoid them.

My mother's favorite phrases are: "I can't believe someone threw this out. It looks like it's brand new" or "Look at this dress, it still has the price tag on it." Somehow it didn't seem quite as embarrassing if something still had the price tag because maybe the person who previously owned the item might not notice you wearing it when you passed them on the street. It wouldn't be like, "Hey, is that my favorite Hawaiian luau shirt you're wearing? I thought I threw that out last month." What could one reply except, "Thanks for breaking it in for me."

My mother's love of garbage has always been a double-edged sword. While we found it embarrassing, my brothers and I did profit from it. The Big Wheel, for example was a huge hit with all of us. She also brought home piles of clothes that she would wash and then we'd try them on to see if anything fit. If not, she'd put them in a bag for the Kidney Fund so someone else could profit from her refuse finds. Even now, I have a clock on my mantle that was from someone's garbage.

My dad wasn't as appalled as my brothers and I were at my mother's love for dumpster diving. He bragged to us about my mother's talent for bringing home other people's cast-off's.

"Did you see that table your mother brought home yesterday? Sure it was missing a leg but I think I can fix it with the chair legs she found last week." I would stare at him in horror as I said, "I've got to go finish my homework" and head for my bedroom where I would daydream about having brand new clothes and underwear.

My mother was like an out of control MacGyver. "We can use this fabric and Velcro to make a skirt for your bathroom sink. That way you'll have more storage space in the bathroom."

"How would you like me to make you a traditional Indian headdress with these feathers I removed from inside a worn out pillow?" My first studio apartment was decorated with my mother's "design for less than a dime" creativity. She found a table and three chairs in someone's front yard, brought them home and we recovered the chairs. Then she brought the entire dining set to my apartment. She pushed one side of the table up against the wall so it would be less noticeable that one of the chairs was missing. She got a comforter and pillow shams from her sister so I could make the utmost use of my twin bed for sleeping and a couch. Over several months' time she was able to amass an entire set of dishes for me, including serving pieces, from a grocery store.

My mother is almost magical, with powers like a modern-day Jesus, giving life to toys from the depths of trash heaps. "Who could throw out this cute little doll?" my mother asked in all seriousness.

"Mother, it has no head."

"Yes it does, it's right here in my pocket, look."

And she retrieved a doll head with one eye all milky, like the victim of a bad case of cataracts. "I'm sure your father can repair the doll if he puts some string through here and runs it up into the head. It will be as good as new."

"Except it's blind in one eye."

"Well, it can use the good eye to see out of."

Eventually my dad was sucked into the treasure find as well, but he could never compete in the same league with my mother. Once he brought me a spindle from a staircase that had been painted maroon and had a square metal plate nailed to the top of it. "I thought you could use it for an ashtray," he said. It was touching – the thought of my parents out for a stroll spying a piece of garbage that made them think of my brothers or me. It reaffirmed my feeling that they really did love us.

We had a cat, Quincy, who joined my mother in the grazing for garbage craze. After roaming the neighborhood, he came streaking across our front lawn with something hanging from his mouth. He ran to the front step and laid it down howling for us to come see what he had risked life and limb to bring us: a pair of little girl's pink panties. I surely hope he found those in someone's garbage.

"Good kitty," my mother said as she patted him on the head. "Some day you'll follow in my footsteps." Then she murmured, "Dear Lord, if I can't teach my children the thrill of the swill hunt, thank you for allowing me to teach my cat." And with that she was off to scrub grime from a Barbie doll that someone had given a purple Mohawk.

---

# Always Prepared
## Christy Lowman

*You never know when nature may catch you off guard.*

"My mother taught me better than this," I told myself as I paced back and forth between my bare cupboard and kitchen window.

It was my first autumn living in Nebraska. We had just got married that August and moved to the Air Force base where my husband was stationed.

The budget was very tight because I was having a hard time finding a job. It seemed as though everyone was scared to hire someone who had just moved from out of state.

Since there was very little extra money, I had put off getting groceries. All we had was a jar of peanut butter, a jar of jelly, and a few spices. I had fixed the last of the coffee that morning.

Autumn had just begun and it was already pouring snow. The sky was dark gray and the wind was frigid as it whistled through the small apartment windows. With each hard gust of wind the lights flickered.

As I sipped on my coffee, I watched the swirls of steam rise out of my cup and thought back to my mother teaching me to always be prepared.

I remembered back to when I was ten years old. The only hurricane "Hugo" came ripping through our backyard. It wasn't even supposed to come to our way, but changed its course at the last minute.

Early that morning mom came in my room carrying a lit oil lamp to check on me.

"It's here," she said as a big gush of wind blew around the corner of the house. "Don't worry. Everything's going to be okay. I just wanted to let you know the power was out. Try to go back to sleep."

The room went dark as she scurried down the hall to check on my younger brother.

I tossed and turned listening to the wind and rain against my windows. It sounded like my room was going to be ripped off from the rest of the house and carried away.

As soon as daylight approached I got up and watched the trees as they tried to stand up against the mighty hurricane.

When it was over, we went outside to see the damage. Our house was still in good shape, except the roof had been robbed of its shingles on one side.

The forest surrounding our house looked like Paul Bunyan had cut rows of trees down with his mighty ax.

We were out of power and out of school for over two weeks, but we never went hungry. Mom worked hard. She kept the old wood stove piping hot and used it to cook our meals. Each meal was made from scratch, and was well planned out to each family member's tastes.

"Pay close attention. You need to know how to cook like this. There may come a time where you may have to do this for your family," she said while whisking gravy in the skillet on top of the wood stove.

She also had biscuits cooking on the inside shelf to go with the gravy.

"I always wondered what that shelf was for," I said as I watched mom in amazement.

Some of the best meals I've ever had came from that stove. The wood stove flavored the food quite nicely.

Mom had stored up so much food in the freezers that it was impossible to eat it all. We gave food to the neighbors, but still lost a lot while the power was out.

Despite the tight budget, Mom always made sure we had plenty of necessities set aside for emergencies.

"Get ready, so we can go to the store," my husband said bringing my train of thought back to the present. Thank goodness he was off that day. He had been stationed here two years already, working outside daily. As a result he had become relatively callous to the harsh Nebraska winters. He was also trained for emergency situations, which made me feel safe that he was there.

As soon as the snow slowed down we put on layers of clothes along with our boots and headed out. We walked just two blocks to the gas station; however it seemed more like a mile. Each step was like pulling yourself out of quick sand.

There were at least two feet of snow already on the ground. The texture was very different from what I was used to. It was fine and looked like white sand.

Once we reached the station we ordered subs for lunch and grabbed the last loaf of bread and gallon of milk to go with our peanut butter and jelly.

I decided from that moment on, every time I went to the grocery store I was going to make sure to buy a small amount extra to set aside just in case of bad weather or a power outage. This proved to be a good idea because that winter was the most snow I had ever seen in one season.

I've continued my routine to this day even though we have moved back home where it rarely snows. I keep a small stash all year long and add to it a little more before the hurricane season and winter months.

After all, nature is unpredictable. You never know when it may catch you off guard. At least next time when it does, I can rest assured that I will be prepared, like my Mom.

*Christy Lowman is a freelance writer from the foothills of the Great Smoky Mountains of North Carolina. Her work has been published in several anthology books. She is married to her high school sweetheart, with whom she has two wonderful sons.*

---

## My Mother, the New Age Pioneer
### Wanda Ryder

*After a life of hard work, a woman in her 70s builds her dream home.*

My mother, Norma, was born in 1904 in a log house on the Manitoba Prairies. When she died – nine decades later – she was living in a solar-heated house that she had designed and built with the help of her grandson.

As the eldest daughter in a family of eight, Norma's early years involved tending to her younger siblings. This commonly accepted role for females of the time, meant that her schooling ended after eight years. It also meant that she was accustomed to taking the lead and assuming authority over the family.

This probably came about from having parents who were less than supportive – an alcoholic father who died at a young age, and a mother who was happy to turn over the family responsibilities to someone else. In any case Norma's brothers and sisters weren't always happy with her "take charge" attitude and, even as adults, often resented her interference in their lives. (In time, her own children occasionally complained about the very same thing!)

This self-confident approach to life stood her in good stead in later years, when shortly after she married a farmer, the depression of the nineteen thirties devastated the country's economy. During those hard times she and my father, Mac, raised one child – me – and also fed and clothed many of her siblings as well as numerous nieces and nephews. How that was done defies explanation for they had little to share, but Norma was an excellent seamstress and constructed, altered or converted used clothing to fit those in need.

By the time the Second World War was upon us, the money situation had eased to some extent, although Norma and Mac were never rich. Also, by that time, two more children had been born to them. Still, as was the custom of rural wives, Norma assisted in much of the outdoor work such as milking the cows, and helping in the field when necessary. Until a tractor was acquired, this latter activity involved using horse power as a means to propel the various farming implements.

In a few years, a larger acreage was purchased and the family relocated to the bigger farm a short distance away. Others might have considered this an "upwardly mobile" move, but Norma grieved over the abandonment of the little house she had carefully and lovingly turned into an attractive and comfortable home. The exchange – a large, drafty house much in need of repairs and updating – was not a joyful prospect, but she approached the job with a will.

Some of the renovations included the building of new kitchen cupboards – a job Norma undertook herself. By this time, I was going to a high school in a nearby town, and no longer at home to help with my brother and sister – ages four and three respectively. A small woman with abundant energy, she managed to hone her woodworking and furniture-refinishing skills while also attending to household tasks and outdoor chores.

Carpentry became one of her passions, and she was of the opinion that it was a more interesting and rewarding calling than housework. Also more fun. The "new" house improved with the passage of time, and in 1948, Rural Electrification brought (besides good lighting) the possibility of power tools!

In 1955, she helped my father install waterworks and a new furnace. These were the last big projects he was able to undertake, for in the late summer of 1956, he was diagnosed with a brain tumor and died that November. During his illness, crops ripened and harvesting had to be done. This was a frantic time for all of us, since Norma had only minimal knowledge of the farm's finances, and no experience in actually running a farming business.

That help came from relatives and neighbors is a testament to the spirit of community that existed in the area. The help might not have been offered so willingly, though, had Norma not shown the determination to learn how to do things herself. And there was much to learn. At the age of fifty-two, she became the owner/manager of the operation.

I was married with children of my own by then, and in no position to render much in the way of physical help or finances. However, a nephew who lived nearby kindly offered valuable assistance and farming advice. A quick learner, she was able to carry on capably by herself for the next few years. Then, when my brother finished school and showed an interest in farming, they worked together.

Now, for the first time in her life, Norma felt free to get involved in other activities which included joining the local Toastmistress Club and taking a position on the church board. She also traveled to many parts of Canada and the U.S.

Still, those activities didn't quite fill the need she had for creating, and when the amalgamation of local schools left the neighboring school house empty, she arranged to buy it. The grounds surrounding the building came with it, of course, and were in dire need of attention. One small chokecherry bush was the only sign of life on the premises – a condition she corrected by contacting the Prairie Farm Rehabilitation Association located at Indianhead in Saskatchewan. Through them she acquired, and began planting, trees. Hundreds and hundreds of trees appeared, not only on the school grounds, but on her farm across the road. Norma planted them all.

In between the tree-planting binges, she worked on the school with the objective of turning it into a house – a revenue-bearing property. During this project, she added to her carpentry skills by doing much of the re-wiring and plumbing herself. This was partly because the trades people Norma hired were not as efficient nor as speedy as she wished – not nearly as devoted to the project as she was. They were possibly also discouraged by her "I'm sure I can do it better than you" attitude.

Her explanation involving one long-suffering assistant was, "He lacked the necessary qualities. He was a nice enough fellow, but he could spend hours contemplating a screw nail while I got on with the job myself. I had to let him go." Eventually, in spite of little professional involvement, the old school was transformed into a quite respectable residence and there was no problem in finding renters.

One of Norma's characteristics was in keeping her long-range plans concealed under her hard hat, therefore almost none of us knew that her next effort was in the planning stages. None, except her eldest grandson who was, himself, interested in both building, and the new concept of solar energy which he had already used to some extent while renovating an aging house. The plot came to light, of course, when she and Danny became preoccupied with acquiring suitable designs – a difficult task when no one, it seemed, (including the government) was interested in conservation. Information was hard to find.

In the end, they adapted such ideas as seemed workable, and construction began. It began in an area that she had carefully mapped at the outset of her tree-planting operations, although it wasn't a scheme known to any one else at the time. The front of the house was to face south, of course, and by this time the trees were beginning to provide good wind-breaks to the north and east. The house was to be built on a slab, with air-to-rock heating being the design of choice. Construction began in the summer of 1978 when Norma was seventy-four years old. It got underway with a bed of crushed rock to be used for heat storage. This job was done manually with Norma doing much of the work. After a slab of concrete was poured over the heat-storage bed, erection of the frame began, and Norma assisted every step of the way – shingling the roof, for example.

According to the plan, the south-facing top portion of the house, would take advantage of the low winter sun, and was to be totally glazed. Then, through the glazing, heat collected from the sun would be transferred by means of a fan to the bed of crushed rock and distributed evenly throughout the building. The installation of electric heaters as auxiliary for extremely cold or cloudy weather was the final task, but the efficiency of the project was yet to be determined.

In August of 1979 Norma moved into her dream home and completed the decorating and finishing touches. The design, as well as the heavy-duty insulation kept the house cool in the August heat, but it wasn't until the winter of 1980 that the real test of the system was known. It worked like a charm. "I probably have the most comfortable and cheaply heated home of anyone I know," she said proudly.

With that large project finished, Norma turned her talents to willow furniture construction as well as the more lady-like hobby of quilt-making. Meantime, Danny bought a sailboat and sailed from California to Hawaii. Of his grandmother, he later said, "I often thought of her when the going got rough."

Norma lived happily in her solar-heated house until three days before she died at age ninety. But her legacy lives on – not in what she said, for she kept her preaching to a minimum – not even in her houses, quilts and furniture. It will live on in those of us who witnessed the determination and strength of character that defined her life. She had the will to push herself to the limit, and the courage and self-confidence to prove herself worthy of the title, New Age Pioneer.

*Wanda Ryder, who lives with her husband in Portage la Prairie, Manitoba, is the author of several books. A social history,* Ghost Towns of Manitoba, *which was coauthored with Helen Mulligan, may be purchased from Great Plains Publications of Winnipeg, Manitoba. Wanda's other books – a short story collection,* From a Distance; *an adventure tale,* Prairie Sailor; *and a novel,* Free to Go, *may be obtained by contacting her at: gnwryder@mts.net.*

*She has also written articles as well as plays for stage, radio, and television.*

# Christmas on Fifty Bucks
## Virginia Settle

*Grandmother guides a mother through a lean Christmas*

One night in late November of 1980, as my husband and I sat together in the dining room, the little ones bathed and sleeping, the teens doing homework upstairs, I brought up the subject of gift-giving. He stood, dug into his back pocket and handed me fifty dollars.

"It's all we have for Christmas," he said.

I heard winter slamming against the shutters as I stared up at him. In that moment, I knew he'd been waiting for the right time to let me know, but there was no right time – in fact, time was running out.

The next day, I struggled with the particulars: Christmas Eve gathering, tree, decorations, window ornaments, gifts for my husband, children, my mother, sisters and brothers, nephews and nieces. I'd saved some wrapping from last year, but would need scotch tape, ribbon and name tags. My notations covered three pages. Dinner – the real family celebration, where we gathered to pray, to be thankful, and to light the last candle of Advent now carried a growing sense of sadness for me.

Somehow, the days passed, but the need to address this problem did not. Start by cleaning the house, I told myself, and clear an area for the tree. That won't cost me anything and will serve to group my galloping thoughts.

As I picked up an old dust cloth, I ran it over the coffee table, the heart-shaped candy dish, and – the family Bible. In moving the old heirloom, a time-aged piece of paper slipped to the floor. Grandma Settle's 1935 Christmas list. Did it parallel my own, almost unachievable list? I couldn't remember.

I unfolded the crumpled page and read the shaky longhand: an apron, rag doll, socks, a scarf, mittens, a braided rug, hats. All items Grandma had made herself. There were no designated sites for bargain-basement shopping sprees clipped from local newspapers, no coupons attached. Written on a long strip of paper which had been folded and put away, it was the only Christmas reminder between those sacred pages.

As I fingered her list, tattered edges flaking, the smell of lavender memories warmed my whole being. Today's cold economics melted under visions of her hands gently smoothing my hair, patting my cheeks. "If you did it, Grandma, you know I can," I whispered. From that moment, her essence preceded my every step, grooming the attitude I would share with my children.

Saturday, as they dressed for a morning in the new-fallen snow, I said, "I have a secret I will share with you on Christmas morning." Their faces brightened.

"Tell us now, tell us now!" Gigi, my second youngest, exclaimed impatiently.

"Oh! Then it wouldn't be a secret anymore," I said, "but until then, you can all do something special for the holidays."

They hesitated at the door. "What can we do?" Narda, the oldest, asked.

"Wouldn't it be great for Mom and Dad," I explained, "to have your help – preparing for Christmas Day? Perhaps we can make our gifts and decorations this year. Why don't you think about it and give us some ideas at dinner, and I'll see what we have to work with while you're out shoveling? Tonight, we'll draw names from the Santa box." This spur-of-the-moment disclosure was a manifestation from above, I thought, because I had no idea what a "Santa box" was.

Cleaning the house had produced a variety of usable leftovers: construction paper, two rolls of scotch tape, tubes of glitter from Halloween, some satin ribbon from the girls' Easter hats and thread. I also had several balls of mismatched yarn, and enough new skeins to knit a pair of socks for my husband. The sewing room had lots of odds and ends – material I'd saved for no reason – bits and pieces from superfluous times. These cards we've received over the years will make beautiful decorations, I told myself. Now, patting my own back, I ceded everything I could find over to creating a new Christmas design.

I imagined Grandma's foot pedaling the old Singer machine – sewing aprons and hats – until, suddenly, I was overcome with shame. I flushed at the site of the new Domestic – a recent, lavish model – with all its design attachments. I pondered the insidious influence of commercialism, how it had spoiled me. I hope it isn't too late to set a better example for our children, I thought. With this prayer in my heart,

I began to crochet bowling vests for each child, one for myself, and one for my husband. If the colors don't match, the patterns will – with stars in the centers, front and back! I'll work on the socks another day, I reasoned. After all, they couldn't be very hard to make.

Although I always look forward to the scent of pine each season, this year, I had my husband take an old, artificial tree down from the attic. We balanced it over a red table cloth. Unsealing the stored tree lights, we sang Joy to the World as they lie across the living room floor, a string of blinking stars. I envisioned the presents under the tree – then, the socks I was attempting to knit. They might not be ready for Christmas, I thought, if I don't spend more time on them.

Projects seemed to come alive as ornaments blossomed under the children's creative touch. The kids tried hard to be secretive while collaborating on cards for myself and their Dad, but the younger ones gave this effort away with their giggling. Pleased in their happiness, I started to comprehend the greater aspects of attitude and how much it affects our offspring. Some part of my soul has been sleeping, I reflected, pushed aside in the business of everyday living.

Planning dinner was as easy as I wanted to make it, and I used the rest of the money for vegetables, dry beans, rice and eggs. Eggs were inexpensive, and we always had plenty of milk. These, and a bit of sugar with vanilla flavoring were all I needed for festive drinks, I mused.

On Christmas Eve, we raised our glasses – filled with homemade eggnog – to toast the Little One born so many years ago, to wish each other happiness and to salute the passing year. As each child hung mightily-crafted ornaments, they gaped at presents wrapped in newspaper comics under the tree. Instead of tags, I'd glued and glittered until all six names bounced off the shimmering tree lights.

Later, I reflected, I'd exchange gifts with my husband, presenting him with one hand-knitted sock. And tomorrow, I'd share the secret inspiration of Grandma Settle's Christmas list with our children.

But for now, I savored the moment and all that had brought me to it. With the children closer to me, my husband at my side, and the mismatched gifts and make-shift decorations to admire, I again sensed the warmth of my find falling from the family Bible only a few weeks ago.

"I knew I could do it – thank you, Grandma," I whispered.

*Born in Springfield, Massachusetts in 1940,* **Virginia Watson,** *née V L Settle, returned to that city in 1962. In 1995, she began studies at Springfield Technical Community College, was enrolled in the Honors Program, named to the Dean's List, and inducted into Phi Theta Kappa. In 1998, V L was awarded a summer C.C.C. residence at Smith College in Northampton, where she began her first book of poetry,* TWILIGHT, *publishing that same year using the $1000 First Place Winner's check for "Five Mile Pond." In 2002, she began a second book of poetry,* GREEN MORNING REFLECTIONS.

---

## Mincey Stew
### B. Lynch Black

It took me years to get it right,
the texture of the peppery stew;
the simple, hearty, perfect recipe
I'd watched my mother make
for all my childhood days.

Failures and almost-rights
at every turn and temperature
dogged my preparation of it,
driving me from the stove
to frustrated phone calls.

What essential element
could I have forgotten?
I'd ask my mother,
angry and bewildered
with my watery results.

She doled out ingredients
and advice, one call at a time.
Did you chop the onions fine?
Is the meat browned properly?
The carrots cooked through?

Then, one day, a casual call.
in which we talked of other things
and I mentioned my intent
to try again.  She said,
Be sure to add the flour.

Ah, the flour!  That simple touch
hardly noticed but essential
– like my mother's love –
that thickens the meal
binding it all together.

The finishing touch
that made my mother's recipe
and mine one and the same.
Perfect.  Our shared pleasure,
our joined past and future.

Now when I make mincey stew,
the last ingredient I add
is my own character;
a preference for more pepper,
brown bread instead of white.

I'm glad my mother stretched it out,
giving me one of detail at a time
connecting our lives and stoves
until the day the stew was completely
– yet, not exactly – like hers.

Perfect.  Food of the Gods.

# Menus for a Real Field Day
**Lynn Veach Sadler**


She had "organizational skills"
before they were in for men,
much less "us."

Starting at 4:30, she cooked
a full breakfast for our family—
"scratch" biscuits included—
and then the barn-day/generic
*field-day* "dinner" before leaving for
the field or tobacco barn herself.

She returned home a bit before noon
to see it served,
cleaned up afterwards
(no paper plates),
then went back to the field.

The family did eat leftovers
for "supper," but they were warm.
Her food was largely
home-canned, shelled, peeled,
laboriously attended.

I learned my organizational skills
from Mother,
parlayed them into
a college presidency.

Call me Doubting Thomas[ine]:

I don't believe perspicacity
first gave computers "menus."
Menus are from others
like my mother—
the purest icons.

Chapter 7

# ASSORTED LESSONS:

## Catch-all stories

# Samurai Mother
## L. Michael Black

*...to have no doubt; to know no fear; to live with honor*

A story dedicated to Single Female Heads-of-Households, the true heroes of this age, and My Mother, my Hero.

Had anyone told me twenty years ago that we choose our parents I would have called that person insane. Had they included talk about 'karma' in the discussion to explain parental choices, I would have called 911, for certain. Today, I'm very open to the possibility that such 'mystic' phenomena might be more real than not. I'm a believer because of the way my Mother, who with the spirit of a Samurai, raised me and my brother. My Mom was a born and bred Baptist with strong Jewish influences in her life. However, from a source beyond anything I could comprehend, she brought forward into the Twentieth Century, the unconquerable spirit of Miyamoto Musashi[i], a Sixteenth Century Japanese warrior of great renown. My life is a happy and successful one because she raised me to be a winner. I was brought up according to the Code of the Samurai: to have no doubt; to know no fear; to see obstacles as opportunities; and, to live with honor, no matter what! In my youth I didn't realize that she was the best teacher I could ever have selected, or that hers would be the most valuable lessons of my life. Not only did she teach effectively, she created an environment that made me want to learn. I survived numerous battles in a time and at a place where many of my contemporaries did not. Many of my childhood associates were destroyed by their environments either in actuality or in principle. I chose the best parent, a Samurai warrior. Contrary to the garbage the close-minded, uninformed majority spews out, there's nothing wrong about being raised in a single female-headed household. In many ways it can be far healthier than growing up in a two parent household. There is no love to compare with a Mother's Love. Any person ever exposed to an environment dominated by an abusive, over-worked and insecure male, who on any given day might direct his anger and frustration toward his family, knows exactly what I am saying. I have never seen, or known my birth father. I am not saying that my youth was, or would have been that a disaster. What I am saying is that I have no regrets about the way my youth was, in spite of the fact that many would have me think otherwise. I am forever grateful to my Mother, Mabel. She only had a sixth grade education, which was more book learning than anyone in our family had to date. Her encouragement, none the less, stimulated me to pursue higher education and subsequently to hold some prestigious positions in my professional life. I know how difficult her life was when she was growing up. She had to be a warrior of the first echelon, and a diplomat, merely to survive in the 'deep South' in those days. She was not allowed to go to school because of her race. She gave birth to two male children. Neither of us ever knew our birth fathers. I was older by eighteen months.

Mabel was born and grew up in Savannah, Georgia. She used to say to me, "Tell me where the Black race came from?" If every person on Earth has some kind of color in their skin and if white implies the absence of color then how can there be any thing like the White race or the Black race? I was taught there are three primary colors; black, white and green. What happened to the Green race?" Her perspective was formed by her father who lived on the outskirts of Saint Augustine, Florida. He owned and operated a small, but profitable alligator farm. He was half Seminole Indian, and half Black-American. I saw him only twice in my life but I will never forget him. The last time I saw him I was ten years old. He was having a disagreement with a White farmer, a neighbor, I believe. Granpop called him a 'Red-necked' old farmer. He called Granpop a sorry-assed, colored son-of-a-bitch. Granpop was a peaceable man with lots of common sense, but he never backed down from anyone, of any color. We always feared that his mouth someday would be his undoing. Today, I thought, the end is in sight.

I firmly believed he was going to be lynched before the sun rose again. That's what they did to uppity colored people down South. I recall Granpop's response to the insults hurled his way that day. He laughed and calmly said to his oppressor, "When I was born, I was brown. I grew up brown. When I'm cold in the snow or hot in the sunlight I'm still brown. When I get sick, I'm brown, and when I die I'll be brown, all the way to Heaven, or Hell. You, on the other hand, when you were born you were pink. You grew up being white. In the sun you turn red. When you're cold, you turn blue. When sick, you turn purple. And when you die, you'll turn a sickly gray. Where do you get the damn nerve to call me "colored?" With that, the farmer cussed some more, glared, turned and walked away. Me, I turned also, scared shitless, and ran like hell! That was the last time I saw Granpop or went down South until I was in basic training at Camp Rucker, Alabama. Incidentally, I found out later that Mabel feared for my life, as well. She prayed for my safety every day until I was home again. Don't tell me that a Samurai's prayer is not as mighty as sword and staff. I had a few close calls in the environments of racism I found in the South; encounters that I survived because of the power of a Samurai's prayers and my "gift of gab."

I believe Mabel should have been classified a "secret weapon." I was never "spanked" for misbehaving. She was an expert at psychological warfare, and had no need for the whip. She possessed more courage and common sense than anyone I ever met. She was a "survivor" and a competent provider. I was born in New York City, before the "Great War," which means that Mabel migrated North in her late teens, pregnant with me. My brother was also born in New York City. By the time I started school we lived in Philadelphia, Pennsylvania, in a public housing project. Determined to see that I received a good education, Mom enrolled me into a Catholic school where tuition had to be paid rather than sending me to free public schools. This has to be one of Mabel's most brilliant strategies because when I entered college I was able to "ace" every exam I took. She purchased a little two bedroom house in the middle of North Philadelphia's battleground at the height of the Second World War. How she pulled it off I'll never know. I believe her mortgage payment was forty-four dollars a month, a lot of money for a single mother of color in those days. I heard later she bartered for and sold ration stamps, in addition to cleaning offices at night and cooking for a Jewish household on the Main Line in the mornings. She didn't holler or preach at me. There was no need. She had a look that could paralyze. She could tell instantly whether or not I was lying. She would stare me down and say, "Don't you lie to me boy!" The truth had to come out. She should have worked for the War Department as an interrogator. We could have won the war without the bomb. She was a tough individual, and I grew up believing in my heart of hearts that she was not to be messed with, no way, Jose!

Mabel kept me straight with her 'house rules' from which there would be no deviation. Rule #1: If you get in trouble in the streets, and get arrested, don't call here 'cause I ain't coming to get you. Rule #2: Keep it in your pants or I'll whack that little weasel off! Rule #3: Don't even think about bringing no ready-made family into this house. I ain't feeding no more mouths, and I ain't washing no diapers. I believed her and wouldn't dare defy her rules. I should have stuck to her rules and not have developed my own code of behavior as early as I did. In fact, I tell people all the time that if I had had any real sense, I would have lived at home until I was forty. But no, I wanted to be a man. I couldn't live the kind of life I craved in Mabel's house. She didn't smoke, drink, party or cuss. She took no sass and always got her point across without using profanity. What is more, she had the fastest backhand on the East Coast. I would swear she worked out as a sparring partner with Joe Louis. Her hands were just as lethal, if not more so. Just let her even hear of me responding to an adult without saying "Ma'am" or "Sir" and I'd be reminded how fast Mabel's backhand was.

Mabel was a proud woman, though not vain in the least. I never saw her step outside the house in hair rollers or a bathrobe. There were always white gloves and two little lace-trimmed handkerchiefs in her purse. She was always groomed and attired respectfully. So was I. We never went hungry or dirty. When I got home from school, I had to hang up my school clothes immediately. I had to be in the house at the appointed time or the door would be locked. I couldn't get in unless my 'story' was really convincing. We all sat together at the kitchen table for dinner every evening. You had to eat everything on your plate and knew that if you didn't it would there at the next sitting. To waste food was a mortal sin in Mabel's house. Many times I heard her say, "It may be beans and hot dogs but they'll fill your stomach and it's nobody's business but ours. What goes on behind these doors, stays in here. Keep it that way! You don't like it, get a job and buy your own food." Someone wrote a song for my Mom. Maybe you've heard it before. It goes "Mabel, Mabel, sweet and able, keep your elbows off the table." I called it her song because she told me almost every day of my young life, "Keep your elbows off the table!"

By the time I was ten years old Mabel would take me along with her to visit the homes of kin folk - that's what she called extended family members, church associates like the Ushers Club, and her woman's social club where they just ate, and ate, and ate some more. These events were intended to showcase one's cooking and presentation skills. Afterwards, for recreation, they played Keno or Pity-Pat, for pennies. This is when I learned what the gloves, always in her purse, were really for. She would have them on when we entered the house. To my absolute amazement, and sometimes chagrin, the woman would actually be finger-inspecting the house for dust and dirt, like an Inspector General. I was so embarrassed that I would be saying silent "Hail Mary's" that she wouldn't be detected. However, it got worse! Sometimes she would ask, politely, if I might go to the kitchen and fetch a glass of water for her. The 'worse' was that I was really being sent on a mission; to inspect sanitary conditions in the kitchen and especially to be on the lookout for "critters" – that meant roaches in her jargon. She was a firm believer that "cleanliness is next to godliness" something I was reminded of frequently. I never told her that I saw critters and I used to fantasize about what would have happened if I had. These excursions stopped when one evening I was allowed to play Keno with the women. I won the "corners' pot" which had more than one hundred pennies in it, the biggest win of the evening. That ended my social life and my kitchen inspection duties. I regretted neither. There was one time though that her penchant for cleanliness had me scared out of my wits. We were on a trolley car headed to her night job. We were seated and there was a man standing directly over Mabel. He gave off a body odor like you wouldn't believe! After sitting there with her faced all scrunched up and obviously uncomfortable for ten minutes, she looked the man directly in the eyes and said, "Look Mister, I don't mean to be impolite but soap is cheap and water is free." I was shocked and so scared that I nearly fainted. I suppose she had her paralyzing look on because the man merely grunted and moved away. We got off at the next stop, unscathed, but I was not unafraid!

Mabel was determined that I would be the family's first college graduate. I was, with her determination and G.I. Bill help. I completed high school at sixteen, and she only had to say it once, "There's nothing for you out in the streets." I enlisted in the Army. She coerced the Parrish Priest into helping and secured a Baptism certificate that made me two years older than on my birth certificate. I was already six feet tall and weighed one hundred and eighty pounds. What is more, I made minced-meat out of the Army placement tests. Being Regular Army, I chose to become an Airborne Ranger. It was not their reputation for heroics that attracted me; it was the additional fifty dollars a month you got paid for jumping out of airplanes. In our house, money was a needed commodity and I was able to send an allotment home

She always bought the Philadelphia Enquirer home with her. It didn't matter that the paper was a day old. The newspaper was how I learned to read and think for myself. She would often have me read for her before she went to work in the evening. That was part of my homework and she asked me questions about the 'news' like I was in school or something. I developed a love for reading, writing, and memorizing things from the tabloid. In truth, I was showing off for her. Majoring in English in college brought back fond memories. She had trained me well and prepared me with a desire to master the English language, enjoy contemporary and classic literature, and to communicate effectively while showing respect to everyone.

We didn't have television at home. Our entertainment was radio, newspapers and comic books. These fed my overactive imagination which later in life took me through South America, Greenland and Africa, where I was privileged to make the climb up Mt. Kilimanjaro. I existed inside adventure stories and romantic radio soap operas. "Stella Dallas" and "The Guiding Light" were her favorites. "Sergeant Preston of the Yukon" and "Jack Armstrong" mine. Today, I have financial interest in a kennel that breeds wolf-hybrids. Our animals are bred to 95% wolf. They are the most intelligent, most loyal and undefeatable canine I know. Sgt Preston would be proud. My personal animal is named Myonechi, which means Morning Sun, in Japanese. My Mother named him and she never told me where she got the name from. But the sun, you know, is important to maintaining life on this earth. We could not survive on this Planet without the Sun. Mabel had a soft spot for animals. She never complained about my dogs, cats, snakes, fish, pigeons or rats, as she called them, as long as I properly cared for them and treated them with kindness. Would you believe that she helped me buy a horse when I was twelve years old? Somewhere in her heart she must have known that every warrior of merit must have a good horse. Wondergirl was an ex race track filly and worked for her own keep by being rented out at the riding stables in Fairmount Park in Philadelphia, where she was boarded. I would walk my dog to the stables, about four miles from home, and ride Wondergirl back to my neighborhood to ride the kids in my street for ten cents - cash, credit, or barter. The only time Mabel ever had to get me out of jail was when Wondergirl and I got locked up for running along beside a trolley car. My biggest surprise was not that Mabel got me released! More amazing was that she actually laughed about it. Mabel didn't have a lot to laugh about in those days. Her greatest joys were realized through her children and our successes. Mabel was in silent agreement with the Samurai axiom, "In battle, keep your horse near and your enemies far!"

Mabel was not against television. It was more like something we could not afford. Few people living in the projects could in those days. Because I boxed in the pee-wee division of the Police Athletic League, whenever Joe Louis' or Sugar Ray Robinson's fights were televised, in summer, winter, spring or fall, she would take me by the hand and we would walk to the television shop six long blocks away to watch the 'Brown Bomber' or 'Sugar Ray' do their thing, standing on the sidewalk, watching through the plate glass storefront. She would comment compassionately, "You be careful, boxing is a sure road to brain damage! You can get hurt even if you're good at it." She was right, of course, and she made sure I would learn the lesson through close-up observation.

So you tell me, what's so wrong about being raised in a single female-headed household where abuse of any kind is extremely rare? It is unlikely that you'll be told, "My way or the highway," unless of course you are there until you're thirty-five or forty. Did you have to watch your mom worry, fret, sweat and cry over a man's whereabouts or mistreatment? Did you ever have to search elsewhere for love, trust and respect? I don't think so. Likewise I don't think anyone could ever have a better mom than mine or the many single mothers I have known just like Mabel. One more thing I want to share. My younger brother at age sixteen became the first boy of color to win the Eastern States Foil and Fencing Championships. I used to wonder how he did that. That was before I realized his mother was Samurai.

© L. Michael Black, Los Angeles, CA, 2007

--------------------------------------------------------------------------------

[i] The Japanese entrepreneur is not nurtured as an Asian equivalent of our Harvard Business School. Instead, he studies, lives and works according to an almost-mythic tome written in 1645, by the great Samurai, Miyamoto Musashi. Musashi was Japan's most renowned warrior. By age 30 he had fought and won over 60 duels by killing his opponents. The invincible Musashi eventually retired to a cave to record for future generations the lessons of his intense life. There he completed, a few weeks before his own death, the classic A Book of Five Rings. He wrote it not only as a thesis on battle strategy, but "for any situation where plans and tactics are used." Not surprisingly, business executives of 20th Century Japan revere Musashi's philosophy as a guide for their daily decisions. They therefore view the running of a business like a military operation.

Musashi was a Buddhist follower of the Nichiren Sect and was the only Samurai ever known to have a "Gohonzon" engraved on the breastplate of his armour. This is not to say there were not others, however, none as legendary as was Musashi.

# A Mother's Voice Crosses the Miles
## Susan E. Méra

*Childrearing messages from half a world away*

I stroked the soft white wool with a gentle palm. Tears flowed down my cheeks and plopped onto the spherical bump that was my unborn baby. Tenderly, I lifted the shawl to my wet cheek and continued to sob.

People talk about love, about sacrifice, about symbols and here in my shaking hands were love and sacrifice, and a symbol so huge that I could barely breathe.

We had never got on. And now that she has "passed over" as they say, we do. Today, five years after she died, and almost 40 years after I held a shawl to my wet cheek, we are the best of friends. Do I have regrets? I regret that I didn't tell her how very much she was loved, but then I didn't know; I regret that I didn't tell her how fond of her I was but then I hadn't realized; and I regret that it took me years to appreciate the many things she taught me.

But this story is not about regrets but about joy, not about "what ifs" but about "what is." It also carries a message to all daughters, which is to look behind the meanness of spirit, the tough words, the rigidity and the apparent self-centeredness, and find the light, the joy and the love.

My Mother was angry. She spent her whole life being angry. She was also neurotic and bitter and difficult and, at times, deeply embarrassing. But hers was also a life of unfulfilled dreams in an era when women lived for their husbands and children and relied on handouts from their spouses for treats that were often very small.

He'd told her very early on in their marriage that no wife of his was going to work. Later he said that women were too stupid to drive, thus trapping her in a friendless home and depriving her of the independence she craved. Of course, she didn't tell me about these, and other things, or indeed of her lost dreams, until years after he died. Even then she continued to cling on to the love she was sure she felt for him, and therefore did, mourned his going and stayed loyal and faithful until, tired of the struggle, she left to join him. At least that's what she told me she planned to do.

I was 52 when I discovered, just by chance, that my mother was a closet feminist and this during one of the last of the relatively cogent conversations we managed before her mind drifted into that other space occupied by a land called dementia. Her openness, the first I had known, gave me hope of meeting my dreams in a world consumed by work and deadlines and little else.

But back to the shawl, which had been knitted by a woman whose gnarled and pain filled fingers would have screamed for relief from the agony of casting every stitch.

It was to be her first and only grandchild and the mother, her unthinking and apparently selfish daughter, was having this baby at the other end of the globe, in Australia. This woman who so loved children, whose own history meant that she could only have two, had spent many painful months knitting a beautiful shawl for the unborn grandchild she would only meet twice thanks to what was, in those days, the tyranny of distance.

On their second meeting, my son, by now an adult, connected with this tiny white-haired woman in a way that I had never thought possible. Tears in his eyes, but his face full of joy, he told me, "She's wonderful Mum, she's so beautiful and she's a lot of fun." I looked at him, Lord Dubious written all over my face and responded as I was supposed to respond, "You're right." Of course, these days I know he was right and I marvel, retrospectively, at his ability to see past and beyond the obstacle course that was the relationship between my mother and me in order to find her true self.

The things my mother taught me really began when I was a small child. But it took the birth of my son to make me aware of the wisdom she had passed on to me. I was in my late teens and married to a man who I already knew was a repeat of the man my mother married. I was 12,000 miles from my family and friends and in my arms was a tiny bundle. They say newborn babies can't see but his face wore the same trusting expression it has always worn for me. At the top of the steps in front of me was the door to our apartment and a lifetime of motherhood. I bent over and kissed him very gently and tenderly on the forehead, "What in God's name do I do now," I whispered. "You're going to have to help me, we're in this together." I felt something touch me and was sure I heard, "No you're not." Shaking my head with a mixture of surprise and denial I carefully climbed the steps.

Bedtime, and I went to lay him down on his back. These days that's precisely how the cot death people recommend you put a baby to bed, but to me my Mother's advice still makes much more sense. "Not that way. Lie him down on his right side and next time his left side, and then do it turn about. If you put him on his back he'll choke if he's sick in the middle of the night."

As I placed my son in his bassinet on his right side I wondered if I was "hearing" this advice through the ether and across the miles from the United Kingdom or was it coming up from the deep recesses of my mind? Was I simply recalling things my mother had taught me?

That first night home from the hospital, he was up and down all night. I'd feed him, I'd change his nappy, I'd cuddle him, but still he cried in between fitful naps. At 4am my head was drooping and nodding over a screaming baby. "He's got wind." "What?" "He's got wind, ignore what those nurses told you about putting him over your lap or your knees. Put him over your shoulder and rub, but not too hard now." Well, miraculously my left eardrum remained intact as a noise of blunderbuss proportions filled the room. He was asleep in seconds.

After that night he slept the sleep of angels, waking only for his nighttime feeds. My newly formed circle of friends wondered at his contentment.

Our daily walk and talk. He with his trusting eyes fixed on mine, me proudly pushing him in the large blue pram with the white hood. "Where's his hat?" "What?" "Never take a baby out in the sun without a hat, they have very tender skin." Back up the steps for the hat.

One day, he cried in a way that was so heartbreaking it was clear he was in a great deal of pain. His face was the color of beetroot, the eyes a tight line, tears flowed down his cheeks. "Gripe water, he's teething." "What?" "Gripe water, put it in a bottle of warm water." Muttering to myself about the ark and prehistoric medicines I slunk into a pharmacy and asked for gripe water in a very soft and embarrassed voice. A smiling assistant, of a somewhat mature vintage, asked me if my baby had teething problems. Astonished and grateful I handed over a very small amount of money in exchange for a bottle of clear liquid. After a few sips of gripe water diluted in warm water my precious baby's face returned to its usual color, he calmed down and stopped crying. All these decades on, I assume that gripe water has been banned or at least is so unfashionable as to be out of use. For my baby's gums and me, it was a lifesaver.

Over the years it continued. When, as a little boy, he was a bit naughty and I was about to send him to his room, no smacking in my home, I heard: "Never send a child to his room when he's misbehaving, it means that he associates his bedroom with punishment, it will affect his sleep you know." Right.

And it was not just to do with child rearing; the range of tips and advice was broad and diverse but primarily focused on housework. Comments included everything from how I cleaned the windows, to ironing shirts and cooking and baking. "Your hands are too hot for making pastry, everything has to be cool if pastry is to be light and crisp." Okay.

As I got older and she got older, I decided to try to mend bridges, to behave as though her venomous letters had never been written, her criticisms had never been made; her accusations about my behavior and habits had never been issued. I returned to the UK for a few years and lived closer to her. Without ever discussing it we made our peace and achieved a gentleness and a knowingness we had never previously experienced.

The last time I saw her she didn't know who I was, so buried were her memories old and new. But she smiled at me and hugged me and her beautiful blue eyes, now faded from the midnight hue of old, lit up. I captured the smile in my memory banks and returned with it to Australia.

When on the following year she died, her grandson and I spent a day doing her favorite things: walking on beaches, looking at the sunset, eating ice cream, listening to music, talking. A very special day, and at the end of it we sent her on her journey to a life that was no longer full of bitterness and anger, but peace and joy.

And those little "nudges," those things she taught me, stopped. No more directions, no more tips and hints, no more suggestions until, that is, a sunny day in France four years after her death.

Decades after the dismal end of my first marriage I had met my soul mate. We are blessed by a love that is pure and whole and complete. I was staying in the lower Alps of France waiting for him to join me for our wedding in a nearby village.

A clear blue Provençal sky stretched to the horizon. A yellow sun tickled the hairs on my neck. I watched butterflies dancing over ripening rye; listened to bird song and smelled the familiar and exquisite perfume of the season's first crop of lavender.

I'd been burnt over the years; an emotional burning that had left me fragile and unsure. And as I contemplated my forthcoming marriage the doubts started flooding in. Was I doing the right thing? What if I was hurt again? What if? What if? What if?

And then, clear as a bell, "Don't be stupid lassie, he's the best thing that ever happened to you."

By now I'd climbed to a village that looked out over lavender fields. The tears flowed down my cheeks, just as they had all those decades ago when I held a shawl to my wet cheek.

As I descended into the fields below, and on to what has become the most beautiful, loving and tender journey of my life, I whispered my grateful thanks.

The shawl, which swaddled my son at his Christening, is stored, carefully wrapped in tissue paper, waiting for any grandchildren that may bless my world.

Thank you mother, thank you for everything, but mostly thanks for all the things you taught me.

*As a teenager, **Susan Méra** followed her childhood dream of becoming a journalist when she joined her first newspaper. Over the years she worked for media outlets in the UK and Australia and more recently in the public sector specializing in social justice issues. Now focusing on personal writing, the 'Wisdom of Our Mothers' contest is her first successful foray into the world of book publishing.*

*Susan and her French husband Henry plan to move to France where she hopes to fulfil her latest dream – writing for a Gallic readership in a language she has yet to conquer.*

---

# Things Mother Taught Me
## Sandra Fischer

*Lessons in many ways – through messages spoken and silent*

Lessons from my mother came in many ways. Some came through her larger, skilled hands cupping mine and moving my fingers with hers, helping me form stitches or knead dough. Others came through messages both spoken and silent, whose impact reverberates in my memory, even now, with the same vibrant sounds and visions as when I first experienced them. Still others were more subtle, taking root in me like small seedlings searching for a place to grow. Some lessons I mastered and accepted easily, without question. Others I challenged. All served to mold and shape me. Through all of them I never doubted the breadth and depth of her love.

Mother's presence was a given. She was there after school, listening to my account of the day as I shared between gulps of milk and brown sugar sandwiches. She was there with a needle to remove a piece of glass from my knee, because the doctor who made house calls was unavailable and hospitals were reserved for more serious hurts. She was there when I tried to hide the matches after a reckless dare, which set my sister's hair on fire. Her close supervision gradually grew less as I grew older, but her availability to listen, to comfort, to encourage remained a part of our relationship.

Some sociologists would have doomed me, as the middle child in a brood of five, to be lost in the shuffle. Adding to that speculation was the fact that my father worked away on the railroad and was only home on weekends, leaving my mother with the unenviable job of taking care of our daily needs. Yet, despite the difficulties of managing a household almost single-handedly, she made us feel special. Somewhere in between the chicken plucking, garden tending, food canning, floor scrubbing, and wringer washing, she took time to give each of us special attention. One vivid memory is of her asking me to model a flowered robe she was "making for the neighbor girl, who was about my size." What a surprise to find the robe under the Christmas tree with my name on it. And, who would have thought she had time to plan a special surprise birthday party for a curly-headed six year old, complete with paper dolls, cake and homemade ice cream? She did such special things for each of us as we grew up.

Mother also taught a class called "Responsibility." She was a charter subscriber to the work ethic ideal. Sharing the load at our house was a *privilege* to which we were automatically entitled at birth. We learned to do most household chores, which included everything from hanging laundry on the clothesline, to filling canning jars, to the lowly task of emptying and cleaning the chamber pot. Even now, the smells of sun drenched cotton, steaming tomatoes, and bathroom odors assault my senses when I recall those tasks.

Age ten was a hallmark in our household. It marked our initiation into the local workforce. Each of us was given a portion of a paper route when we reached that ripe old double-digit age. Each morning at 4:00 a.m. Mother would awaken us and ply our sleepy senses to life with milk-diluted coffee. After the paper truck arrived, we would fold the dailies into neat little squares and count out those needed to fill bags for our designated routes. Off we'd go, trudging through rain or sleet or snow or whatever weather, to serve our patrons with the latest news. We learned how to keep sales and expense records as well as to budget and save. Out of our earnings we were expected to buy our own shoes, mother's way of allowing us another family privilege – helping to underwrite the meager wages of our hardworking father.

Mother's life required inner strength as well as physical stamina, since she carried the daily load of training and discipline. She was tough. She tolerated little nonsense and, when we deserved to be punished, used a small, leather strap across our behinds to impart a stinging reminder of who was in charge when father wasn't there. Fortunately, those occasions were fairly rare and the corrections were done in the spirit of "not spoiling the child." She did, however, spend a great deal of time encouraging us to do our best, whether in school, completing a 4-H project, or simply playing a game. She believed *in* us. She also believed in miracles.

One of her favorite hobbies was hunting mushrooms – the spongy morels that graced Indiana woodlands each spring. We were all recruited for such "hunts," after school or on weekends, enjoying the fruits of our labors in various culinary forms from mother's kitchen. One year, because of surgery, mother was unable to go to the woods and was a little depressed, until one morning, while enjoying her flower garden, she noted a curiosity – morel mushrooms growing among the tulips! "You see," she said, "God sent the mushrooms to me, since I couldn't go find them!" That was the only year mother couldn't go hunting and the only year she found mushrooms in the garden.

Our father planted a large vegetable garden each year, but the majority of weeding, picking and preserving fell upon mother. We had fresh tomatoes, green beans, onions, carrots, potatoes and corn in season and we canned extra for our winter table. We also gave some of the produce to our widowed neighbors or to those folks who had no space for a garden. While I know it took management ingenuity to provide for a family of seven, my mother never hesitated to share or to show hospitality to others. Many times I would hear a voice outside our back stoop saying, "Thank you, ma'am." Peeking out, I would see one of the vagrants who rode the nearby railroad freights munching on food my mother had given him. Sometimes they might offer to split wood or bring a hopper of coal up from the bin, but mother fed them whether they worked or not. She said anyone could fall into hard times and might need to depend upon others for help. Caring for others whether family, friends or strangers was natural for her.

As I think about the things my mother taught me, I begin to perceive their dynamic in my life and the lives of my own children. They continue to manifest themselves in various ways, almost too numerous to count. It has been said that daughters "become" their mothers as they grow older, and many times I will catch myself reflecting the same qualities of my mother. Most of the time I feel good about it – particularly if I am displaying the aspects of her character as revealed in these glimpses. Nothing would please me more than to have my own daughters say they saw the same qualities in me – that I was available, resolute, devoted, diligent, encouraging, faithful and caring. Then, as a successful student, I will have passed on the valuable lessons of my own teacher, my mother.

*Sandra Fischer taught high school English in Indiana and owned a Christian bookstore for several years. Most of her writing is devoted to stories from her experiences growing up in the Midwest. She has been published in* Guideposts, *trade journals and more recently in* Faithwriters Magazine and Faithwriters.com *online. Sandra is retired and lives in South Carolina with her husband, Craig, where she continues to write.*

---

# Mother Knit Wisdom
## Pat Richards

*Knitting provides lessons for living one's life.*

The title Mother is usually attributed to one's own mother or adopted mother. But one must not neglect another mother: mother-in-law.

Much like Robert Fulghum's observation, *All I Really Need to Know*

*I Learned in Kindergarten,* I learned everything I need to know from my mother-in-law, Mary Frances Richards, and her knitting life example.

**Tangles:** In the seventies my husband gave his mother huge cartons of tangled yarn… a bargain at two dollars a box. He carted his "find" all the way home from a mill in Uxbridge, Massachusetts.

Mother R. was thrilled. With Gidget the dog resting comfortably at her feet, Mary Frances spent untold hours untangling those skeins of yarn. It provided the largess for a winter's worth of knitting.

Sometimes when my life snarls like those tangled skeins of yarn, I conjure an image of Mary Frances rewinding yarn into fat fluffy balls… and following her example, I try to remember that sometimes you need to be willing to unsnarl a web one tangle or knot at a time.

**Patterns**: Life doesn't always follow a pattern. Most days one must take up pointy sticks (needles) and available yarn and improvise. Mary Frances didn't rely on commercial patterns, other people's configuration. With a lifetime of knitting experience she made up her own patterns, making adjustments or revisions as she went along.

**Fabric:** A fine gauge yarn and small sized needles worked rhythmically with persistence and patience will produce a sturdy long-lasting fabric. Patience and persistence is key.

**Originality**: Mary Frances designed an afghan knitted with a strand of wool and a strand of crochet cotton to create long sturdy rectangles that her grandsons dubbed "shiver blankets." On below zero Adirondack mornings the grand boys would wrap up in these heavy blankets… much like Arctic sheiks to stave off the cold.

Once Mary Frances took a beloved rag doll aptly named baby… that was losing its stuffing and its head… she knitted the doll a sweater and leggings and reattached its head. Baby lives in a trunk in our house… although the toddler who loved her is grown and gone.

Mary Frances' creations warmed the feet and hands of many a grandchild as they skied the Adirondack mountain on blustery snow days.

**Shaker Simplicity**: All Mother R's knitted garments could be deemed plain. Stark you might say. Beautiful! Intuit the message: Keep life simple.

**Color**: Mary Frances often added a tad of color... a thin or thick stripe to a sock or mitten. How remarkable to find that the addition of a small bit of color will uplift the grayest day.

**Raveling**: Thrift and recycling were part of Mother R's heritage. She loved to unravel a sweater found at a jumble sale and knit a new one.

Raveling makes sense – more easily accomplished with a knitting swatch than some of life's thornier problem – but still like Frances: starting over, making new, generates enthusiasm... even hope.

**Gifting**: Gifting is essential to the good life. Mother R. kept long lists: of mittens, socks, caps given to friends and family or sold to a few favored customers... much like Grandma Moses.

Even lacking the prerequisite (made by Frances with love) tag: it was obvious... all her knitwear was stitched with loving care.

Mary Frances' knitting legacy lives. We still cherish her handiwork. We (her heirs) try to follow both her knitting and life lessons.

May Mary Frances' wisdom endure!

*A fiber artist, author, veteran blogger, and genealogist, Patricia Richards lives with her husband in Kingston, New York and Sarasota, Florida. Her nonfiction book,* sassy pat knitting: a memoir, *debuted at the Chronicle Book Fair 2008. Pat will be teaching a workshop titled* Blog to Book *in the coming year. With a young adult novel,* White Plague, *in the works and a collection of monologues,* Irish Muses, *in the hopper, the coming year should prove to be a busy one.*

*Visit her at sassypatknitting.blogspot.com.*

# My Mother
## Sheila Sievewright

*Honest love, with no illusions*
*From Ireland*

I see her now – all 12 stone 5'2" of her, her large bosom covered by the apron she always wore.

I see her full red cheeks and her smiling, friendly eyes.  But sometimes there was a deep sadness in those bright blue eyes.  She wore her white hair combed back from her face and tied in a bun at the back of her neck.

My mother – who loved romance and musical comedies.  After seeing "High Society" she knew that Grace Kelly and Bing Crosby were in love.  They should be married to each other.  While Nelson Eddy and Jeanette McDonald singing Rose Marie was what romance was.

My Mother – who welcomed everybody into her home with a cup of tea and home-baked bread and cake.

My mother – who baked every day so there was always the hungry-making smell of home baking in the house.

My mother – who made all our clothes, and showed endless patience in trying to accentuate my 21" waist to my satisfaction, and still make room for my ample hips.

My mother – whom all my friends loved and whom people of all ages confided in.

My mother – who, torn between loyalty to husband and father, abandoned both and lived her life through her children.

My mother – whom I found it difficult to forgive for denying me my father. He became a stranger to all his children.

My mother – who was proud of her well shaped legs, who bought an expensive tailored suit and wore it for the next 20 years.

My mother – with whom I had an argument before I went to school. When I returned at dinner time, full of beans, I was met with a stony silence and a stony face, which plunged me into the dark place where she had spent her morning.

My mother – who listened to me, to whom I could confide all my dreams, and who encouraged me in my dreams.

My mother – who listened to me.

My mother – who got fed up of her young children squabbling, put on her hat and coat and said she was leaving and never coming back – walked out the front door and closed it after her. She left at least one little girl terrified that she would never see her mother again.

My mother – after an incident, I, a young child, locked myself in the toilet and was overheard saying, "Poor little Sheila, nobody loves you." For years afterwards, my mother would say "Poor Little Sheila" to me until tears welled up in my eyes. She seemed to get pleasure from this.

My mother – who confided her anxieties and fears about the rest of the family to me. I became the caretaker of her emotions.

My mother – who collapsed and died on the street. Later a piece of paper was discovered in her pocket with her name and address in case she collapsed and died on the street.

My mother – who adored her only son. We teased her by singing "My son, my son, you're everything to me" to her.

My mother – who had very little education and yet possessed a great wisdom and understanding of other people.

My mother – who related so well to people, yet I never heard her call her husband by name, or touch him.

My mother – who washed, cleaned, scrubbed, polished, and yet had a drawer which was never cleaned and held such interesting odds and ends

My mother – who was human.


*Sheila Sievewright is 72 years of age and has just started her writing career. This is the first writing she has submitted for publication and she is very excited. She left school when she was 15 years of age and went into secretarial employment, where she remained until she married at age 26 years. Twelve years and three children later, she resumed full-time study at university, worked as a social worker, qualified as a psychotherapist, studied art and is now a fairly good djembe player. She still has three children, six grandchildren, and lives with her husband Declan in West Cork, Ireland.*


## Portrait of the Artist's Mother
### Fred Evans

*Homespun wisdom on a variety of topics*


The time: The Great Depression.

The place: Redmond, Washington. Not today's Redmond, the Software Capital of the World, but a frontier village on the edge of the Washington wilderness, where my mother grew up in a humble home with an outhouse and a wood-burning stove. At a time of material poverty, wealth lay in the bonds of family, friendships, and community.

From this setting came my mother's values, which she has tried to pass on to me, on the rare occasions when I have been wise enough to listen.

**On relationships:**
Used to be when groups got together, the women would sit in one corner and talk about relationships, families, and babies, and the men would sit in the other and talk work, sports, and cars. I don't see what was wrong with that.

Any woman who thinks her husband should communicate needs a good girlfriend.

Make your career the center of your life, and your relationships will fall into place around it.

I know how hard it is to be young, single and celibate, but the emotional swings of sex outside marriage are even harder.

**On religion:**
There's a lot of nonsense taught in churches, but you learn better values there than in the bars.

Don't marry a woman who thinks more of Jesus than of you. You'll always suffer from the comparisons.

**On children:**
A baby sets the agenda for a household.

A child is what's left of you when your body is dead and gone. Neglect your child and you neglect your hereafter.

**On economics:**
People think that money in the bank is security. Real security is a plot of good ground, garden tools, seeds, and the strength to plant and tend them.

**On leadership:**
I don't care what the Republicans say about Franklin Roosevelt. He made us feel like we were all in the Depression together, and working together, we'd all get out of it. That kept the Blackshirts and Communists from taking over.

Whatever people may say about John Kennedy, he made people want to be better and made them feel they could change the world for the better. That's what a leader should do.

**On drugs and alcohol:**
The body is the temple of the spirit. Hurt your body and you hurt your spirit. Take care of it, because you only get one.

**On objectivism:**
The profit motive is morally neutral. Good or bad depends on what you are doing for profit.

**On ecology and the environment:**
People who think the Hereafter is all that matters are blasphemers. God made this earth and it's our job to take care of it. Whether by God or our descendents, we'll be held accountable.

*Fred Evans is a middle-aged accountant and occasional freelance writer living in Bellingham, Washington.*

# The Lesson I Refuse to Learn
## Michele Graves

*One can accomplish what one sets one's mind to with constancy.*

The man actually stopped on the side of the narrow, windy road and got out of his PT Cruiser to better yell into my mother's face.

My mother shouldn't have been riding her bicycle so close to the fog line on that steep hill he began, before he got to the crux of his complaint and revealed the real reason he was foul. "I just bought this car and it's having trouble getting up this hill!" he shouted.

I doubt my mom had much empathy for his situation since she had just climbed the North Cascades Highway to Diablo using no other power than that of her 58-year-old legs.

Normally, hearing about this affront to my mother would have made me vicious. And in fact, I still shoot darts at PT Cruisers with my eyes just in case. But then, around the dinner table, I laughed.

I was just happy to have my mom safely home.

When my mom first announced that she was going to spend the summer bicycling from Washington through Montana I greeted the announcement with skepticism.

"But Mom, you don't even own a bike!"

My brother was immediately concerned. He didn't like the idea of his mother riding so far with my Aunt Beverly and just three other women companions. He and I debated the wisdom in telephone calls.

"It's dangerous," he said.

"Don't worry," I said. "It's January and she still doesn't have a bike."

Then, Mom asked me to go bicycle shopping with her. She picked out a purple Bianchi touring bike. When she took the bike for a test ride she wobbled a bit getting on. It had been awhile – decades – since she'd ridden.

Then she bought racing shoes, toe clips, panniers and a front pack – all the gear she'd need for a long trip.

That evening I told my husband that Mom was still talking about going through with her plan and now she'd spent a lot of money on a bike.

"Are you worried?" he asked.

"She doesn't even work out," I said.

Then Mom joined the gym. I went to aerobics class with her. None of the women in the class were larger than a size 10, their stomachs were toned and they moved smoothly through the steps.

Mom struggled. She grunted when she lifted weights. She wiped sweat off her brow repeatedly and laughed at her awkwardness.

Afterwards, I reassured her.

"You know, they make it look easy," I said. "But what you don't know is that all of those women have the routines memorized. They come to class every single day."

Mom came to the gym maybe three times, maybe two times, sometimes just once a week that winter. It was more exercise than normally fit into her schedule. Mom is an elementary school principal. She taught for 20 years and then went back to school to get her masters' degree. She spent long Sundays working on her thesis. My brother and I brought her coffee and licorice.

Even with the degree, it was tough for a woman to get a job as a school administrator in our conservative Eastern Washington town.

"But you are such a great teacher," they told her when she interviewed.

But, with perseverance and a move across the Cascades, mom finally got a position as vice principal, and later, when the district decided to construct a new school they made Mom principal. She got to pick out the colors of the carpets.

It is tough to get a hold of my mom in the evenings during the school week. When I call, often my father will tell me she is at a school board meeting, a music festival or some other event. Sometimes I call and she is home preparing reports and projects for a big day tomorrow at the school. The work and the excitement will keep her up until early morning. If I call her at the school where 840 children learn, she sounds bright, happy and busy.

When I reach mom at home on Friday night she's too tired to hold a conversation.

In early spring in preparation for her trip, mom rode her bike on the weekends, when she could, sometimes just a couple of miles.

She'd have to ride more than 450 miles before she even got to Montana.

I well remember Montana's long roads from the time we drove across the state on a family trip. On a flat, seemingly endless stretch my father couldn't stand any more of my brother's teasing and my whining. He reached back and pinched my brother's knee, stopped the car and threatened to leave Marc there. I imagined what would happen to my brother if he was left alone with the bored and still buffalo and the bored and racing drivers alongside that road.

The prospect scared the joy of teasing out of him and the little sister righteousness out of me.

Now, I couldn't imagine Mom cycling that far on that road.

But in June, on schedule, Mom hopped on her bicycle at Bay View State Park in Washington and began her adventure.

While she was gone, whenever I talked to anyone, I included an update on my mom's progress.

"Can you believe it?" I said. "My mom's in Coeur d'Alene."

Mom rode for more than a month. She went through Montana and kept going. She made it as far as Grand Forks, Minnesota and then had to take the train home to be back in time for the school year.

My dad and I met her at the station. Her hair was bleached white by the sun with blond highlights in it to match her yellow top. Her skin was dark from the edge of her biker shorts all the way down her firm muscular legs. She looked aboriginal, tough and serene.

She wasn't different at all.

Mom does what she says she will do. She lives with passion. She makes things happen. She has taught me this many times.

In 1980, Mom drove from Washington to Michigan with two children ages 8 and 12 and a friend who was disabled.

When I was 16, my mom, who had never traveled overseas, sent me on a trip to Germany. I didn't believe it would really happen until the plane was in the air.

When I joined the Peace Corps and lived 10,000 miles away in Africa my mom told me there was no way she'd spend two years without seeing me. She came after a year and took me on a safari.

In 28 years as my mother and in 36 years of marriage to my father, Mom has shown reservoirs of willpower in her commitment to physical, mental and emotional feats.

But I was still surprised at her latest achievement.

The ride wasn't easy for Mom.

"I should have trained more," she said when she returned.

She cried along the way at times from loneliness when she fell behind the others, exhaustion and pain. She watched a dog nearly get sideswiped by a truck. She fell off her bike at one point bruising her entire side.

But Mom's willingness to experience the gamut of emotions, positive and negative, makes her a true adventurer. Risk the trouble, reap the rewards.

"Cycling is a phenomenal sensory experience," Mom said. "You see hear, smell and taste everything."

After a long day of cycling, a drink of water "fed all my senses," Mom said.

Mom enjoyed the scenery and countryside. She helped a cowboy herd his cows using her bike. And she had the satisfaction of saying at the end that she pedaled more than 1,000 miles.

My mom has shown me that one can accomplish what one sets one's mind to with constancy.

"I never think, 'I can't,'" she said.

By rights if my mom flipped at random through the Guinness Book of World Records, pointed to a page and said that would be her next task I should take it as truth without flinching.

My appearance, mannerisms and expressions mirror my mom's and her philosophy has influenced me strongly, but I am probably her most stubborn student. Perhaps, because I love this particular lesson of hers so much, I often refuse to admit I have learned it.

Recently, Mom announced her plan to ride in the Seattle to Portland trek – 200 miles in just two days. This time she is training by riding 25 to 60 miles every Saturday and Sunday with my brother.

But I just shake my head.

Show me again, Mom. Show me!

---

# Bikini
## Sally Bellerose

*A French-Canadian lesson in modesty…or lack thereof*

Mom was a housewife and a factory worker who wore a bikini in broad daylight in our back yard. This was 1961. Working class western Massachusetts had a dress code. Skimpy bathing suits fell outside of that code. Perhaps my maternal grandparents, who were Quebecois, failed to impart full knowledge of American mores.

Maybe it's because both his parents were Quebecois that my jealous father never seemed to mind that his wife would occasionally step into her tiger-striped suit and out into the yard where she was surrounded by the picket fence he had built with his own hands.

Neither of my parents was hysterical about nudity the way some of our friends' parents were. If one of us kids, say, opened the bathroom door as Mom or Dad happened to be stepping out of the tub, it was no big deal, rating only an irritated, "How many times do I have to tell you to knock?"

This reaction was nothing compared to the overwrought embarrassment I witnessed when Mrs. Gilmartin's boob fell out of her sensible one piece bathing suit while she was hoisting herself out of the public pool. There was downright drama when Mrs. Kallowitz found out that Susie Kallowitz and I had witnessed drunken Mr. Kallowitz peeing on a rhododendron. His wife berated him up one side and down the other. This didn't seem fair. How was he to know we had snuck out of the house at ten o'clock at night? All three of us would have gotten away without a word of reprimand if Suzie and I had been able to contain our eight-year-old glee. Until his wife started screaming, I thought peeing on a bush was funnier than a banana hammock.

So why did Mom wear a bikini? A Hollywood star like Bridgette Bardot could get away with it. But Bridgette Bardot had exaggerated womanhood, fame, wealth, and an agent to protect her. She could flaunt her body, not with immunity exactly, but she didn't need to be a lady the way regular women did. How Mom got up the nerve in the summer of 1962 to carry a glass of Tab with such nonchalance across the yard while wearing next to nothing, is to this day a mystery to me. We lived in a neighborhood of two story houses with small back yards. Anyone who happened to be looking out a second story window in any of the four houses adjacent to ours could peer down and see every inch of her skin except the part covered by the scanty tiger-stripe bra and panties as she plopped herself down on the chaise lounge.

We girls were thirteen, eleven, and eight. We were all home for summer vacation and never knew when we might walk out into our back yard to find Mom unveiled. Any one of our neighbors could gain access to a one dollar pair of opera glasses at LeVignes corner store and peer luridly down at her. We knew because we had three pairs ourselves and kept vigil from our own second story windows. When one sister was posted in the bedroom, one in the hall, and one in the bathroom, we had the immediate neighborhood covered. The view, we figured, was roughly the same from any of the neighbors' second floors.

On one particular hot morning, all the stars aligned and the pay-off for our surveillance arrived. It was too early for spying, but I happened to be seated in the upstairs bathroom. More out of habit than curiosity, I peeked under the shade. There she was, cleavage greatly exaggerated from this angle, cup of Sanka and the morning paper in hand. My sisters hadn't even rolled out of bed yet. I pulled up my baby doll pajama bottoms and flew back to our shared bedroom. My sisters refused to get up. I took up my post at the bedroom window. Soon, I saw a mailman who was not our mailman coming down the street carrying an over-sized sack.

"A man," I said into Kathy's ear, not loud enough to be heard through the open windows. "Mom's out in the bikini."

She gave me a filthy look and sat up in bed. All three of us peered at the man through our opera glasses as he took a big book out of his sack and stuffed it in the LesPerence's mailbox.

"Phone books," Kathy said knowingly.

"How's he going to get that big book in our mailbox?" Janie asked. It was a good question. The LesPerence's had a mailbox big enough to accommodate Mr. LesPerence's mail order model airplane hobby. We had a normal mailbox. The fat phone book would never fit.

My older sister dropped her opera glasses. "Stay put," she commanded. "Don't take your eyes off him." She bounded down the stairs.

I didn't want to stay put. I left Janie with the same order Kathy had just barked at us and ran to the hall window to watch Kathy warn Mom that a strange man with a phone book was on the loose. I could see from way up there that Mom was not impressed with this information.

Kathy's mouth tightened and her hands went to her hips. Mom laughed. More than anything Kathy hated to be laughed at. I laughed, too. Mom turned toward the window. "Quit spying and come out here."

Since I'd been caught red-handed, I waved at them. Mom waved back. Kathy stared at Mom's bust line and scowled.

Mom rolled her eyes. "I am in my own back yard." She pointed to the towel draped over the back of the chaise. "I have a towel." It was true she always had a towel with her even though she never got wet. "How did you girls get this way?" But what if she wasn't quick enough with the towel?

I thought I heard a faint knock at the front door. I definitely heard the back door slam. It was Janie running out into the yard, gesturing toward the front of the house. I bolted down the stairs. There was no one at the front door. I grabbed the afghan off Dad's Lazy Boy as I ran through the living room on my way to the back yard.

I almost crossed paths with the guy as he came through the side gate saying, "Good morning. Glad I didn't wake you folks." The disgrace of it, the danger, the adrenaline. I rushed to join my two sisters who were already standing at her side. We created a screen of daughters to block his view. He was looking down at his bag, pulling out the phone book, saying, "Got your new telephone directory."

Mom had already twisted around and was smiling. Thankfully, she stayed seated in the chaise lounge. "Oh, thank you. Would you just leave it there on the picnic table?"

We held our breath. Was the threat avoided or did he see? Would he tell the tale all up and down the street? He left the book and turned away without making eye contact with any of us. I collapsed crossed legged to the ground next to Mom who was now frowning with her arms crossed, still firmly seated.

Mom stared at his back as the gate squeaked shut. Finally, she looked embarrassed.

Kathy glared at her.

Mom didn't notice. She was still staring at the gate. "Oh, shit," she said. Mom, who never said, "shit."

Janie sat tentatively on the end of the chaise. When she was not shoo'd off, my little sister put her head on Mom's thigh. Mom stroked her hair absentmindedly. "I hope he didn't realize I recognized him."

Kathy's mouth relaxed a bit. She squinted as if this would help her hear what Mom was about to say.

Janie lifted her head off Mom's thigh. "Who is he, Mom?"

"He used to work with your father." She seemed so sad. "He got let go."

"Fired," Kathy corrected.

Mom shook her head in sympathy. "Poor man. Two kids in diapers. How much can he be making delivering phone books? He must be so embarrassed." She looked seriously from daughter to daughter to daughter. "Don't marry heavy drinkers, girls. No matter how charming or good looking, do not marry a man who drinks too much." Her eyes landed on Janie, who sat up and looked back at her earnestly. Mom stroked Janie's hair one more time. Then shook off the phone guy with a forced smile. "You girls are up early."

Kathy's eyes drifted to the afghan on the ground next to me. I pulled the blanket to my lap so that Mom wouldn't notice that it had been touching the dirt. Kathy locked eyes with me and nodded at the afghan. I knew what she wanted. I wanted it too. I never would have had the guts to do it without my older sister's silent instruction.

Suddenly, with great dexterity, Kathy grabbed the afghan and threw it over Mom. Then with perfect timing, like a female tag team on world wide wrestling, we were on her. We wrapped the blanket around and under her. We would have stopped if Mom had ordered us to, but she squealed, laughing like a teenager getting thrown in a pool.

"What are you doing?" She could hardly get it out, she was laughing so hard. When it was absolutely clear that Mom was not angry, Janie joined in. The three of us carried our mother, who was fighting like a banshee and screaming with laughter, into the house.

I can't exaggerate how much fun this was; Mom allowing us to pretend we are saving her from herself. Mom laughing at us and herself and her own flesh, laughing wrapped in an afghan crocheted by our Memere before she died, laughing as if some things that are usually not allowed, are sometimes not only allowed, but allowed to be laughed at. It was maybe the most fun I'd had in my career as a kid up to that point. Between orders of, "Watch her head," and "Open the door," even Kathy was laughing.

*Sally Bellerose writes: The themes of my work often involve sexuality, illness, and class. I've been writing about family lately and find the themes haven't changed much. The older I get the more interested I become in using humor and absurdity in my art.*

*I have received various grants and fellowships including an NEA, the Barbara Deming Fiction Prize, and the Rick DeMartinis Award. My recently published work can be read in* Rock and Sling, The Binnacle, The Journal of Humanistic Anthropology, Boston Literary Magazine, Passager, Cutthroat, Saint Ann's Review, Per Contra, *and* Memoir (and). *Please email me at sbellerose(at)comcast.net.*

## A Mother's Love
**Patrick Hurley**

Sit up straight!
Clean your damn room!
Did you remember
to take your medicine?
Congratulations,
now don't blow it.

Is your homework done?
You call this clean?
Did you remember
to take your medicine?
You are definitely
not going out in that.

Don't do it half-assed.
Why don't you let me cut your hair?
Did you remember
to take your medicine?
You're so handsome,
if only you'd shave once in a while.

It's about time!
Can't you see I'm on the phone?
Did you remember
to take your medicine?
Honey, always remember,
that Mom loves you.

**Chapter 8**

# HERITAGE:

## A sense of the past

# Wigilia
## Erin Lawlor

*A Grandmother's Christmas Eve traditions from Poland*

The picture of the Black Madonna hangs nobly in the hallway, guarding the kitchen, now pouring out scents of pierogis, latkes and golonkis. At the other end of the hall you can hear broken English being shouted over old Polish uncles, all mumbling, talking, chatting in their loud Dombrowski voices. I hover with my brother over the trays of kruschiki that sit on the kitchen table. We wait until Mom leaves the kitchen, then stare lovingly at Babcia, "Quickly, but just one," she says, guarding the door for us as we each snatch one of the powder sugared cookies. We giggle and run across the hard wood floors, dodging aunts and uncles, ducking under serving trays, and squeezing between adults in the midst of conversations. We lap around the coffee table, laughing at the way the aspic jiggles when we dash past, Connor is grabbed by one aunt, while I leap into the arms of another.

This is the time of night that is different from other Christmas Eves. We are all standing in the living room, the TV is turned off and the music hushed, Babcia is at the front of the room holding a small envelope sent over from Poland. She calls Connor and me up to start the Oplatek. We each take a sheet of wafer, and exchange with Grandma. "Merry Christmas Babcia," we say, breaking off pieces of the thin white bread. Soon everyone is walking around the room, hugging, exchanging kisses, and wishing each other season's greetings and good luck in the following year, the ones who remember the old country wish each other a plentiful harvest. When you've gotten everyone, and your wafer is done, it is finally time to eat.

We sit, at the long table set with the good China. We fold our hands and bow our heads. There is an empty setting at the head of the table, just in case He comes tonight, and the wheat is in the corner of the room, hopes for a good crop, even though no one in the family farms anymore. Babcia and the aunts bring out trays and plates of blessed food. The savory smells of an old country invade the room. From my seat I can see the glow of the Christmas tree reflecting off the front window, and I can see the whole family, all sitting together. But that was then, that was when I was little and the world was innocent. Then, Babcia died, and all we could see was our Polish heritage slowly disappearing. And, maybe it would have, maybe we would have had turkey on Christmas Eve, maybe we would have left the picture of the Black Madonna in the hall closet, maybe we would have been your average American family. But, as long as my mom had anything to do with it, we wouldn't. That's when the short, blond-haired, Irish in-law stepped in. Because my mom wasn't born Polish, she married Polish, and even if you asked her, you wouldn't know the difference.

I can remember the first Christmas Eve without Babcia, I can remember it being different than all the ones before, I can remember a lot of crying, and I can remember my mom not sleeping for nights before. And I remember our crowded house, jammed with aunts and uncles, everyone carrying in trays of food, everyone worried that Patty might mess something up. And the truth is, I think she was the most worried of them all. I can remember standing next to her in the kitchen on the morning of Christmas Eve, her counting the list of relatives over and over again, making sure there would be enough food. But, most of all I remember looking up at her, confused and concerned. "Mommy, why are we doing this?" I asked, holding out the bowl of shredded potatoes as she peeled more and more. "I guess, sweetie, it's because I don't want this to die." I can remember seeing the tears building up in her eyes, and not knowing what she was talking about because Babcia had already died. She must have seen the perplexity in my face, "I just want to make sure, that when you and your brother get older, you have the same traditions your dad had, and that when you have kids, they can have some kind of tradition too." I never really thought much as to why my mom wasn't concerned about her family's traditions, until I got a little older, and realized that her family didn't have those traditions for her to save. And I don't know if she taught it to me in the kitchen, that first Christmas Eve without Babcia or sometime later in my life, but my mom has instilled in me the importance of family, and tradition, and heritage. And maybe it's because her family lacked the customs my father's has, or maybe it's because she wants something better for me, or my brother, or my children, but no matter the reason, as long as the importance of tradition continues, I guess that's all that matters.

*Erin Lawlor graduated from Red Bank Regional High School in Little Silver, NJ in 2008. It is here where her passion for writing grew. Under the instruction of Dr. Gretna Wilkinson, Erin's creativity and imagination were able to flourish. Erin was a winner of the 2008 NJ High School Poetry Contest, funded by the Geraldine R. Dodge Foundation. After high school, Erin attended Georgian Court University in Lakewood, NJ. Erin credits her family and friends for their support and Dr. Wilkinson and her Creative Writing Family for their inspiration which allowed Erin to develop into the writer she is today.*

---

## Bread Making...a Rite of Passage
### Sylvia Bright-Green

*...more than just the making and baking of homemade bread.*

As I stood there looking into my mother's cedar chest, I fought back tears. Eighty years of my mother's life was represented in this mahogany box she referred to as her "Hope Chest." And now, weeks after her funeral, I was the only one of my twelve (fourteen in all) remaining siblings who would take on the task of distributing all of mom's accumulated and handcrafted items. Yet somehow I managed to get through the task without shedding a tear; and then lost it when I got to my mother's cookbook from her mother.

Sobs spilled forth as I held that old cookbook. My first ceremonial baking lesson came from this book by way of my mother fifty-six years ago, when I was twelve years old.

I can still hear her gentle voice saying to me: "Learning to make bread is a rite of passage, a journey back to your family history. So today we are going on a journey," Mom said.

She spoke of how her journey with her mother began much the same way, as they, too, stood at an old wooden kitchen table wearing an apron her mother also made from a flour sack.

"You take this much flour," she instructed. "Dump those six cups in a large bowl. Then you add one cake of yeast... crumbling it into the flour. Take the cooled two cups of boiled milk in which we melted the 1/4 cup of lard (butter), and mix this with the flour and yeast. Here, now you do it," she added.

Using her wooden spoon to mix this gooey mess, I had no idea what I was going to end up with. Certainly not bread at this point, I thought. Yet, I knew my mother would give me a hint when I got to the right stage in the process.

After all the ingredients were blended, mother said to me, "Now you must turn this dough out onto the floured table and knead it until smooth and satiny, about eight or ten minutes. You do that by 'working' the dough. Working the dough means rolling and folding it over and over using your hands like this."

While mother had me working the dough, she put the teakettle on. This meant my journey was also going to be a lesson in listening without interruptions.

She began by speaking about her farms days and how the town's folks considered their family to be poor, due to having ten children. But the family never let those remarks bother them because they never felt poor, nor did they really lack for anything, mom quickly added.

"In fact, we were always dressed nicer than most. That's because my Mom (your grandmother) patterned and sewed all us children the latest fashions she saw in the catalogs. Mother had a knack for re-patterning old clothes and flour sack material to create us the latest styles. She also had a knack for creating tasty meals from fresh or garden canned fruits and vegetables, wild game, chicken and beef, farm fresh milk and eggs which produced homemade pies, cakes, cookies and baked bread. Bread that my mother taught me how to make from her handed-down recipe, taught to her from her mother's mother," she noted.

"Speaking of bread, Mom," I said, hesitant in wanting to interrupt her reminiscing, "it's been ten minutes. You need to inspect my kneaded dough."

Mom ran her hand over the dough's surface, and murmured, "Very smooth. Just like what I was taught from my mother. Now you must place the dough in a greased bowl, turning once to grease the dough's other side."

After doing that, I covered the bowl with a clean, damp dishtowel and set the bowl in a warm place for the dough to rise, doubling in bulk, per my mother's instructions.

While the dough was rising, we sipped tea. And mother continued telling me about her world growing up with her nine brothers and sisters on a 120-acre farm in Wisconsin Rapids. She talked of games they played like "Red Rover, Red Rover," and "Ante, Ante Over" during her one-room school days. She described her one-room school much like the "Little House on the Prairie" book. She recalled how each row of desks represented a grade, and how they had to wear coats, hats and boots in school during winter due to the room not being insulated and only having a small wood-burning stove.

"In fact," she added, "chopping ice off our drinking water in the school room during sub-zero temperatures, or running outdoors to the outhouse to relieve ourselves, would be considered a cruel hardship for the children of today," she said, with a chuckle in her voice.

On and on she went relating stories of her prairie day existence about how she helped plow the fields, plant crops, bale hay, milk cows, slop the pigs, feed the chickens, gather the eggs, pick berries, and all the other fun and adventure they had mixed in with the dawn to dusk farm work.

As she continued talking about those days, a rosy blush covered her makeup-free face, and her hazy eyes sparkled and danced. It was plain to see she genuinely enjoyed all the good times of her farm life, even though there were many manual hardships.

"Landsakes," mother gasped. "I almost forgot about the bread dough. Bread dough, you know, is a lot like life," she added. "If you allow things in your life to get out of control, they can consume you."

With the bread dough being doubled in size, almost spilling over the bowl, mother showed me how to punch it down again and set it aside ... but this time for only thirty minutes. During that time, mother also revealed some of her childhood antics of tossing live chickens at her brothers when they walked around the corner of the chicken coop, scaring the "hellion" out of them. Or, sneaking up on her brothers, tossing a buck of water over their heads so mother could hear them cuss, and punish them.

Again, Mom got so into her life story that she forgot about the bread dough that was ballooning over the bowl and I once more had to interrupt her.

"Gracious me," she said. "I'm getting just as long-winded as your granddad with the spinning of his yarns. But lordy, time sure has a way of slipping by a person. I guess that's why we should see and seize the best in every moment. Hurry child, we need to shape this dough into loaves, place them into two greased bread pans, and let them rise for thirty more minutes."

As soon as the dough rose above the sides of the bread pans, with me being anxious to see the "fruits of my labor," I hastened to place it in the oven at 350 degrees. Thirty minutes later, I removed the bread from the oven to cool. Seeing the two perfect loaves of bread, Mom gave a sigh of satisfaction, and, looking over at me with a grin, said, "There... now that's a job well done."

And somehow I knew, she meant more than just the making and baking of the homemade bread.

*Sylvia Bright-Green has been writing for twenty-nine years and has been published over 1500 articles, columns, photo-features, and short stories in local and national publications. She has also been published in seven anthologies, a* Famous Wisconsin Mystics *book by Badger Books, co-authored the* Sheboygan County: One Hundred Years of Progress *state historical book, hosted a cable talk show, and taught writing and parapsychology at conferences and colleges in her home state of Wisconsin.*

# Momma Was a Storyteller
## Shirley Anne Cox

*Heritage – family and spiritual – in the mountains of Tennessee*

Momma loved music. When she was younger, I can remember her singing as she washed dishes, or did the Spring cleaning, or washed the laundry on the wringer washer, or as she hung sheets on the clothesline. She loved to have the radio on as she worked. It seemed to fill the room with a sheltering calmness. We knew Momma was happy and everything was right in our little world.

These were the times when Momma would tell her stories. I never remember her sitting down and telling them. She was always about doing something that needed doing. One such day lingers forever in my memory.

The air was scented by the freshly ironed, delicately flowered, sheer curtains as the gentle breeze blew through the open windows. The bright sunlight streaming through the white Venetian blinds made patterns on the wallpaper and the linoleum rug.

This was HOME to my younger sister, Linda, and me; a small four-room house on the Weaver Pike. We sat in our little rocking chairs facing the "entertainment center" which in the fifties consisted of a four-foot tall wooden radio/record player console. It was much taller than we were. There were slat-covered speaker slots in front and the top lifted up to change the records or the radio station. It sat catty-cornered in the living room over from the front door.

We could see and hear Momma in the bedroom just through the open doorway. Momma was singing as she smoothed out the knotted white bedspread she always kept on the bed. She sang along with Jimmy Dean to "Big, Bad John" as she told us stories of her father, our grandfather we never knew, who was nicknamed Big John Nichols. Her stories described the working conditions of his job in the coal mines which was the only way to feed and clothe his family of twelve children. Momma told of the penetrating coal dust which settled deeply upon the miner's clothes and bodies. Everything in their homes, even the innermost parts of their being was coated with the ever present black dust. Her father and my Daddy's father would go into the mines before daylight and come out after dark, living without seeing the sun, day in and day out.

The next song was "Sixteen Tons" by Tennessee Ernie Ford. Momma told us that he was from our own hometown, Bristol, Tennessee. She explained to us what the company store was and how the miners were paid with script that could only be spent there. If you went in debt there, you stayed in debt and could never get ahead. When Momma went to buy groceries, she always referred to it as "going tradin'." She never asked for a bag, she always called it a "poke."

My mother was a story teller. These stories gave us our first glimpse into our family's past. Through Momma's stories we learned about her life before our family of four. These accounts of our "people," that is her term for our kin folk who were raised in the coal mining towns of Virginia, would be the only way we would come to know our maternal grandparents who had died when Momma was very young.

Momma was faithful to recount these and many more as we grew older. I wish I could hear her tell them to me just one more time.

As Christian mothers we are to tell our children of our spiritual past, also. We need to tell them how God has worked in our lives. We must set up memorials in their thoughts that will point them to the Truth, Jesus Christ. How faithful as storytellers are we to tell our children of their Spiritual heritage?

Deuteronomy 6:6-7

And these words, which I command thee this day, shall be in thine heart: And thou shalt teach them diligently unto thy children, and shalt talk of them when thou sittest in thine house, and when thou walkest by the way, and when thou liest down, and when thou risest up.

*Shirley Anne Cox lives in Bristol, Tennessee and is a housewife of thirty-seven years with three grown children and three grandchildren. She has taught Sunday School, Children's Church, and a Lady's Bible*

*Study. Now because of failing health, Shirley is able to put her efforts into writing as the Holy Spirit guides. It is important for each of us to leave behind written memorials for the generations to come.*

*Many of her stories can be found online in e-zines such as: eternal-ink.org, sermonillustrator.org, christianonestop.org, christianvoices.org, heartswithsoul.com, write2theheart.com, frontporchinspiraions.com, and grandparents.com.*

---

# Yom Kippur, circa 1962
## Roxanne Hoffman

*On a holy day of penance, Mom adds a touch of fun.*

It's dark in the little tunnel of a room I share with my big sister. I'm seven, sprawled out on the top bunk of the bunk bed, fasting for Yom Kippur. No lights are switched on. The drapes are drawn over the one window that would normally brighten the room. But it's overcast anyway. Already looks like nighttime outside and it's not even noon. The rain is beating Taps against the window, a down pouring of boredom on this saddest of days. Yom Kippur.

Sylvester is not chasing Tweety on this TV. I'm trying to identify the reflections on the darkened monitor to pass the time. Get into it. Get out of it. Get bored again. No cowboys giddy-yapping in here. In fact, nobody is yapping. Not even my usually giddy sister, now fast asleep in the bunk below me. Nada. Just the tick-tick-tock of the clock counting off the seconds and the muffled drumming of the rain outside to pass the time, occasionally punctuated by the seesawing of my sister's soft inconsistent snores rising from the lower bunk and the claps of thunder. I try humming to distract myself, rollover and stare at the wall. Make clicking sounds in my throat like the pounding hooves of horses. Stare at the dimples on the walls. Count the dimples. Play connect-the-dimples, dragging my index finger along the wall. Spot a hole in the wall where a picture must have once hung. Try to crawl into it with my fingernail.

Can't quite fit. Can't remember exactly what was hung there, either. Watch the shadows from the potted plants and toys, atop the windowsill, dart along the drapes and walls as the lighting strikes, briefly illuminating the room.

I perk up a little at the sound of Mom's bare feet slinking across the carpet like the padded feet of a cat. She climbs up to my bunk and squeezes in next to me, strokes the back of my head, gently tugging my braids. I feel her hot breath against my neck. She tickles me between my ribs. I turn to face her. We stare at each, curled up face-to-face in fetal position, knees-to-knees, nose-to-nose for a while. Make fish faces at each other. Blow fish kisses. Then we flip onto our backs, side by side, holding hands staring at the ceiling. Twin fishes gliding in sparkling sea of blue-gray green sheets and walls. We're both Pisces: her birthday on March 7th; mine, just two days later.

We watch the shadows and lights of the outside world dance across the ceiling together. Imagine the stars twinkling above us. *Twinkle, twinkle little star.* We each make a wish. *But don't tell or they won't come true,* Mom warns. Mine: Dad comes home from Yonkers with burgers, fries and milkshakes. We float, still thinking of our wishes.

Mom whispers, tells me about another dark-eyed, dark-haired little girl, as she strokes my bangs. One, brave enough to stay quiet in the dark and wait all day to eat. Mom knows the story by heart. And suddenly, it's a game. We're in the attic with Anne hiding in the dark to stay safe. A little hungry, but safe for now. Waiting for Dad, the Water-Bearer to come home. His birthday, a month earlier than ours, in February.

It's quiet. Peaceful. We sleep. I hear the rush of gas. Wake up. Heart-racing. Panicked. Mom's snoring beside me. Then I realize it's just the steam rising in the radiators. Wonder about Anne. How old would she be now? Sleep. Dream. *Twin fishes gliding in sparkling sea of blue-gray green.*

# Grandmother
## Roberta Filzer Pearl

*The memories of Perele Kordamer Golokow, a Russian immigrant mother*

My grandmother brought me up until I was ten years old. She died in the early 1970s. In the last year of her life, at the age of ninety-four, she told me again the stories I had heard all during my childhood. They were stories of shtetl life: The Cossacks, the pogroms, the stoning and the killing of the Jews, her dreams of a different life, of an education, of courtship, her marriage, and finally, of her escape from Russia.

These stories and her life have been an inspiration and have guided me throughout my life. She cared deeply about her family and about education. Though she never had a formal education, philosophy was her passion and she wanted to share her ideas.

She wanted people to know who she was and what she cared about. I do too.

These are my memories of my grandmother's stories:

"The wedding lasts a week. There is a dance and food and the religious ceremony. So, after he gives the ring, so then you go to a private place with him. But I didn't know what it meant. So when we were private, this was something terrible. I didn't know what has to go on. And I pushed him, pushed him, pushed him, he should leave me alone. I didn't want that. This was terrible to me. This is animal life, not human beings. You can laugh – how little I knew what life is, at that time. And I was bleeding and bleeding and bleeding, and I didn't know what to do. So, I went to a doctor and he examined me, and he said, 'Who did this to you? Who did you marry? Was it a soldier?' You understand what he thought. He thought my husband was a big man, a strong man, that he could do this to me.

"But he wasn't. He was little, and weak, a coward. But he could do that to me. And after, I went to my father. I said, 'before the wedding, he couldn't touch me. He couldn't even hold my hand. And now, for this little ringele, for this little ringele on my finger, he could do that to me?'

"My father, what could he say? He said nothing. He turned away. So, then I knew. So, this means, this is life."

In the early 1900's in Russia, my grandmother was the young mother of two daughters and pregnant with a third, my mother. She was the proprietor of a small inn on a busy way station. During a particularly dangerous period for Jews, she refused to serve two Cossacks who made anti-Semitic remarks to her. Enraged, the Cossacks threw her against the wall and beat her in front of her mother, who pleaded for her pregnant daughter's life. The Cossacks finally left, threatening to return and kill her. Neighbors hid my grandmother under a feather mattress until the immediate danger was past.

After the birth of my mother, as soon as she was able to travel, my grandmother began her flight to the New World, her two toddlers under her cloak, and the baby wrapped in her petticoat to muffle its cry.

My grandmother and her children joined a small group of Jews traveling to America. During their flight the group encountered a large body of water which had to be crossed. Since they had to go in darkness and secrecy, they could not hire a boat and had to cross through water up to their necks. The current was strong and the children and the women had to be carried across.

My grandmother came from a deeply religious family and the thought that she would be carried by a man other than her husband was shocking. She felt she could neither submit, nor go back. She sat at the edge of the river trying to come to terms with her dilemma.

Frightened by the delay, the group threatened to leave her behind. My grandmother rose up, handed her children over to the men to be carried, and agreed to be carried herself, saying: "So, all right. So, God will have to be satisfied."

"They took us to a barn to stay the night, and at two o'clock in the morning they came for us. On the border, we knew, were soldiers – with guns. And if they hear a little noise, they shoot. The babies were sleeping and the men had to pick them up and carry them. But I was sure they will start to cry.

"I was wearing three petticoats. I took off my three petticoats and covered over their faces, each with a petticoat. I was afraid they would feel the wind and wake up, and start to cry. And this is how my three children were carried. And I was afraid they will smother. And so, that is how we went to America."

"I worked so hard in America. I sold things, ladies' things on a pushcart. The women liked me. They trusted me and I made a little money. So then, later, I rented a little store. It had a room in the back with a little kitchen and bath. For the family. So soon, I had five children and I still had to work all day 'til night in the front, in the store. I cut up all the vegetables for dinner every day, but I couldn't be in the store and in the kitchen at the same time. Esther was the oldest, but she was slow, so Sarah, the next oldest, she had to cook the dinner. And she was so little she had to stand on a chair to reach the stove! How did she do it? Such a little one!

"And the boys? The boys ran wild in the streets, and I was so worried, but what could I do? I had to make money to feed the children. Shimmon? He was out playing cards, women, who knows? And at night, after I closed the store and washed the children and did the laundry, and scrubbed the floor, Shimmon would come home and want a wife. You know what this means? And I was so tired, but he wants. He wants.

"When you work so hard, from early morning 'til late at night, and the children are running, running and crying, and there is no money, and from your husband never a kind word, never a gentle touch. I was so afraid the children will get sick and die, like my brothers and sisters in Russia, and then, you have no life, no joy. I felt so helpless and empty, so empty.

"Later, when we were already becoming Americans, I got a letter. A letter from the shtetl. The pogroms, the Cossacks, they took care of my mother. The Cossacks were stoning her. She had to run away from the Cossacks. She thought she could save herself. The lake was frozen. She ran out on the ice. The ice broke in, and she drowned.

"What could I do? I could cry. I could cry. And that's all.

"One night I ran to the window. I would throw myself out the window. I couldn't take it anymore. And I see my mother's face. 'Perele! Perele! You do this? You would do this thing?' My mother! My poor dead mother's face! No! I couldn't do it. My mother! I couldn't do it. I went back in.

"And Shimmon? Shimmon? He curses me.

"I got sick. I was bleeding and bleeding and it wouldn't stop. My head hurt so much, I thought I was dying. A neighbor lady called the doctor, and he came. He told Shimmon I had a fifty-fifty chance. He told Shimmon he should buy a certain medicine. After the doctor left, Shimmon threw fifty dollars at me, and said, 'So. Go get medicine. Would another man do this?'

"He meant would another man give so much money for his wife to get well. So, when I was better, I took the five children, and we went away.

"In America I taught myself to read English. I love to read. I have to read. And little by little, when the children were grown, I found people who like to discuss. People who also love books. I read Tolstoy, Dostoyevsky, Spinoza.

"And Tolstoy and Spinoza, they were my friends, my best friends.

"You know, it is very hard to leave everything behind – my parents, my house, everything! But I must save my children, and myself. The Cossacks, they were going to come back and kill me! I wanted a safe place to raise my children. America. There was safety in America. There was a way to make a living in America. There were doctors in America. I wouldn't have to watch my children die, like my poor mother did. And you know, everyone who has come here from somewhere else, that is why they come. Who would want to leave their country, their parents, everything they know, to come to a strange place, with a strange language if they could be safe in their own country? It is not easy to be a refugee. I knew I would have to work hard. Work? I was not afraid of work. I was afraid my children would die. That is why, when I see someone different, a different look, a different religion, a different way to do things – it doesn't matter. I know what they go through. I know they fear for their children! And I have to share. It could be a little soup, a place to sleep, a gentle word. I know what it means to be a refugee. It happened to me."

# An Irish Trilogy
## Liz Dolan

### Mother Crosses the Ocean

Master Breen poses in the top row,
his hands folded across his chest like Cuchulain
the tips of his handle-bar mustache brush his checked cravat,
My mother – just a girl – stands to his left
in a coarse wool dress she sewed herself –
lisle stockings and clutie brogues.
Her auburn hair about her face, she beams.
At half ten each morning she serves the master his tea.
I beg her, stay in Tullaree forever.
You will miss the warmth of the cows' udders
and the bleating sheep in the upper pasture.
You can touch the stars here.
Don't cross the sea, Mama. You'll scrub
until your knuckles bleed pink tears on our white blouses
You will dust shelves and polish floors to pay our school tuitions
with Yeats turned to stone in your chest.
Your son's head will be crushed by a truck, three infants will die.
Your husband, a master you'll serve for thirty-five years,
will wax as thorny as pyracantha.

Daughter, at Eastertide they shot sixteen patriots in Dublin.
I am a papist scullion in the six counties
which will be chopped off like a gangrened arm in '23.
The oldest son will inherit the land. You have never been starved
by the raw wind from the banks of the Bann.
You choose your masters in this life.
Our whispered faith, sustained as we knelt on nettles,
will gird me like the radiant skin of a snake.
And you, my child, will write this poem.

**Lessons**

In her cabbage-flowered housecoat she holds
the silver canister beneath her heart,
to toss a fist full of leaves into the Delft pot, then
douses them with boiling water.
"You have to let it brew," she says.
Her hands round the Blue Willow
cup painted with two Chinese lovers
plotting on a wooden bridge,
she mostly listens.
Then she tips my drained cup:
in the leaves a black-haired man

I will someday marry and the blood-red boat
we will sail on in and out of seas
and over weeks and years. It is good
to wait and to be silent.
Tranquility has given her ninety-six years
and when, near the end,
her lungs bloated with fluid,
a nurse serves her piss-yellow tea not fit for pigs,
in the leaves a howling wolf,
she turns her cup upside down
and sets its rim in the round lip of the saucer

**Perhaps Forgiveness Sustains**

My god, the woman could forgive anything:
my boyfriend blotto in a backyard chair,
his forearm gashed, his pristine Karmann Ghia totaled.
Too bad he wasn't totaled, I said
A man has to be able to take a drink, she said.
She'd tell us to respect our father after a tirade
over a missing watch, because he's your father

and you don't know everything, Miss. Your father
peddled apples during the depression.
Decades later she still wet leaves
for his tea, peeled spuds for his supper.
She even forgave God for taking four bairn:
each night on calloused knees, she fingered her black-thorn beads
Above her bowed head,
Magdalene Touches the Foot of the Cross.
At ninety-six, still sharp, after relishing chicken salad,
Mother died,
her heart still as big as a blue whale's.

---

# A Mother's Memoir
## (Dictated to Her Daughter)
## Rita Janice Traub

Hiroshima and Nagasaki
brought an end to the Second World War.
I spent a whole month at a sea resort
only twenty years before.
The happiest month of my life it was,
by the beautiful Baltic Sea.
I was very pretty and seventeen.
Young men were courting me.

The sea air was a joy to breathe
that June I was away,
to swim and dream and just relax.
The sun shone every day.
Close by were groves of evergreens,
their fragrance a delight.
I'd chat with friends, and read and think.
The future seemed so bright.

My dreams were hazy, crudely formed.
What lay ahead for me?
I wanted love and a settled life
with a husband and family.
The next year, though, we sailed away
from that very Baltic Sea,
my parents and I, to America,
where everything changed for me.

From that Baltic shore, in Baltimore,
a woman I soon became,
and the strangers mocked the way I spoke
and gave me a foreign name.
I worked and studied; I earned a degree.
Wife, mother, and widow was I.
I've lived on the East Coast and the West.
Now I think of my life gone by.

So many people needed my care,
and I gave all the help that I could.
Sometimes I've been envied, and other times scorned.
I've been too often misunderstood.
I once had some good friends; they now are gone.
My daughters were never like me.
My husband was loving but soon fell ill.
We spent years in poverty.

I never once visited Israel
and now am too ill to go.
My thoughts at night return to my home,
land of amber and flax and snow,
and that wonderful month at the Baltic Sea,
and the horrors that lay ahead:
how in fifteen years the Holocaust
would leave all my dearest ones dead.

They murdered my people in their homes,
in the streets, river, fields that I knew,
and they slaughtered more at that Baltic shore
by the waves of glittering blue —
as my girls played hide-and-seek and catch
in their backyard in Baltimore.
Then with Hiroshima and Nagasaki
came an end to the Second World War.

*Rita Janice Traub writes:*

*I am a professional writer and editor in Fulton County, Georgia. I started writing rhymes at an early age and have been a creative writer throughout my life. After obtaining my law degree, I spent many years in California law firms preparing briefs and motions. When we relocated as a family to Georgia, I went into business for myself, specializing in marketing research and information technology. By far the most rewarding career I've held to date has been that of caregiver to my mother and sister.*

# Chapter 9

# LOSS:

## Learning from mother's absence

# An Ordinary / Extraordinary Day
## Iona Carroll

*Mother and daughter re-unite after thirty-three years*

There was once a hospital and a healing. And wisdom.

I never sat on my mother's knee. Lessons I might have learned, I never learned. For thirty-three years where there should have been words, there was silence. Until one day our separate lives changed and neither of us, mother or daughter, were ever the same again. Could ever be the same again.

It was an August day. I walked through the hospital grounds and saw a line of wheelchairs in which motionless individuals sat captive and dependant upon others. I counted about twenty people there in the sun - some reading, some talking, others just sitting, expressionless, dreaming. And in one of those chairs, staring Buddha-like with her hands neatly folded in her lap, was the mother I had never known. It was her arms, browned under the Queensland sun that I noticed first. These arms had held me, a baby, for four months and then let me go.

I wonder still what force coursed through me, for at that moment of great stress, I was guided safely and surely to the certainty of my next action. Without pausing to think, although my heart pounded in my chest and my knees grew weak, I walked straight up to this "stranger." Guided by an inner knowledge and gaining courage as I did, I gently placed my hand on hers. Immediately, and without embarrassment, there was recognition in her brown eyes, too. Those arms that I had sensed I knew were around me. I leaned down to her, holding her too, and all the years of not knowing disappeared.

Her words tumbled out. Words that told of sad circumstances, of ignorance, of decisions hastily made and deeply regretted. A tale of two countries. No fault or blame in the telling, just facts as they were remembered. My mother was married. My father was married.....but not to each other. Divorce, because of Church rules, was out of the question. A child was conceived and a mother panicked. This was the end of the 1940's, not 2008. In some parts of the world, women didn't even vote. Their bras had not been burnt! This was another time. My mother fled. I have no idea how she could have kept her condition hidden from my father, her widowed mother, her four sisters and two brothers, but she did and, when she was nine months pregnant, booked her passage across the Tasman Sea from New Zealand to Sydney, Australia. Three days later, she gave birth to me, in Brisbane. She had an aunt in Brisbane whom she thought might have been able to help. I became an Australian by three days, it seems! What happened during the next four months after my birth, I do not know. All I can surmise is that my aunt felt my mother could not cope, alone, with a baby to care for and adoption was the only solution. All the secrets, long kept from me, answered at last. The riddle solved. My mother kept talking and talking. I was her only child. My father her only love.

Around us, curious faces strained to hear but this was neither the time nor the place, to be subject to stares and conjecture. My mother's next words to me were worth more than all the wisdom contained in books. I believe what she said to me was true. I have no reason to doubt.

"I have prayed for you every day." Thirty-three years of prayers for her baby. Seven simple words.

That someone could pray for me every day still seems like a miracle. To have prayed to see me again and believed she would *is* a miracle. How many times, through so many difficult days, must she have prayed? What else can I be but humbled as I think on all this?

When faith sometimes seems to be a dead issue or at best, not proven for we are admonished in this increasingly secular world to believe only what we see, I remind myself of those seven simple words. My mother's life, despite all its difficulties, was lived by faith and love, too, for isn't love greater even than faith? She had been confined to her wheelchair for eight years not able to move a muscle in her legs. But what happened next confounded both doctor, nurse and everyone else because she rose from the prison that was her wheelchair and stood again on legs that were weak from lack of movement. Stood, and then a stumbling step....... and then another.

My mother continued to walk, unaided but courageous to the end. It was important to me to find out more. I crossed the Tasman Sea again, to the New Zealand that was so nearly my birthplace. There I was reunited with my mother's brothers and sisters and their families. A few months later I crossed the world. I had a sea voyage to make too, and a passage already booked. I sailed on the "Canberra" to Britain, to ultimately meet my husband and raise a family of my own. In Britain I was able to make a new life for myself so far from the mother I knew for such a brief time, just four months, too. Three years after that first meeting at the hospital grounds, my mother passed away. I am almost as old now as my mother was then.

I am a writer and words are my business but I know that these words I am trying to write here are inadequate, insufficient things and can never fully describe the healing that comes with reconciliation and forgiveness. As I look back on my life, with all its joys and sorrows, ups and downs, I believe without any doubt that my mother proved to me that there is wisdom beyond words and there is always hope, regardless of outer circumstances. And it is my hope that I can, by word and deed, give to others what was given to me on that August day, at a hospital where once there was a healing.

*The events described here took place in the grounds of the Princess Alexandra Hospital, Brisbane, Queensland, Australia on 20th August 1980.*

*Iona Carroll has published features and short stories in literary magazines in Australia and the UK. At present, she is working on a family saga contained in three novels, "The Story of Fr Vic," which span over fifty years and set in three countries. The first book, "Choices and Changes," begins the story in the 1950s/60s in a fictional town in the West of Ireland. The other two novels, "Familiar Yet Far" and "Homecoming," conclude the trilogy.*

*Iona is currently the Secretary of the Borders Writers' Forum www.borderswriterforum.com and is a member of the society of Authors www.societyofauthors.org.*

---

# A Mother's Love
## Jean Noble

*What is it like to grow up without a mother's love?*

The year was 1946. She was my mother and only twenty-five years old; I was only three. Her second baby was due that day, but God had other plans. Late in the night her screams became evident that something was terribly wrong. An ambulance was called, but by the time she arrived at the hospital, she and the baby were gone. A cerebral hemorrhage had taken both of their young lives, leaving me without a mother.

Alone, without a mother's love, my life moved forward. Yes, there was my father, much destroyed by his (our) devastating loss. There were grandparents, aunts, uncles, cousins, etc., but the mother love was gone forever.

After a couple of years there was a new stepmother, stepsister, and three years later a half brother. My father had become invisible, still in the household, but never really there.

Life did go on. Always troubled by losing the mother love, my life took the direction of a child growing up under those conditions. Since my stepmother had her own two children, my maternal grandmother would remind me to never forget that "Your mother is in the ground." With that as a constant reminder I never felt that I fit into the new family. I was a very troubled youngster, hungering to fill a void, yet too young to understand. I then became a troubled teen, acting out at home, in school, and finally being expelled in my sophomore year of high school. It continued to influence me into my adulthood and my entire life as a whole.

I often asked myself the question, "Why did no one try to console me?" My stepmother did the best that she could under the circumstances. There were never many displays of love or affection from her or my father, such as hugging or being told "I love you." If there ever were any confidential talks when I was troubled by something, I have no recollection of them. My sister and brother were her own flesh and blood and somehow, even as a young child, I felt the difference. So I learned that by acting out I could get attention, and that is exactly what I did. It did not give me the kind of love that I was craving, but rather negative attention. But then even negative attention was better than none at all.

What is it like to grow up without a mother's love? In giving this much thought the questions came to me, such as: who was there to teach me how to be a young woman in a child's growing body? Who was there to hold my hand when life's heartaches came my way? Who was there to teach me how to be a good wife and mother, or for that matter to find a decent husband? Who was there to teach me how important an education was? Who was there to direct me in ways that would help me create a successful life, financially as well as emotionally? Who was there to hold my hand when I was about to deliver my first child, (my husband was in the Navy and overseas) or my second child? Who was there to be a grandmother to my children, or for that matter to teach me, by example, how to be a good grandmother? Who was there to teach me how to cook or take care of a home and a family? Who was there when I needed a mother's shoulder to lean on through life's trials?

My mother's death left a hole in my heart, down to the very core of my being, a hole that has not been filled no matter how hard I have tried. I know that she is always near, on the other side. I know that she knows everything that I have experienced during my life, but it is not the same. I have tried and tried and yet can not fill the void of being a motherless daughter.

By chance, or by the grace of God, I was able to give birth to two beautiful and healthy children. I was able to raise them by pure instinct, (no motherly guidance and no tools to speak of). I fumbled my way through motherhood and made mistakes that have taken their toll on my children until this day, thirty-eight years later.

Through the years of searching, and then finding the church that became my spiritual home, I found an inner peace through finding God. I had not only found God the Creator, my Creator, but also my God within. Finding this inner strength and faith gave me an added peace that I had not known before, yet the place in my heart and life that my mother would have filled has never and can never be replaced. My inner child, to this day, still cries "Mommy, Mommy," 55 years later.

Yes, I admit that there have been many people on this earth that have had horrendous experiences even though they had their mother through their lives. I admit and acknowledge the fact that there are many people who have suffered and do suffer far worse things than losing their mother at such a young age. All these things are true. But does this fill that emptiness? Does knowing this replace the emptiness that I have carried through my whole life? No.

Is this selfish? Is this unreasonable? Where is the answer? I have not been able to find it yet. Even though I had a life before having children of my own, it is as though my life somehow began after I had my own children. I then tried to be the mother to my children that I never had. Yes, I made my mistakes that in retrospect, were due to not having the mother role model. Yet I must admit that through my experiences, I did learn to be a survivor. I learned that I did have an inner strength. I may have grown up without a mother's love, but I did learn how to be a good mother to my own children. I gave my own children everything that I would have wanted or would have expected my own mother to give me.

I can now see, hindsight being as it is, that my whole life, filled with a myriad of experiences, prepared me to be the caring, loving, compassionate woman that I have grown to be, a carbon copy of my own mother, from what those that knew her have told me.

I know there are those that have experienced the same loss and can identify with me. In the meantime, may God bless us all and help us to find our own answers.

*Jean Noble writes: I am a grandmother of four, living in Camarillo, CA, working as a part time crossing guard. I am sure there are many that can identify with me and I hope that my story will touch another's heart.*

# A Motherless Daughter
## Melissa England

*An always disgusted-mother, or an always-smiling mother, leaves a child confused.*

I'm a member of a club. The name is "Motherless-Daughters." It means the most significant person in my life is dead. It's an inevitable loss for all of us. For years I never consciously thought about her. It was easier to pretend she never existed. I dreamed of a mother who was tender and compassionate, more god-like than human. The woman who gave birth to me was Mary England; at least that was the name on her death certificate. Her mother had named her Impy, a Finnish name that other children found an easy target for ridicule. Her older sister gave her the name Mary her first day of school. She never looked back.

I've had strong feelings about the woman who gave birth to me. I loved her, I hated her, and I was terrified of her. I thought there was nothing more frightening than the line that ran down the center of her forehead when her mood darkened. It was that face I tried to bury in my sub-conscious. It took 40 years to come to terms with her. Like the rest of the family she had a Scandinavian beauty; like the rest of the family she shared in a mental illness. Her own mother was capable of outrageous atrocities toward children.

Mary didn't want children, but life has a way of happening, she did, and she proved to be good "baby mother." She was the kind of woman who liked infants, not children. I grew. A baby brother replaced me. She was in total control. I think my mother was through with me when I started saying "no." She was my first catastrophic loss. She broke my heart, and I longed for her.

I turned to my father, he seemed to be able to hang in there with my emerging personality, but like myself, she was the true object of his desire. I wished her gone. I wanted him all to myself.

She was dead before I was seven. I didn't cry. I knew deep in my heart it was my fault. I knew then I must be evil. I deserved to be abandoned. I wished her dead and it happened. I thought my wish got out of hand because it killed him too.

I carried the guilt and shame of my feelings for an eternity. It's amazing to me how death never really ends a relationship.

Then I gave birth. I became the fantasy mother, the one I wished I had. I loved my children, but I couldn't discipline them. I was afraid they would hate me, the same way I hated my mother. I rarely said no to anything. I was the parent the rest of the parents were disgusted with. I didn't make bedtimes, didn't insist on chores, and didn't back up teachers on their need to fill in for my own inadequacy. My overwhelming fear was that my children would leave me in the same permanent way my parents left me.

My less-than-ideal childhood helped create a less-than-ideal childhood for my children. But I am a work in progress, and I learn as I grow. I have come to understand too much constraint and none are extremes that damage a child's need to explore this world safely. I have also come to understand that an always disgusted-mother, or an always-smiling mother, leaves a child confused about the depth of love being offered. I understand my mother more; she was 31 when she died, truly a child herself. I've framed a picture of her and placed it on my dresser. I see her face every morning, this face that doesn't age. I have grown fonder of her eyes, fonder of the struggle in her soul.

I am grateful for her strength, her independence. I am grateful for her creativity, for her ability to rearrange the physical world. I am grateful she was real, not a fantasy-perfect-picture, but a woman who made mistakes. My mother was hard, she struggled against an even crueler background.

Today, she gives me permission to be real, to have all my feelings, to make mistakes, to address my fears, to fall down and to try again. She gave me all the tenderness she could give, I am grateful for that also. She came from nothing, and gave me a place to begin.

Her name was Mary; she was a wife, a mother, and an artist. She was 5'4"; she had beautiful legs, delicate fingers and green eyes. She has taught me something about life that is not taught anywhere but in the pain of her loss, and God, in his infinite wisdom, has allowed me to walk in her shoes.

Today is the first time I can say this with meaning,

To my mother,

Thank you for my life, and yours.

---

# Mother's Day
## Jacqueline Seewald

Mother –
moldering in the earth these many years.
How very much I miss you!
As I stare at uneaten oatmeal thickening in old bowls,
memory washes over me
like Wolfe's eternal river,
a beckoning brook
meandering through timeless shoals
and mossy, macerated rocks.

Mother's Day should be special.
I have it on the good authority of every greeting card.
Mother – why do they refuse to eat their oatmeal?
What would be your words of wisdom?
Don't throw out the love with the oatmeal?
Yes, that is just what you would say!
Part of me was buried with you;
part of you lives on in me –
Mother.

**Chapter 10**

# THE DARK SIDE:

## Learning from bad examples

# Meet My Mother
## Rheana Lee Campbell

*What can one learn from the worst experiences?*
*Reader discretion advised.*

She stood over me sneering and told me when I was six that I couldn't borrow her jeans cause I stank down there. It took me almost 15 years to be comfortable with someone going down on me. Probably not the start of what sounds like the fondest ode to motherhood. Yeah, well life isn't always nice and sweet and easily swallowed, some of the things we swallow make us sick, others kill us.

I have been writing the same poem, the same story asking the same questions now for twenty eight years and still this knot of discontent rubs my skin raw, pulls at me. The first time I can remember having to save my mother's life I was only six and she had left to live with a guy named Dwayne who had gone awol from the army and was currently living at his dad's house in La Grange up in South Bend.

My mother went from one guy to another, but she did it with a method. If this one had a better job he was the one for her, if this one had a better racket going on then she would make the first one crazy, use it as an excuse and have the next dupe ready to charge in and save her.

This night in question they were all downstairs partying, beer and crown and weed and loud music and laughter. This is what I grew up to it's what I thought I wanted sitting in the front room looking through pictures of my drunk mother in a smoky basement at a concert. I wanted to be that cool, to be that carefree. I wanted to be like her, standing at the bathroom door taking in the sounds of her getting ready, the anxious wait for her to get out of the shower, followed by the Q95 blasting through the house every window open the sweet grass cut smell of summer zipping through with promise.

I remember standing at the bathroom door watching her wind the towel around her head, I can still see her young in my head and as much as I loved her and looked up to her, even then it felt like unrequited love. How was I to know I ruined her life and that I was just extra baggage?

I was in love with watching her get ready, the sound of first the towel running over her head brisk magnified in my pulse the sound of the hair dryer comforting as a lullaby the smell of it heated and safe, the heavy earth smell of base and eyeliner the inky scent of what it must be like to be a woman, preened and cleaned and ready to roll.

I loved my mother and since she was 17 when she had me, we grew up together and I'm sorry she had it as rough as she did. How do you cram a whole life of things that never seem to balance out into one letter into one life, into one narrow vein?

I love my mother even though sneaking into her stuff I found she had boxes of true crime books about serial killers I still feel she fell in love with the sexual horror of it and only masked it with saying how great the cops and lawyers that caught them. I still feel my mother was training me to grow up and be something that would make her proud a fucking killer.

Anyway I've rambled away from a simple story. I was six, mom was forever 29 to me younger or older it didn't matter I suppose. But she had been down in the basement partying with her boyfriend and all his friends. There was this fellow named Rocky, I'm sure it wasn't his name but you know, whatever. So the party is winding down and mom has been flirting with rocky, cause while Dwayne was her meal ticket at the time she rarely wanted to fuck the guys she was using. It was like she looked down on them for being dumb enough to be taken in.

So of course he needs a ride home and of course my mother is happy to give him one. Whether she slept with him or not, I don't think it really matters. I so think she slept with him. My mom could never seem to turn away from anyone that was willing to worship her. I know I wound up sitting at her feet listening to her cry about the 19-year-old boy she married who was cheating on her. I could only feel it half-heartedly cause he was the same 19 year old boy she let abuse me.

So every life time story has to start somewhere, so she takes Rocky home and is gone a long time even for drunk dark country road standards, in this time and this is where my mom screws up, she gives these guys time alone to think…her spell starts to wear off and she's lost them to reason.

He sits on the couch waiting and drinking since that clears things up in no time, and thinks to himself, what do I really have to offer her? I don't have a job, I live in my dad's house, and she's gone with another man. Did I mention I was asleep in the next room?

I was fine, I was used to dodging stupid rage even then, I popped out of the womb equipped for it. I thank my mother and God for that. Anyway He's on the couch drinking and thinking and thinking and drinking and it was good he did a lot more drinking cause being the "I want to defend my country and carry big guns." Until of course he realized it was work and ran off, he never went to jail so I assume they thought it was for the best, so of course my mom chose him.

My mother taught me a lot about what to look for in guys, Or what to look for to avoid guys. Is he homeless? Does he have an I.D? Does he do a lot of drugs? Does he want you to do a lot of drugs? Do you get sick to your stomach just standing around him? Does he think of no one but himself and finally is he going to be the biggest rock star in the world as soon as his luck changes and people start to see what he has to offer the world?

I know this cause I followed right down the path my mom did… only I got rid of mine a little faster and I only had one boyfriend who wore my underwear and skirt and tried to cut my head off with a cheap sword from A&K. She helped save my life that time, but I think it was only cause mom likes to be in the spot light and if someone wasn't trying to kill us… I think she got bored.

Back to the story, where were we? Yeah, he being the big shiny gun toting type started to get wise in his stupor and realize mom was playing him, and he couldn't be played he was a man and she was a whore. So he slipped the gun under the pillow and waited. Truth be told my mom has the luck of well every good criminal, she can get caught but it's never her that gets hurt bullets would fly off her lying smiling teeth and lodge in someone else's heart whom she would hold until the ambulance came to take them away and then have a story about how she saved someone's life.

So what I meant by that was… The fact she was probably doing this guy made her late enough just long enough that Dwayne got drunk enough he forgot where he put his gun. SO when mom walked in and I'm still alive, though I think she would have breathed deeply if I had died. She would have been rid of me, which would have freed up time and effort and she would have been loved for having a dead daughter. But I fucked up her plans.

She walked through the door and he looks at her and she looks at him and they know what went on and he reaches for his gun and can't find it, so instead he launches himself at her and knocks her down. My mom can scrap, she has such a rage inside of her that she pretty much offers everyone to fight, picks and prods and pokes and blames it on you.

One day I walked in front of her to hand her a brush and apparently I handed it to her in a aggressive manner and she looked up at me and I saw it… funny that when people try to kill you more than once you can see they all have the same demon. I saw it in my mother all the time. Anyway she looked up at me smiling the edges of her lips pressed white and said. " Oh so you wanna hurt me, anytime you think you're big enough."

She either had epilepsy today or she's faking it. My mom is real good at faking it. But she would have a "seizure" and fall to the ground; I never once got a hammer and cracked her skull open so she should have left me alone when I was younger. But I don't think the demon in her would let her love herself or anyone else. She had one of the biggest holes in her chest and nothing stopped it from seeping out its poisons all over every one she touched.

It's funny how the past won't let the present alone you know? So they look at each other and he launches and gets her down and presses his thumbs into her eyeballs, or that's what he is trying to do. I know this cause I wake up and walk into the room, of course something inside me was already hip to this if you will.

I walk in shake the sleep from my head and don't even scream or maybe I did, but it felt pretty calm to me at the time, it never got better, and it's been the same with mom two or three more times, same shit different players, different guy different struggle, same goal. Mom could never just break up with a guy, which would be far too anti-climatic.

So I walk in and mom is used to being beaten and choked from her step mom and from the times she had been raped, me I was lucky to only have been raped once. Now I just don't trust anyone or anything I drink. But that's not about that right now is it?

I look at my mother on the ground under this crazy drunk guy who right now I understand what happened and why, mom could twist the places that hurt the most and then twist even more by berating you for letting it get to you. Bitch worked for Hitler in a past life. Hell he lost his cool after he met her more than likely. Okay a little far fetched, but met my mom and then decide how far.

I come in there's my mother struggling for her life and I wonder now if part of me would have rather he killed her and then killed me. I mean how horrible would a strangling death been compared to what she and her second husband put me through?

Mom just won't die, I mean I'm pretty sure she can, and it will be something simple, gout or cancer or just old age finally stops her from living, but it won't be huge… something safe for the picture frame as Tori Amos puts it.

Mom is bucking up and thrusting against him trying to dislodge him and his fingers slip and she looks at me white and blue lipped to run up and down this country road with like three houses and yell fire cause no one will come if they know its trouble.

Just like the solider she made me I do just that book out the door screaming fire! Fire!

And two gay guys who saved our lives that night come out and say honey what is it and I tell them that Dwayne is trying to kill my mother and they look at each other like they he had a few screws loose and we all run back down to the house and by this time my mother with the lucky of the unholy has made her way to the front yard where Dwayne tackles her and goes back for her eyes.

I don't remember how they got him off her if they threatened if they had to touch him or if just showing up stopped him but I do remember running back to their house with my mom in tow and Dwayne right behind us. We stayed in their den that night and all that night Dwayne howled around the house banging the windows and screaming baby I love you and baby come back and baby it's okay if you slept with him I forgive you.

Cause my mother, man you know she's poison but she was addictive, my mother might have given heroin its zip, or maybe it was tar that ran through her blood. I don't know. I wanted her to love me, I wanted her to be proud of me. I wanted her to not hate me. I never got any of those things.

Now I don't want you to think that my mother was all terrible. Let me explain. Like a wife explaining her husband pissing in the fountain at a company party. My mother is the reason I have Ritz tattooed on my left forearm.

When my mother wasn't with a guy she was the greatest person in the world. We would watch movies and we would laugh and we would sit in the kitchen and eat a big box of Ritz crackers and easy cheese. There would be parks and rides and when she was with her girlfriend

Even though they weren't having sex, I'm gay I know what a girlfriend is. There would be ice cream and taking her truck as fast as she could over the tracks and there was freedom and freedom so deep and rich I could forgive her for anything and I did.

Part of me still does. I remember the excitement of breaking away from her husbands and boyfriends. I remember sleeping in the front of the truck, I remember being so tired there was no way I could drink all of that 16 ounce glass bottle of doctor pepper, but I wanted to be grown up enough to try, and she always let me. I remember sunrises on highways going to start over again.

I remember gas stations at one in the morning the darkness creeping in and being held back by all those headlights and the gas stations lights were halos.

What did I learn from my mother, well hell, what didn't I learn from her, good and bad, I learned that just because it's family, it doesn't mean love, I learned most people are full of bullshit though most desperately don't want to be. I learned the cops do not come to the rescue, that government buildings do not hold hope and no one really gives a damn and the people that do go home at night feeling like shit cause they can't do a damn thing.

My mother abused me horribly, not like these kids that are put in bags and burnt and savagely beaten. That was never my mom's style she left the beatings to my step father who didn't want to really get in trouble so it was toned down. Pinched and shoved and picked up by my neck and more ass beatings that left me bruised and unable to sit down for weeks.

My mother taught me forgiveness cause if I didn't forgive what she did where would I be? Not writing this piece that probably won't make it anyway. I learned from her I am not a killer, I am not a violent person. I learned from her, you have to not take everything so personal and if someone treats you like shit bide your time if you have to and get out of there as soon as you can, be ready to pick up and leave everything behind parts of yourself if need be.

My mother also taught me to care for the poor to take care of the sick to help those that are older and to respect other people. I guess that went for everyone but herself and her kids. Yeah I have a sister, we don't talk, if we did mom would come fuck with our heads and hearts some more and now my sister has a baby so I love her from afar. She grew up with me, she understands.

The one thing that hurt the most was mom said I was lying, one more story and I'll go on send this forget about it, hope it helps, someone something somewhere. What hurt was when I was looking through mom's stuff to find out who she was, to get close to her, to be cool like her, I read those books about those serial killers and each and every asshole was abused and looking down the list, we shared a lot those sick boys and me.

One of the most painful things was and still is if I ever let myself feel it… When young kids are abused severely and mine was mostly mental. It doesn't leave traces, the young body is still learning to regulate itself and abuses will cause the inability to control one's bowels. In other words, I couldn't stop shitting myself, didn't do it at school, just at home.

I'd be standing there feeling it, knowing it was happening and couldn't do a damn thing.

My mother would beat me for that, and make me wash my panties out in the toilet that the man who was making me shit myself would have his weekend beer dumps in. Did he think it was normal or right? Prick.

Anyway I think my mom knew she was abusing me, I think she didn't care, she talked to others about how horrible it was that kids were abused and how I was so lucky and how I was such a bad daughter, always running away. I ran away 14 times before I was 14. It's still in the books somewhere I assume.

Anyway that was the part that ate at me… she wasn't stupid or ignorant, she did it cause she liked it. Hurting me turned her on, made her marriage better, even though she blamed it on me that they fell apart. Had nothing to do with the fact she only left when he hit her, one time.

Like I said that one story and I'll leave you with the only thing my mom could offer to make up for all the wounds, which have made me a more compassionate if not leery person. One time after the last man that went nuts… we were in the parking lot of taco bell leaning against my Buick and she had for years told me I was laying about being abused. Well you might not know if I'm telling the truth, but I do… and when we all die if you wanna go find the footage in some angels bedroom go ahead watch it.. I bet it's pretty fucking exciting. Oliver twist ain't got shit on me and mine.

Anyway (and man I love that word cause it's what it means, you got a broken heart, live anyway, or this horrible shit is happening, well life goes on anyway doesn't it?) she lit a cigarette after our meal and out of nowhere, but my mom had her life planned down to my responses as well… she goes, " Rheana, you wanna know how to be the best liar in the world?"

Something inside of me said "listen, this is all you're getting." So I did. She butts her cigarette out and I watch it fly across the lot and it feels like my heart I suppose. She blows out the last vestiges of smoke and says, "no matter what they say, or what proof they give, you just keep lying, that simple." And I knew my mother in that moment. If you asked me to explain her you and I would have to drink a fifth of crown and listen to ac/dc and Aerosmith's rag doll and remember what it's like to really be free. What it's like to really for one second in spite of it all be happy.

# A Brand New Woman
## JaeLynn Conrad

*A "tomboy" rebels against her mother's teaching*

Like other years before, I stood in the field, waiting for the signal. My feet, tender from a winter of thick socks and flannel sheets, ached in cold rubber boots as I watched the sky above me from between the little rivers of trickling snow-melt. I breathed lightly, quietly, straining my ears for them.

I usually heard them before I actually saw those rounded bodies and slender necks flying high overhead. The honk of the Canada goose heralded the awakening of my grey-brown earth, soon to turn purple with crocuses. Only then, though the gravel might cut like shards of ice, could I begin.

The field seemed to rush under and away from me as I raced breathlessly back to the house to shed my boots and socks before heading out again. Shivering, I peered at the stumpy blue toes beneath me before beginning the surreptitious barefoot walk up the driveway to build the calluses on my feet.

Weeks passed, then months, and I watched little grasshoppers leap to become giant scythe-jawed monsters. I once felt my mother watch me too; I heard her muttered *oh, bah*, as she turned from my strange, single-minded trek.

By the time we gathered for the midsummer family picnic, the bottoms of my feet were thick as rawhide. My bare-chested cousins tried in vain to hide their admiration. Their bantam egos wilted in the sun as they watched my brave, falterless summer tromp through Canadian Thistle, burrs and little prairie rose bushes. They strutted through the back forty like puffed-up minicocks; tail feathers up, trying not to wince on the balls of their virgin feet. I ran away strongly, invincibly, laughing wide-mouthed, tasting the hot wind-grit between my teeth.

Hunger eventually steered me closer to the picnic area. My mouth watered, muddying my teeth, at the sizzling farmer sausage in the fire. The picnic tables were laden with potato salad and melting Jell-O in big green Tupperware bowls, fresh-baked buns and real butter pudding soft in the sun, rhubarb pie still steaming from my mother's oven, and mounds of fresh baked *rollkuchen* to compliment the mountain of sliced watermelon dripping its sugarblood under the table to the tongue of an eager dog.

Above these aromas wafted the pungent smell of sweaty, fussing cooks who were busy slapping hungry hands, shooing flies and reaching to open plastic lids that strained to burst in the midday heat. Their aprons clung to lumpy *schinka fleisch* thighs that jiggled like the half-melted Jell-O when someone knocked the table.

The sweatier men smelled like their pig farms and sat on sagging lawn chairs, watching the preparations of their flushed female counterparts. Their stomachs rumbled lazily as they sucked on wet toothpicks and snorted over falling hog markets, grain handlers and ornery bull calves. If I got too close, I could almost see the stench escaping from the oven of their leather boots.

Smudged and sweating, I skulked dusty-footed past the lawn chair jury: the oldest of the aunts, the matriarchs who earned their leisure by birthing the harried women and sweaty men. I tried to skirt their gnarled, claw-like hands as they grasped for the flaxen curls that swayed against the points of my shoulders.

"Such a waste," one muttered, shaking her grey head at me.

*"Tomboy."*

She spat the word like a peppercorn, spiking my brain like the thorns that attempted to pierce my feet. The old hens just nodded and clucked as they watched my friends springing, bounding and yelling. Hot wind chaffed my cheeks as I ran away, cursing the fate that gave me a body so different from my shirtless friends who ran as they willed, bronze from the waist up, basking in the glorious summer heat.

The silly girl cousins sat primly, their legs defined by white stockings. Paralysed with fear of smudges or sweat, their bone and muscle was reduced to mere pedestals on which to display still, Sunday bodies, perfectly poised heads and carefully placed curls. I cursed their uselessness and determined to prove rank among my brave comrades by jumping further, running faster and bruising quieter than any of them.

Years went by, each one stretching the gap between my mother and I until we no longer recognised any similarity in each other. In the heat of one of many heart-searing rows my mother cursed me:

"I hope you have all *girls*."

She spat the last word like a peppercorn. The heat of her blast reddened my cheeks as I walked away, and knowing my despicable lack of femininity, I felt confident in the ability to bear only sons.

Time conspired against me and I began to understand what a tiresome business it was, this useless competition. I could still climb high, but not as high, as I was reminded by my now baritone friends. I still ran fast, but not as fast. (I still bruised quieter than they ever could, although no one ever noticed.)

Except for loving one man and bearing my beautiful sons, my femininity was a disadvantage without purpose. I decided that for my new friends, these beautiful sons, I'd have to change the world in order to fulfil myself, and them, within it.

Then came the evening when a man in a green mask sat poised between my knees and my yelps of pain became screaming curses against womanhood. With my husband's taught face close to mine I writhed in agony, hearing the distant echoes of old peppercorn curses turning into deafening screeches around my head. Round and round they swirled, tighter and tighter, thunderous in my ears until at last they were sucked into a whirling vortex as the man in the green mask looked up from between my knees. In one life-defining phrase, he refocused the world within me to a pinpoint; silencing the screams, sealing the vortex, and relinquishing me from my mother's curse that so long ago enslaved me:

"You have a daughter."

A mild summer breeze whispers softly tonight as I watch my baby girl. In sleep her fingers slowly stretch and curl, and her brow furrows as a flock of Canada geese fly overhead, honking gently. Her delicate feet are soft, untouched by calluses; her cheeks are not flushed but pink like a fresh prairie rose blossom.

I look at her, and amazed, I realise that within her tiny frame she embodies all strength, femininity, vulnerability and promise – she is the very image of a woman.

I have a daughter.

I am no longer compelled to change her world. I am empowered to create it.

---

# The Motherhood Myth
## Lynne Daroff

*Motherhood is learned, not instinctive*

Pregnant at 25 years of age, I was at once elated and fearful. Mother dismissed my worries and declared that Motherhood – with a capital M – was the natural state of women who are preternaturally equipped to take on the role and do it well. I accepted this Motherhood Myth and swallowed back my anxiety. But, the more I thought about it, the more questions surfaced.

It was strange, I thought, that my own mother seemed to have eluded the Motherhood metamorphoses. She was not like the tender, loving care-givers I saw on television and movie screens – no crisp, neatly ironed apron, no plates of homemade chocolate chip cookies, no soothing kisses or gentle hugs. She never cared to hear about my day, help me solve a problem, or review my homework. In fact, she had been severely deficient in the whole Motherhood department. Only as an adult, did I realize what a deprived, neglected and abusive childhood I had experienced. I couldn't help wonder: Why?

I faced the painful truth. Married at 19 and a mother by 20, my mother deeply resented the burdens and responsibilities. She had hoped for a different life – a college education, career, accomplishment and even, perhaps, fame and fortune. Instead, barely out of her teens, she was trapped in a drab life of marital and parental bondage at a time when married meant forever. . . and women didn't win college scholarships. Her early disappointments festered and transformed her from a hopeful young woman into a bitter, angry and depressed matron – all before her twenty-first birthday!  Needless to say, mother lacked even elementary parenting skills.

When my first daughter was born, I, too, was a naive and insufficiently prepared mother, dependent upon the Motherhood mythology which promised a miraculous appearance of superb parenting skills.  I waited for something to "click" and release those "innate" instincts.  But, Motherhood skills did not come naturally to me either.  Instead of joy, I experienced rancor.  By the time my baby was a month old, I had my mother's unsmiling face and harsh, impatient voice.

My throat echoed mother's acidic voice and the sound made my soul tremble.  I did not want to be the same kind of "natural" mother she had been, nor did I want my daughter to live through a repeat of the horrors of my own childhood.  I pledged to do better and immediately set about to learn how to be a good, loving and nurturing parent.  Books and magazines piled up on my coffee table and I welcomed personal advice from women whose parenting skills I admired.  I read; I asked; I learned and...I incorporated every technique I thought warranted merit.  Unlike my mother, I also satisfied my hunger for education and career which dissolved any personal frustrations.

When my younger daughter gave birth to her first child, I did not tell her the Motherhood Myth.  She doesn't expect to be mystically or supernaturally transformed into a wonderful parent.  She takes a modern approach as befits a certified Web Master.  Where books and magazines were my main information source, for my daughter, the Internet reigns supreme with its access to the world's libraries, dedicated parent and health sites, and uncountable chat rooms where young women compare notes with contemporaries around the world.  The computer is her tool, her link to the world and the cornerstone of her home business.  Understandably, my daughter has been able to embrace Motherhood with a verve and enthusiasm unknown in prior generations of our family.  She has found what it took me a lifetime to learn: Motherhood can be as natural and satisfying as purported in the Motherhood Myth – not magically, but through knowledge, preparedness and hard work.

To her last breath, my mother believed she was a great parent, completely unaware of her inadequacies and the suffering she inflicted on her unhappy daughter.  I do value, however, what gifts she was able to bestow.  She taught me to cook, sew and read, all important skills, as well as how to enrich life through an appreciation for music, literature, art and theater. The most valuable lesson I learned, however, was to reject the Motherhood Myth, think for myself and work diligently to become a mother my two daughters would cherish.

*Lynne Daroff is a political activist, freelance writer and grandmother ... not necessarily in that order.*

---

# Radiance
## Liz Allen

*"...role model, support, fan club, best friend...and antagonist."*

Radiance by definition: *the quality of being bright and sending out rays of light.* Radiance was also my mother's name. Yes, her *real* name; christened so by my forward thinking grandmother in 1925. Beginning life with such a spectacular label proposed challenges, but Radiance was up for them.

Mom was beautiful, theatrical, vivacious, creative *and* high-maintenance. She aspired to be an actress but her career only bloomed locally on the community stage. She was, however, magnificent. She was my role model, my support, my fan club and my best friend. She was also my antagonist.

I was the final product of Mom's fifth and last marriage. Amongst this woman's many loves, she captured the hearts of five men who found her too irresistible not to marry. Conversely, each one was eventually overwhelmed and blinded by her brilliant light, ultimately leaving her to shine alone.

But role model she was. I observed my Mom's technique to suffer, beg compromise, negotiate and manipulate men – my father in particular. And I learned. I watched her desperate attempts fail to produce the results she sought. And I learned. I watched my Dad try to smother her with a pillow and I believed her when she caught her breath and calmly told me and my brother they were rehearsing a scene from a play. I watched her survive. And I learned. Radiance was nothing if not a warrior. She had dreadful judgment regarding which battles she picked, but she fought valiantly and she survived.

My parents divorced when I was twelve years old and I lived with my father for the next four years. By sixteen, I was terribly in need of maternal love, attention and guidance. Much to my mother's elation, I returned to the warmth of the womb. What I didn't anticipate was the role reversal; Radiance was just as needy for the same. She became helpless and clingy. She displayed weakness, dependency and anxiety with regularity. I became impatient and angry with her behavior. I felt overwhelmed; not safe and secure as I had anticipated. She was forcing me to surrender my childhood to become *her* mother! Ah, *there's* that blinding light that drives everyone away!

I was a terror throughout my teens and blatantly tortured my mother. I showed her utter disrespect; I spoke harshly to her without reservation; I avoided her; I told her I hated her. I broke her heart countless times and each tear she shed empowered my aggression. But somehow she survived my attacks and belligerence. She *never* gave up on me and she never stopped loving me. And I learned. I learned what *unconditional* meant.

I didn't lighten up on my Mom until I came home one day from high school to an ambulance parked in front of my house. There was a small crowd of neighbors all whispering that the "little lady who lived there had jumped off the roof." We had a two story house. I was charged with the intense level of fear and terror that adrenalin can stimulate. I pushed through everyone to my Mom being carried out by paramedics. She was alive but crushed. She didn't *jump* off the roof of our house, she fell. She lost her footing while – brace yourself – vacuuming leaves off the roof. Radiance didn't always employ the most sensible judgment when it came to certain ideas. This was clearly not one of her smarter plans. But she survived and I learned.

Don't vacuum leaves off the roof!

Once we were past the crisis, I collapsed emotionally, rattled with the panic of how close I came to losing Mom. Amazingly, she recovered from a collapsed lung and multiple fractures. Eventually my fright gave way to appreciating her, but before long, the conflicts were queued up again.

By the age of seventeen, I was dating a thirty-two year old divorcé with two small children. I moved into his house, but Mom tried everything she could to keep me close. That summer, his eight year old daughter, Debbie, was visiting. My boyfriend had to go out of town for a business trip leaving Debbie fatherless with a teen guardian.

I tried to plan fun activities and called Mom for suggestions. She had planned to drive to Atlanta to see my sister for a few days and asked if we would like to come along. She sweetened the deal by offering to pay for a day at Six Flags over Georgia. This was ideal timing. It would be nice to see my sister too.

I can't remember the last time I was in a captive situation for *hours* with my mother. We were all going to be in a car for at least seven. I tried not to anticipate the worst, but Mom did not disappoint. Debbie and I packed a few things, swung by to pick Mom up, and began our trip to Atlanta in my Gremlin.

Ninety minutes out of Tampa and Mom is already *languishing* from the heat. I ran the air conditioning but it wasn't freezing enough for her.

It starts. The more she whined and overdramatized how she was *melting*, the more she amused Debbie, who had never seen a grown woman bellyache so much. The hilarity would be short lived as my Mom would morph very soon into a shrike (a brown or gray songbird with a screeching call and a hooked beak that eats insects and small animals that become impaled on sharp objects such as thorns.) We pulled over and bought a bag of ice so Mom could dab a washcloth into the ice water and use it to keep her cool.

We had only driven as far north as Gainesville when we stopped for dinner. We'd lost an hour of drive time, so Mom decided we should stop for the day and stay at a hotel.

The evening was relatively uneventful. Mom was in total fantasy land as she regaled Debbie with tales of *our* wonderful relationship. In the morning, we had breakfast and hit the road again. No more than twenty minutes crossing the Georgia state line, Mom started to bristle her quills. We had been playing word games like Password, twenty questions, etc., and Mom decided to introduce a *really fun concept...Let's name the presidents and state capitals!* I was a pretty decent student, but I couldn't name presidents in order (still can't), and truth be told, I'm still challenged with at least half the state capitals.

The game began. Mom zeroed in on Debbie and started grilling her. Debbie tried her best, but with every incorrect answer, Mom made her feel stupid and insignificant. Mom had a mean streak in her that was rarely shown, but when she was bad, she was *horrible.* I had grown up with her so I had the tools necessary to handle her episodes. Debbie, on the other hand, was a complete innocent. She didn't understand what my mother was doing or *why.*

So once Radiance was on a roll, she wouldn't stop. She criticized Debbie, her education (or *lack* of it), her parents, her looks, *her weight…* She surpassed the boundaries of tactlessness and indecency.

Had my dear mother completely forgotten what this little girls' situation was? Had she forgotten the purpose of this trip was to cheer her up since her dad ditched her?

I drove while this assault unfolded. Debbie was weeping and Mom literally told her to suck it up. I was desperately trying to stop the attack, but Mom ignored me. She had her fangs deep into this victim and was intoxicated with the taste of blood.

Debbie was my responsibility and I had to protect her. Mom wouldn't stop. It was weird – like an avalanche that couldn't be thwarted. Debbie was pleading with me to make her stop and kept imploring, "Why does your Mom hate me??????!!?"

I pulled over on Interstate 75 and stopped the car.

We stopped on the median. *That* shut her up. I demanded she apologize to Debbie. She would not. I felt like a mother tiger protecting her young. I told Mom to get out of the car. She turned pale (as did Debbie) and then started to laugh (as did Debbie). I wasn't kidding. And she knew it. She had gone too far. At that point, I didn't care if she apologized. I wanted this toxic troll out of the car. She had spewed her venom for the last time.

I was livid and even though she became penitent, I was too far gone. Again I insisted that she get out of the car. Mom gave me an adrenalized stare and then tried to get tough.

"You can't do this to me. I'm your *mother.*"

"I know who you are. Get out."

She wouldn't budge. I took the keys from the ignition, got out, and walked around to the passenger side. Mom locked the door and held the handle all the while screaming, "Stop it! Lizzie, honey, PLEASE!"

I put the key in her door and firmly pulled the handle while turning the key. She fell back away from the open door as she clutched her purse. I grabbed her arms and literally pulled her out kicking and screaming. (My adrenalin was pumping too, but she only weighed about 90 pounds, so the extraction wasn't too difficult.) Once she was out, I locked and slammed the passenger door shut. Walked around to the drivers' side, got in, and drove off.

I'm sure Mom thought I was bluffing in order to scare her. Debbie sure thought I was. Until I picked up speed and *really* drove off. I briefly saw Mom in the rearview mirror, shocked and defeated. We were too far away to see the transition to fear and panic.

The expected thing to say now would be, "I'm not proud of what I did," but that would be a lie. I was *very* proud of myself, then and to this day. At such a young age, my maternal instincts had kicked in, and I did what I believed necessary to protect my young. I will admit that tossing my mom out of a car (at least it wasn't *moving*) probably didn't set a good example for Debbie, although she idolized me as a result. She was somewhere between stunned and exhilarated from my actions.

Even now, I teach my teenage daughter about abusive relationships. Regardless of personal or professional, it you are in an abusive relationship (physically, emotionally, psychologically), try everything you can to heal it. If it cannot be healed and you remain in danger, remove yourself from it. Period. Both parties must be willing to do the work; you can't do it all. Besides, you can't heal the abuser. That's not your job; it's *theirs*. If you can't see clearly, remove the obstacle. God, I hope my kid doesn't throw me out of a car some day. Now *that* would be karma.

*  *  *

Mom was fine. I never had a doubt her resourcefulness would see her through this little adventure. Someone picked her up within minutes (I can just hear her telling *that* story) and took her to a gas station where she called a taxi. The cab took her to the Atlanta airport; she booked a flight home and was back before dinner time.

Debbie and I went on to Six Flags and had the time of our lives. Being Radiance's daughter, I was resourceful too. I had brought cash, *just in case.*

By the time we returned to Tampa, Mom had left nearly a dozen messages on my answering machine. They all said the same thing: "Please forgive me."

Wow! I dumped her like garbage on the side of the road and she asks *my* forgiveness. I suspect this was some weird twisted reverse psychology, but *I forgave her.* We would talk about this episode for the rest of her life. She would continue to ask me, right up until the moment before she died, if I had *really* forgiven her.

Radiance did her best. She was the best mom *she knew how to be.* She had learned from *her* role model and hers before her.

Mom died before my daughter was born, but the baton had been passed. I knew what kind of a mother I hoped to be. Radiances' legacies were her survival skills and unwavering love. She had an insanely high pain threshold and, while she would wince, she would always rise above. In fact, even in death, she lives on. Her brilliant light did not go out when she died; it's just shining somewhere else.

Whenever my daughter mouths off to me or says something hurtful, I turn to the light and I *know* Radiances' granddaughter still loves me.

*Liz Allen writes:*
*I grew up in Tampa, Florida where I attended the University of South Florida. I moved out to California in 1990 where I met my future husband whom I married in 1992. In 1995 I had a child and in 1999 post-traumatic syndrome brought on by three earthquakes forced me back to Florida. My first book* Who Got Liz Gardner *is available on www.elizabeth-allen.com. My second book* Discovering Arugula *which is a sequel to* Who Got Liz Gardner *will be available in summer 2010.*

# Messages from Mother
## Madeline Steeg

*A victim of patriarchal religion*

As I near my 69th birthday, my mother's messages still ring loud and clear. They had a profound effect on me and my eight siblings. They shaped our psyches like nothing else, shaped us into her beliefs and her experience of life in the early 1900s, as they had shaped her mother's and the women before her, ever backward through the centuries of recorded history. They said that all mankind was worthless, but woman was even more flawed because she had disobeyed God in the Garden, and that woman's work on earth was to serve God in man, bear and care for man's children.

She was a curious mixture: on one hand caring for us from early morn till late at night, finding food and clothes enough for us, keeping us clean and off to daily Mass and school on time, attentive to our ailments as best she could. She never forgot a birthday – how she found the money for this and for a Christmas present or two, and an Easter basket for each of us – I do not know. It was Depression years and money was scarce.

But on the other hand, there were the truly cruel and destructive messages that we heard every day: "You'll do as I say, or you'll be pushing up daisies," "Don't tell me what you want...I'll tell you!," and "just who do you think you are?" "I can make you sorry you were ever born." Not healthy messages for a child, but I'm sure she wasn't aware of this back then. She had heard the same from her parents.

Obedience was high on her list of demands along with the Sixth Commandment: "Thou shalt not commit adultery." This was really crazy-making for youngsters – because nothing was ever explained to us – what were they talking about exactly, we wondered. But some part of childhood's intuition came to the fore and told us that our bodies below our belts were evil, must be ignored, must never be touched by ourselves or anyone else. Also, we must not discuss where babies come from or anything else on that subject, beware of "impure thoughts," and remember that all sins against purity are mortal, not venial, and if you die with a mortal sin on your soul you will burn in hell for all eternity. No ands, ifs or buts! Hugging, kissing, touching of any kind (except spankings on various parts of one's body) were something we children never saw in our home.

Mother did not feel good about her sexuality and she passed this on to us. Out of the nine of us children, only three married, two went to the convent and one is an ex-priest. Even as I write this, I am in awe of the insidious power of religion's beliefs – how they can eviscerate the young, impressionable child. But my mother was obsessed with her Catholic religion. So when I told her my fantasy or becoming a nun someday – like those we lived next door to and who taught us every day in school – she was delighted. I was only fourteen but the nuns had recently begun accepting girls of high school age, so without really knowing what I was getting into and never having been away from home before, I was put on a Greyhound bus and driven hundreds of miles away from my home to become an "aspirant" to the Religious Life of the Sisters of St. Angela. I knew from the first hour on that bus that I wanted none of this. I wanted to be back home – I had to get back home! But it was not that easy.

There were five of us aspirants. We virtually lived the lives of the nuns around us. I missed my mother and family terribly and when we were told we could go home for ten days over Christmas, I made up my mind that I was staying there. But after a few days, when I worked up courage to broach the subject, her eyes turned dark, she grew sad and I knew the next phase would be her anger – much banging of pots and pans, stomping of feet, muttering to herself about "ungrateful, good for nothing children." And her black mood would invade the entire household and the other sibs would draw away from the perpetrator – Me! She had greeted me so warmly at the bus station and written loving letters every week about how she missed me...but the truth was, she didn't want me home. She wanted me in a convent, a nun. That meant everything to her. I contracted laryngitis the next day and could not speak above a whisper for the remaining days of my stay.

I wanted to be home with my girlfriends, to go to parties and dance with boys, to go to movies and take long carefree walks. Most of all I wanted to be near my mother. I needed her presence – without it I had a pain in my heart, a real, true, physical ache there.

Suffice it to say, now, as I am starting to wander afield – my mother was a valiant, strong woman who loved us, I know, but she became ever more obsessed with her Catholic faith. To her, it was everything. She valued it above any person or any pain or any contradiction....beyond reason itself.

I finally found my way home after five long years, crucial teenage years. Much of my life has been spent in seeking mental health. She felt, when I did come home at last, that I was doing this to "hurt her."

I long ago came to terms with my anger about this, realizing how she, like most women, was a victim of patriarchal religion, patriarchal society. I know she did her best with what was given her. But we truly never enjoyed each other's company again through long years until she died.

There was one moment though, that I remember with joy – I'd come from far off for my father's funeral. She was in a wheelchair then, nearly blind, deaf. I knelt beside her to tell her goodbye, my eyes full of tears. She said, "You loved your dad, didn't you?" and pressed my head against her breast and I felt such a warmth and comfort there – some great fire from long ago – perhaps when I took root in her body, beneath her heart. An older sister said, "Enough of that now, let's not get into a crying jag here!" I felt so sorry for us all.

---

# At My Mother's Knee
## Jean M. Hendrickson

There was a time,
long after I should have known,
when I dared not deviate
from Mother's rules.
I took her prejudices
and wove them into my hair;
wore them like raiment;
learned them by heart.

Mother taught
with a toss of her head,
punishing sighs,
the set of her jaw,
with muttered slurs,
her rigid stance
a turning away.

Mother said

girls with
long hair are cheap
short hair, mannish
without girdles, loose.
Artistic girls are deluded,
athletic girls, unfeminine
smart girls, unattractive
popular girls are immoral.

Mother said

Catholics are idolaters
Jews, heathens
Negroes and Mexicans,
ignorant and dirty,
Chinese and Russians,
Communists,
and all Japanese are evil.

Mother's rules were hard and glossy as anthracite.

One day, I walked out of Mother's house
into a sweet spring.

I heard blaring horns,
tatters of music,

curse words,
saw men and women,
arms entwined,
happy children
with dirty faces,
and the conceit of sunrise.

I saw an uncorsetted girl
with flowing curls, rouge
and an artist's palette
under her plump, bare arm,
skip down the street,
singing a raucous love song.

I sat beside old men
playing checkers in the park,
rescued a three-legged cat
smiled at strangers
entered a synagogue
--and a Catholic church—

I smelled Thai, Mexican and Cajun food,
Chinese, Italian, and Indian food,
Kosher, Japanese, and Soul food,

and I breathed, laughed,
sang, and ate,

until I was full.

*Like many daughters, when **Jean Hendrickson** was in her late teens, she and her mother clashed over rules and ideals. Fortunately, she learned to respect their differences and to love her mother for the wonderful woman she was.*

*A year to the day after her death in 1989, Addie McLeod visited her daughter and left her with the last in a series of "mother poems."*

*Jean Hendrickson's book,* Tiny Poems for Women Who Think They Hate Poetry, *can be found at http://www.hamptonroadswriters.org/jeanhendrickson.php. Additionally, she has had thirty-two short stories and poems published in literary journals since 1993.*

---

## Photo Synthesis
### Beverly Jackson


She was prim, my mother,
in her respectable clothing,
flipping my photo album pages
as if her eyes could play catch up
by just staring at snapshots
of my life,
years lost like buttons
between us.

One photo – a college fraternity party:
I wore the tops of his pajamas.

Two photos – two different weddings:
I was bride in both.

One nude or nearly so – panties airbrushed out.

She never blinked;
pages flipping soundlessly
under her long, white fingers.
Her face a gentle mask of tolerance,
curiosity, or indifference.

One photo – in a bikini on the dancefloor –

gripped by strong, black arms.

She turned to me, disdain across her face.
– They don't respect white girls, you know.
the daughter idea dimming
in narrow eyes,
dying
at once
for good.

# Chapter 11

# FROM OTHER LANDS:

## Motherhood around the world

# Always, Mama
## Dalia van den Boogaard

*An immigrant mother gives her daughter a distinctive view of the
world*

A Saturday morning in a quiet Indiana town finds it the very picture
of the apple-pie normalcy of the American Midwest. It's the late 1960s,
but none of the heated clashes between youth and the Establishment that
have burst forth across the country have surfaced on the tree-lined streets
of suburban Munster. There is something brewing, however, at Burger's
Market, and it's not the café-chic espresso you'll find there forty years
later. Some kind of face-off is about to take place between two distinct
generations and mindsets, a confrontation we can only hope will not
erupt in the hurling of cantaloupes willy-nilly across the produce
department.

"*Viktorai! Dalia! Kur jûs rupûþës pabëgot?*" yells our mom from
over near the melon bins, loudly enough that my brother and I hear it all
the way back in the candy aisle, where we have camped out to evade her
and to gaze at all the Jujubes and chocolate cigarettes she will never buy
for us because, she often states flatly, "American kids eat too much
candy."

"Good 'N Plenty, Good 'N Plenty, Good 'N Plenty," I murmur,
shaking the box one last time before putting it back on the shelf.
"C'mon," my older brother Viktor says, tugging my sleeve and leading
me towards Mama's voice, still calling us in Lithuanian at foghorn level.

Our approach is met with both relief and irritation. Viktor, age ten,
is mustering up the courage to insist to Mama that in public she speak to
us only in English, but she has already launched into a scolding in her

native tongue. I can see that my brother has resigned himself to silence, perhaps for fear that any pleas on his part will only result in a further barrage in a language peppered with the strange rhotic-trilled *r*, as well as fricatives and affricates like *č*, *š*, and the dreaded *ž*. Both he and I look over our shoulders, praying not to find any kids from school snickering at us.

The uprising has been averted. We meekly follow Mama to the check-out line, where our father is already removing a loaf of rye bread, a jar of horseradish, and tins of Baltic sardines from our cart and placing them on the conveyor belt. We take over that task, glumly adding cans of pickled red beets and sauerkraut to the bevy of items that will comprise tonight's supper. Mama takes a deep breath and finally smiles at us. There will be no mutually satisfying resolution to our conflict today, but at least there will be no further spectacle regarding our disobedience, either.

*   *   *   *   *

When I was a kid, I knew my mom stood out as being different, and it often bothered me. Let's face it: it embarrassed me. While other mothers would take their daughters shopping at Marshall Field's on a Friday afternoon, my mom – who never learned to drive a car – took me into our garden to plant snapdragons and recite poems together. My friends all had Malibu Barbies in mini-skirts and go-go boots, but I was not allowed to have fashion dolls ("Such bosoms they have!" Mama would say) and had to content myself with freckle-faced, flat-chested Chatty Cathy. I also missed out on the rollicking pillow fights of sleepover parties, which I was not permitted to attend because Mama worried, "What if the parents smoke? What if the whole house burns down in the middle of the night?"

I was mortified at how overprotective she was – until I became a mom myself. Funny, how her fears no longer seemed irrational, how her view of the world suddenly seemed to make sense. Yet I've tried to extend the boundaries a bit with my own children. Mama taught me to guard them, but she unknowingly also made me vow – by curtailing my opportunities – to let them experience certain traditions of an American childhood. The tough part is agreeing to things I immediately regret, and then stressing out until my kids are back home, in one piece, and safely tucked into their beds.

As I grew up, I began to appreciate just how much Mama's unique qualities made her beloved among friends and family and unforgettable to people who knew her only briefly. I didn't always understand her, but I always loved her. Now that I have children of my own, I realize how much she molded me into the mother I am today.

Mama sang all the time, everything from Lithuanian folk songs to Italian operettas to Harry Belafonte's "Day-O." In order to make her endless housework seem less of a chore, she played records and sang along as she waltzed through the house with her bright orange feather duster. My friends would come up to the screen door and, before they could knock, drop their Bazooka-clacking jaws at this scene.

On top of that, we were known as The Family That Sang in the Car – in four-part harmony, no less. My brother and I were not formally taught to harmonize – we simply picked it up by listening to our mom blend melodies with our dad. All of our voices chiming together, especially on journeys to and from Wisconsin Dells, is a memory I cherish – though at the time, I would always slink down in the back seat of our beige Chevy Impala when Dad turned onto our street for the home stretch.

One of the reasons that music was always flowing through our house was that Mama saw no reason for us to buy a television set. We were the only people on the block, if not in the whole town, without one. My mother had seen enough TV programs to come to the conclusion that few were truly worth viewing. She'd rather that we spend evenings reading or playing Monopoly, while Nat King Cole serenaded us from the stereo. Along with the over-consumption of sweets, Mama felt that "American kids watch too much television."

Only on Sunday nights were we treated to TV after our weekly dinner at our grandparents' house in nearby Hammond. Their television set was a polished walnut Motorola console that stood at an angle in the corner of the living room, and we all gathered in front of it – adults on the sofa and chairs, cousins overlapping one another on the shag carpet – to watch "Bonanza" and "The Ed Sullivan Show." But during the rest of the week, as our friends were glued to "Batman" and "Bewitched," I was practicing my piano lesson, while my brother struggled to churn out fast-paced polkas on his shiny red accordion.

That's right: his accordion. This was the instrument of choice – Mama's choice – for a young lad with a European heritage. While other boys his age were banging on junior drum sets and spending their allowance on hit 45s, Viktor was pumping decidedly less-groovy Stan Yankovic hits on his accordion. He would trudge down to the basement rec room to practice, hoping no one on our block would hear him. Mama would go downstairs, nodding at him in approval and sometimes even doing a few impromptu heel-and-toe steps with the laundry basket in her arms. When she'd open up the basement windows to air out the dampness, the whole neighborhood would sure enough thump with the accordion's oom-pa oom-pa beat. And there was no end to the teasing Viktor's buddies subjected him to over this.

I've tried to soften these indignities in raising my own children. The current tally at our house is:

Televisions: 3

Accordions: 0

I've insisted that the kids all learn to play the piano, but the boys also thrash at the guitar and drums. And I'm guilty of letting them all watch their fair share of mindless TV shows. During the school year, however, I remind them – as they roll their eyes and play air-violin in the background – that I grew up in a household that for many years did not even have a TV. My simple rule is this: no zoning out in front of the tube on weeknights. Instead, we talk, read, or even pull out that old Monopoly game. This is Mama's influence upon me.

Regarding unrestricted singing: I'm guilty of that, too, and so is my daughter. Either that's genetics at work, or my daughter simply grasping the joy of allowing music to burst forth from her own internal boom-box. From time to time I am conscious of other drivers peering into our car as my little diva and I belt out "I Will Survive." She blushes and ducks. I do not. I will survive their stares. I do, however, make sure all the windows are rolled up.

People used to comment that our family had not only an impressive collection of records, but enough books spilling off our shelves to open up a local library branch. Mama was responsible for this. From her earliest days, she immersed herself in the world opened up to her by literature, even being whipped with a switch by her Papa whenever he found her reading by candlelight into the early hours of the morning.

Among the few items that our mother brought with her from the old country was a pile of treasured books, several full of poetry she'd largely committed to memory. Some of her favorite poems to recite were "Trees," by Joyce Kilmer, and – with somewhat melodramatic flair – Alfred, Lord Tennyson's "The Lady of Shallot."

For my brother and me, memorizing poems was more of an uphill battle. Oddly enough, I found myself writing poetry after awhile, especially when creating construction paper cards for Mother's Day or for Mama's birthday. The tears in her eyes let me know that my syrupy verses meant a lot to her. Little did I know that poetry would become – and remain – my favorite form of literature, and that the poems Mama loved would become the poems I love to this very day.

Like my mother before me, I ask my kids to memorize poetry from time to time. All three can recite "Trees," Robert Frost's "Stopping By Woods on a Snowy Evening," and – this one of their own choosing – Clement C. Moore's "The Night Before Christmas." I want to open them up to the limitless possibilities of where poetry can lead them. I want to let them in on the secret that Mama shared with me long ago: that good poems are simply good for your soul.

Whether it was due to all the reading she did over the course of her life, or to some magic streaming from her soul to her pen, Mama had a gift for writing. In fact, an essay she wrote while at Washington High School in East Chicago, an essay composed in a language she was still painstakingly trying to learn, earned her a full scholarship to study English Literature at Indiana University. The students were asked to write about the meaning of freedom. For a girl who had survived so long without it, the topic held a particular resonance. Her words rang true and flowed directly from her heart.

Many competing students resented her for having won the scholarship. After all, here she was, Erika Franckevičius – mocked as "French cabbage juice" – the daughter of an immigrant foundry worker, a soft-spoken girl with a heavy accent who came to school in outdated dresses that a teacher had donated to her to replace the rags in which she'd arrived at Ellis Island. She made few friends at school. Most were black students who sensed that she was, like them, an outsider.

Maybe because she herself was scorned as a third-class citizen, my mother felt empathy for minorities and treated them with kindness and respect. Since she spoke six languages, she helped other "displaced persons," young and old, complete homework, write letters, and apply for jobs in their new country. Parties thrown by our family always felt like international festivals, with Spanish spoken at one end of the house, German at the other, and Russian, Polish and Lithuanian everywhere in between. I may not have understood most of the chatter, but I soaked up the atmosphere: the music, the dancing, the laughter, the ping-pong table covered with a giant white tablecloth and crammed with a vast array of proudly-prepared ethnic dishes. Welcoming people of all countries and colors was our way of life, and we learned from Mama that everyone, even from the humblest of backgrounds, had a meaningful story to share.

When we were old enough to realize that her own story – and the way she told it – was remarkable, my brother and I repeatedly urged Mama to write her autobiography. She always had a ready excuse not to, such as "*Jûs iš proto išėjot!*" ("You have lost your minds!"), or "As if I have the time!" or "Who on earth would want to read about me?" Mama considered writing one's memoirs a bit self-indulgent, unless, of course, one was as illustrious as Jackie O or Elizabeth Taylor. But our dad pulled us aside and told us that the real reason she would never write her own story was that the unspeakable hardships that she and her family had suffered during the war – the terror, the famine, the death among her own siblings – were too emotionally harrowing for her to relive, in their shocking, detailed entirety, for a book.

Instead, tending to her family and keeping a spotless house and picture-perfect garden were Mama's constant focus, and what remains of her writing is largely correspondence. I sometimes re-read her letters and marvel at how poignantly she expressed her feelings, how enchantingly she described the events of an ordinary day. Her sense of humor, mainly aimed at herself, still leaves me grinning. She closed her letters to me with "Always, Mama" – and really, this sums up her presence in my life. Even today, almost ten years since she's been gone, hers is still the voice that guides me, laughs with me, cries with me, and – always – comforts me.

Of all the things she wrote, my mother's descriptions of simple gifts of nature in our own backyard inspire me the most. She was happiest in her garden, and I sense her joy as I plant ordinary seeds and watch them turn into extraordinary flowers. Mama gardened every day, rain or shine, even when her arthritic hands failed her. She bound herself to the good earth long before she was laid to rest in its cool bed of soil. Like Emily Dickinson, she did not let things like a May flower or a summer shower escape her notice. And on a gray, wet day, she was always the first to spot the rainbow.

The 1970s astrology craze left me with the notion that Mama exhibited many of the polar-opposite traits of the sign of Cancer: she could be emotional and loving one minute, overemotional and touchy the next. She wasn't perfect; she was human. She recognized her own faults and always apologized if she flew off the handle or gave us an occasional, old-fashioned spanking. Happily, she dispensed hugs far more freely, and there was nothing better than being surrounded by her soft, warm arms, which had the gentle scent of Avon Topaz cream sachet. While I can't say that I consciously always try to be like my mom – on certain levels, I try to act just the opposite – I can't deny that I walk most roads directly in her footsteps. And I'm proud of that. Mama was the single greatest influence on my life.

One of the lessons I've learned the hard way is that my parenting style, which purposely differs in some ways from my mother's, is not nearly as effective. Mama may have understood the value of freedom, but she also understood the value of discipline. She had a no-no-nonsense approach to teaching her children right from wrong and to accept the responsibilities that would help them grow up and thrive as independent adults. Her "no" was simple and firm, not wishy-washy and over-explained. If my brother and I misbehaved, we faced the consequences, leaving us feeling very unhappy, but never unloved.

My "no," on the other hand, has often bordered on "maybe" and occasionally slid into "yes," and if there's one way to teach your kids to walk all over you, it's by not defining "no" from the very start. Frankly, I've tried to be a less restrictive, "cooler" mom than Mama was, but that has led me to draw an often-blurry line between what is acceptable and what is not. I am still learning from Mama, sometimes by going out of my way to take a different path and then realizing that her way was, after all, best.

There are so many things Mama taught me, some that she articulated, but most not. I think the things my mom lost in the war were the things she placed so much value upon in her new life in this country: Family.

Freedom. Education. A home and garden to call one's own. These good, basic values she passed down to me.

Being Mama's daughter was taking a course in accepting life's challenges and persevering with hope and vigor to get through them. Being her daughter was learning to sing when the work was done – or, when possible, while doing it. It was learning to celebrate the natural beauty of the earth. It was allowing language, allowing literature, to open doors to people and places I might not otherwise have gotten to know, to even open windows into my own mind and heart. It was learning to be kind to those that society shunned. It was learning that saying "no" to your kids is always difficult, but often best. Being her daughter was learning – above all – how to love.

There's just one more thing:

Being her daughter was learning to breathe deeply on a bleak, rainy day and not to miss the rainbow. Because always, Mama – just as you taught me – there's a rainbow.


*Dalia van den Boogaard is very much her mother's daughter. Her family comes first and spending time with them is what she enjoys most. When she's not watching a good film with her husband, chatting with her son about college life, watching her younger son play baseball, going to the beach with her daughter, or wrestling a tennis ball away from her dog, she might be fiddling around in the garden or at the computer, or sharing a bottle of wine with friends. A resident of Southern California (but a Chicagoan at heart), Dalia writes regularly for* Live OC *magazine.*

# Tiger-Eyes
## Dmae Roberts

*A 99-pound Asian tigress*

She got out of her deathbed to help me buy a car.

In the last two years, my mother has almost died twice. It's been a long and arduous journey for us beginning with an email in Taiwan from relatives I didn't even know telling me Ma was sick and needed to be taken home to Eugene, Oregon.

Our relationship had always been stormy. She was always a 99-pound Tiger-woman to me. A survivor. A fighter. Ma had been sold twice to work as a bonded servant when she was just a baby, an Asian form of adoption called "Sim-bua" (adopted daughter). A way of getting rid of unwanted daughters still practiced in Asia. Her abandonment at such a young age had shaped her to be in survival mode throughout her life.

Ma suffered abuse and starvation from her "step-parents" and survived during World War Two by running away at the age of 16. She escaped bombs and gunfire from American and Japanese planes, crediting Kuan Yin, the Buddhist goddess of compassion, for saving her life. Throughout my childhood, I heard about this goddess who I nicknamed "Lady Buddha" that Ma worshipped.

After the war, Ma got jobs to support herself and met my dad who was stationed in Taiwan. They married, and Daddy moved her, my brother and me to America, where she thought she would live the good life.

But there was never enough money, and they fought constantly. Daddy wanted to be a salesman. She wanted something more secure for the family. So finally he gave in and got a job at a plywood mill. She eventually got a job there too so they would have more money.

When he died from heart failure, the battle continued with her and me. Mostly, she wanted to keep me at home to be with her. To read for her, translate for her, handle her finances and legal business. To be the filial Chinese daughter. Mostly, I wanted to live my own life and go to college to become someone.

Through the years, the conflict never let up. I was her like her in many ways and had a bit of the Tiger in me, too. Sometimes we got along. Sometimes we would go for years not speaking to one another. Always my brother stayed with her, never having a chance to go to school or get a decent job. But he was there. And I was the selfish American daughter who had left home to live in Portland, two hours away.

When I got married at the age of 40, our relationship improved a bit. She loved my husband, a good, kind man who knows how to fix things around the house. When he volunteered to help her with home repairs, that helped Ma and me to mend our emotional fences.

After she retired from the plywood mill, Ma wanted to go traveling. She decided to return to Taiwan to visit her last surviving brother and his family.

Four months later, I got the email from a cousin I had never met saying she was sick. On a weekend, I flew to Taiwan and brought her home. During the flight, I thought she might die. She had a severe infection and coughing fits, and was receiving "energy shots" which I suspected were cortisone.

Not understanding the language or the Taiwanese medical system, I risked bringing her back to an American emergency room. Within a week she was better and at home, but still coughing.

In six months, she was diagnosed with breast cancer that had spread to her lungs. She had already had a mastectomy 10 years earlier. The cancer had returned and was in her lymph nodes.

We tried tamoxifen, a cancer drug and tried a dose of chemotherapy. She responded well without any side effects. We though she might beat the cancer. One afternoon, I got a call from my brother. Ma was acting weird, he said and passing out. I told him to call an ambulance. I drove down to Eugene that day. The doctors said she might not make it through the night. She had pneumonia from the one chemo treatment. I stayed a whole week at the hospital, sometimes driving back and forth from Portland to Eugene to try to tie up my job obligations.

She seemed to get better and wanted to leave the hospital. When they discovered she had fluid in her lungs, they kept her a few more days. She went downhill and demanded to go home to die. I called hospice, and we had aides round the clock. At one point, she was vomiting and unable to eat. She kept losing weight and was crying often.

I told her, "Ma, you have pneumonia. People can live a long time with cancer. You have to decide if you want to live or die."

She looked at me with a fierceness I had not seen for a long time. I couldn't tell if she was angry with me or with the illness.

But she beat the infection and recovered. A few months later she "graduated" from hospice. Nothing short of a miracle. Again, Lady Buddha, Kuan Yin, saved her life.

I drove down to Eugene every week, then every two weeks, then every three until I got into a car accident and totaled my car. When I told her I couldn't find another car like my previous one that I could afford, she told me she'd find me one.

We went to a dealership by her house. She always loved bargaining with salesmen, especially for cars. I hated the game-playing and would walk away disgusted and angry. But she thrived on it. So we found a car I wanted and she said…

"Let me do the talking."

Ma cut me a good deal within an hour. We looked at each other barely able to keep from laughing. What a fighter! Her drive and ferocity were traits I learned to help me to go to school, become a radio producer and to run the non-profit I now head. Her energy and ability to survive any setback, I also got from Ma. My success at anything was always due to her. I knew this though often I didn't want to recognize it.

After shaking hands with the car dealers, Ma looked at me with her big, gorgeous smile. She had won. And she liked winning.

I remember when I was five we were traveling in Taiwan and someone stole our suitcases. She raised such a ruckus at the police station that passers-by were peering through windows to look at the Tiger-woman who was giving the police such a hard time. Through the years, this Tiger-woman and I fought many battles with each other. But the battle against the cancer forged a new admiration, a new relationship between Ma and me.

We drove off in my new car that Ma had helped me get.

"I did good, huh?" Her Tiger-eyes radiating.

"Oh yeah…" God, I was proud.

Ma and I are planning a trip to Canada in that new car. She still has cancer for who knows how long. But this I know. The Tiger-woman is back. She was never really gone. And never will be. Not as long as I'm around.

---

# Prayers and Other Ofrendas
## Andrea Hernandez Holm

*Spiritual wealth from a culture of poverty*

Children of the Fifth Sun

I.
Tonatiuh used to hang
in my parent's bedroom.
Resplendent
in his ceramic mold,
ominous
against the beige trailer walls,
his glory shining forth
in rural Arizona.

He took our privacy
in small sacrifices,
greedily swallowing
tears, anger and guilt
we tried to hide under the bed.
He sneered at us,
challenged us to jump into the burning fire.

II.
They were fighting
because two jobs weren't enough

and we paid for commodities anyway
and the car payment was late again
and the last time the kids
had seen the dentist
was in the grocery store
where we stood in line
buying beans and rice
and a cart full of things
that sank in our stomachs and boiled in our minds.

III.

Dad slammed the door,
and turning to look at him,
we heard the crash, a crack
like the dry desert earth outside
splitting open.
We heard Mom's gasp
through the thin plywood walls
and we ran to see her kneeling
on the itchy brown carpet,
pieces of Tonatiuh cradled
in her trembling arms.

We backed out slowly
as dad joined her on the floor.
We scattered, hid under covers
and in closets, expecting his wrath.

We hadn't noticed that our names
rolled off his bladed tongue
and he already clutched our hearts in his hands.

We lived in Maricopa when the town was just a small dot on the map, if it was featured at all. You had to cross through the Ak-chin Indian Reservation and onto the unpaved desert roads to find our house.

Now, Maricopa is a booming city, what economists might call a bedroom community of Phoenix. As I was growing up, there were few people in Maricopa, and very few jobs to be had. Poverty was an institution, and if you didn't own the farms or cattle ranches in the area, you were probably imbedded in it.

I remember times at home when we had no money and weeks felt like decades on end. I don't mean no money to buy new toys or to go to the movies once a week. I mean no money to pay all the bills and buy groceries too. My dad could be working and my mom could be painting crafts and we still always seemed to be living from paycheck to paycheck, always come up short.

"Everything will be okay," my mom would tell us – even as the Final Notice bills began to arrive and due dates drew near and worries that my parents tried to keep to a whisper in the bedroom sneaked through the air conditioning vents and followed us around the house. My mom would keep telling us to have faith and say our prayers. "Remember God in your actions and your thoughts."

I would try to follow my mom's directions but I often forgot my prayers or asked for things that only fourteen year old girls have the audacity to ask God for.

I remember a day that my parents only had twenty dollars between them. Those twenty dollars were supposed to buy groceries, gas for the car and maybe pay the water bill too. I remember that a woman came to the door of our mobile home that day, slight except for the tender roundness of a pregnant belly. She spoke a Spanish unfamiliar to my ears, maybe one raised in Guatemala or Ecuador. She motioned to her husband and two small daughters sitting in the car that served as their home as she told my mom how she had found her way to our doorstep.

They were working in the fields, laboring as migrant workers across the southwest. I wondered if I had seen them as we drove by the farms. In the early hours of the day, you could drive past the acres of fields and see men and women stooped to gather vegetables that were too tender for machines to pull or handfuls of cotton that had escaped the claws of the harvesters. My parents had both worked the fields when they were young, joining their fathers and brothers and sisters as they filled heavy burlap sacks with cotton. My dad's family and my mom's sisters had even traveled across the southwest and up the northern coast too, working in orchards and farms that grew crops that wouldn't flourish in the Arizona desert. When we drove past fields of workers I often tried to visualize my parents or my *tías* and *tíos* working away like ants.

As the time drew near for our visitor to bring the baby inside of her to light, she and her husband were trying to find more permanent jobs that would allow them to stay in one place. Relying on the protection and assistance of fellow laborers, they had been directed to my parents' house, having been told that Señor and Señora Hernandez always helped when they could.

So my mom invited them in and shuffled us all around until there was enough space for their family at our dinner table. She made our pots boil enough rice and beans to feed us all and when we were done eating, she directed us kids to gather clothes and toys to send with their little ones. As the family started their weary little car that night and directed it out of our driveway, I saw my mom press ten dollars into the woman's palm.

For the first time in my life, I was genuinely furious with my mother. I didn't understand how she could give away our money like that, as if we didn't need it. But when I asked her, she said,

"God will take care of us *mi'ja*, so we must take care of others." And that was that.

She was right. The ten dollars – and more – came back to us from somewhere, just when we needed it most.

Learning to follow my mother's example has not been an easy lesson. I realize now that she when she challenged me to remember God in my actions, she was not only guiding me to develop a relationship with the spiritual realm, and she was challenging me to incorporate those elements of spiritual values and beliefs in to my daily life. She was working to instill in her children the value of living a life of reciprocity – if you want others to treat you with respect, you must treat others with respect; if you want the world to be merciful, you must act mercifully; if you want to be forgiven, you must forgive; and if you expect compassion, you must act with compassion – the universe will take care of you if you take care of the universe. To live this way is hard work. It is often much easier to be judgmental, to dwell on frustration and anger, and to ignore the needs of others, even if you don't do so maliciously. I admit that I can get caught up in the trivial comforts of this American life, so caught up in fact that I begin to think of these things as necessities and work hard to attain them instead of focusing on how I treat others, myself, or the world I live in. But I remember my mom's example and her words and I'm working on it, trying every day to model the love that my mom lives, a love for herself, her family, her community, and her world.

I'm walking,
walking
and *"La gente están cambiando"*
is whispered on the wind,
the words landing quietly in my ear.

I stop,
slowly,
and reach for the source.
There is no one
– a blonde Betty Boop
Who can't hear Spanish –
and a dark-skinned *hermano*
Who pretends he can't hear at all.

There is movement,
swift and methodical,
raking, chopping, clearing.
*Mi abuelo, mi tío y my papá*
look at me through a gardener's
chocolate brown eyes.
They ask me
if I remembered to pray thanks
to the earth, the sun and the moon,
or have I been too busy today?

In the solemn regard of their stare,
the arrogance of my stance
melts into the warming cement below my feet
and I stand like a child,

scolded and shamed in a puddle of my own tears.

Flashing disappointment
and stern reminders my way,
the gardener blinks at me
before moving on, and I silently
start slowly
with the weight of history on my back
and the stories of my people on my tongue.

Tonatiuh dries my tears
and his burning rays
draw a prayer from my soul.

*Andrea Hernandez Holm is a long-time resident of central and southern Arizona. She was born and raised in the Casa Grande area. Her family arrived in the region in the 1940s, on a journey that began in their homelands of Chihuahua, Mexico. Her heritage is mestizo of Tarahumara, Nahuatl, and Spanish ancestry.*

---

## Excerpt from
# The Ignoble Insult
### Deepanjolie Sonya Figg

*A lesson from India in Cookery, Insults and Love!*

"Y'know…e'n the flies are not sitting on the gobi and rice…" The still, small voice that spoke to me didn't come from my heart – it was from my four-year-old, that little rascal, Donny!!

Don had plaintively asked for some dal so I warmed up the little that was there from yesterday with a 'chchauck of desi ghee' while synchronizing stirring the gobhi-alu sabji on the next burner and rolling out chapattis on the first.

The meal had started off all right with my husband Dexter threatening Don of dire consequences (those who don't finish their meal won't go out to play in the evening) and my informing the little chap of all those millions of starving children who beg on the streets for food.

His father (fie, shame and all that), damn the man, tucked his head somewhere into his tummy, a-la - Swami Ramdev stunt-like and signed out from the sad story while I couldn't believe my ears (my own flesh and blood so ungrateful …mmph….so funny….the cheek of the child….manner-less creature (an old favorite from convent school days of early learning the English language)!
…awful…incorrigible…mmmph….heee..hee..hee..haa..haa.)

I didn't come emerge from the privacy and comfort (free laughing zone) of my kitchen till Dexter had resumed a more human pose and his mantle of Glowering Chief and Authority Figure for Fiendish Four-year olds who fuss over their food and insult their mothers (who've slaved over a hot stove to prepare the ghoulish meal …)!

Don finished his food quietly (I'd like to think he understood what his Daddy explained about food being made with love and for him, though only he can truly say what got him to finish every last) and came to me to ask for help with 'picking up the last few bites' as 'the rice wasn't listening' to him (getting scooped on his spoon instead of rolling this way and that on the thaali).

So I did. Despite the ignoble insult ringing in my ears. Or perhaps, I meant, even with.

Mothers can't help hurting but still loving: love is not If (If you get a good report card, bring me gifts, do things my way…I will love you) or Because (because you are pretty, because you are popular, because you make me feel good about myself…I will love you), but In Spite Of what you do – or don't do, understand or don't, feel or don't feel, abide by or do not…I will love you.

I guess that's what my own Mother was trying to tell me so many years ago when I fussed over eating vegetables, the gravy not being right or a special meal not being saved up for me to have a second helping of at night or simply showing the dumps because some other family member's food choice was given preference over my favorites.

Except Ma never carried it with her till the next day like I am prone to do (see, I'm even writing about it to rid myself of some of the shame of it all).

She simply took the ignoble insult and assigned it to the flames of forgotten words (of course she also took the food I'd fussed over away and never once coaxed me into eating it or advertised its goodness or the time/love/effort taken in preparing it – only the defeated look on her face was enough to cure me out of my sightless-ness) that shouldn't come back to haunt any relationships with love in it.

Just like the little bit of dough that the Paharis of the Himalayas assign to the chullahs (cooking stoves) as an offering to the Fire god before making the first roti bread for the day – as a thanksgiving that they were given their daily bread – is what is needed of us to do with ignoble insults – even ones that are true. To understand that we're really not all that great that someone should love us, but that someone does, is something to be grateful for indeed. And to be able to love someone in turn, or even out of it, is more than what most hope for – so, should we get the opportunity to love or be loved, we needs must assign to the flames of forgetfulness all that is unworthy of enduring love.

And, I guess that's what I'll do: Love despite all Odds.

(And remember to throw away the score-card).


*Deepanjolie Sonya Figg is a young mother ("though the brat is fast-aging me") and is also a full-time freelance writer who works from a home-office in the foothills of the Himalayas or back in the city-lights of Pune, near Mumbai, India. Her recent articles have been featured in Marwar (Jan 08 issue - Spirituality), InsideTrack (March 08 issue-Pritzker Prize winner feature), Home Review (April 08 issue - feature on The Straf hotel, Milan.)*

# Tales beside the Grinding Stone
## Oluwafemi Reis

*A fable from Nigeria*

Beside the grinding stone in our smoky kitchen, is where I did most of my growing up. I keenly watched this woman whom I simply referred to as "mama," as she moved from corner to corner like there were wheels placed beneath her feet. Between the grinding stone and the cooking pot, she always found time to tell a tale. Most of them I have forgotten, but the clear picture of one, I can still recall. Amidst the aroma of frying stew, which swept my attention from mama's tale, I was trapped in a dilemma of making a choice; either to use my ears rather than my nose, or to use my nose rather than my ears. I made a wise choice that beautiful night, as I courageously decided to use them both.

She told me this story about an ancient animal kingdom, where the elephant claimed to be the wisest. He went around the kingdom making his boasts, telling the animals that none of them was half as wise as he. News of the elephant soon reached the tortoise, who was so upset by the elephant's boasts; the tortoise was out to prove him wrong, and he took the task upon himself. Very early the following morning, the tortoise set out on a journey to the faraway human kingdom where he learnt they had lost their king. The people were shouting and crying, and singing a song that interested the tortoise: "Who will be our king? Who will be our king? The river has swept Oba Adewusi away; none of our people is bold enough to step into his empty shoes. Who will be our king? Who will be our king?"

Mama sang to the rhythm of the grinding stone, or rather, she ground to the rhythm of the song she sang, then she got up and served me a bowl of stew and roasted yam, which made the story even more interesting — like we have it in the cinemas today. As she served another plate for papa, I almost thought she had forgotten our tale, but soon she returned to the grinding stone, and continued immediately from where she stopped.

The tortoise told the people not to worry, that he could get them a huge, strong, bold and wise king from the kingdom from which he came. He told them the king would lead them forever, and no mighty flood could ever sweep him away. The people were happy with the tortoise's offer; they were glad that the gods had sent them an answer from the animal kingdom. The following morning, before anybody woke, the tortoise dug a big pit and covered it with beautiful mats, he told them this would be the king's palace, and no one should walk in it until he came, and then he left again for the animal kingdom. On his arrival to the animal kingdom, he met the elephant still making his boasts, and he said to the elephant, "Wise elephant, wise elephant, the humble tortoise has been away in search of a kingdom for you to rule with your great wisdom. I have found you one, and they've made you a throne." The elephant was happy, and he set out with the tortoise the following day. As they arrived at the human kingdom, the people rushed out to meet them and they danced and sang a joyful song, "Here comes our king, here comes our king, huge as a rock; sent from the gods. Here comes our king, here comes our king, mighty and strong; beyond any flood." Then they ushered him to his palace, and just as he was about to step in, out of excitement, the people lifted the tortoise and placed him on the elephant's back, and then came the huge crash as the elephant stepped on the beautiful mats.

Neither the tortoise nor the elephant got out of that pit, and the people buried them there and went away in search of another king.

My yam and stew was all gone at this point, and my plate was a shiny as new. I knew mama had a moral to teach so I waited and watched as she put more firewood under the pot of stew. "Don't claim to be wiser than your friends, child," she said, "or you'll fall for the slightest trick. And don't dig a pit for anyone, or you'll fall in right after them."

I tried to look into my mother's eyes, but the smoke won't let me see. And now it was time to go to bed. She pulled the burning woods from beneath the pot and used a bowl of water to put them out. That was it for that beautiful night; I went to my room and laid in bed, as the rhythm of mama's song filtered through my head. Tomorrow night we will convene again, beside the old grinding stone where I grew.

## The Black Pride
**Aderemi Adegbite**

Be proud my child, be proud
Of your endowed black shining skin,
Glistering like the sparkling stars
Above in the glooming sky
At arrival of the glowing moon.

With pride my child, with pride
Must you display your beauty hue
Along city streets
Of Africa - land of bounty and splendor -
From coast to coast in the wider world.

You are black-skinned my child,
Yes you are dark-skinned,
Yet the sparkling makes it lovely
Whilst gleaming with sprinkles of adoration
Across the vast coasts of nations.

My child, be proud with your pride,
For your black, dark shimmering skin,
To the world is symbolized as power,
Strength, manipulation of creativity -
You're an unquantifiable paragon of beauty.

# My Mother
**Flavia Cosma**
*From Romania*

My mother did not play the piano;
She couldn't find a purpose for
My growing fingers, outstretched,
She wouldn't guide them;
She was unaware
Of the lofty sense of flying,
She had no daring.

My mother did not read
Scholarly books or great literature;
Poetry made her by turns
Laugh or cry;
She would sit quietly humming
Melancholy songs about Jesus,
While the fold on her brow
Obstinately deepened
And her face became
More and more pallid.

My mother didn't know much
About the affairs of this world,
But her smile, like a lamp's flame,
Knew all about everything,
Before fading away, much too soon,
Leaving us holding
All the boundless and hungry darkness
In our arms.

My grandmother knew even less.
But her hands, those sorceresses,
Alternately plaited and unbraided our lives,

Like a transparent kerchief,
A magic word,
A flowering dream
Stretching over the world,
Like a light, gentle breeze.


**Flavia Cosma** *is an award-winning Romanian-born Canadian poet, author and translator. She took her Master in electrical engineering at the Polytechnic Institute of Bucharest. After that she studied drama for two years. She has authored twenty books, of which fourteen are poetry collections. Her poetry book* 47 POEMS *(Texas Tech University Press, 1992), won the prestigious ALTA Richard Wilbur Poetry in Translation Prize. Her documentary* Romania, A Country at the Crossroads *won the Canadian Scene National Award. She was awarded Third Prize in the John Dryden Translation Competition-2007, for co-translating* In The Arms of The Father, *poems by Flavia Cosma.*

# Chapter 12

## Postscript and Preview:

# SURVIVING DOMESTIC VIOLENCE

*Half of my profits from sale of this book have been pledged to shelters for women and children escaping domestic violence. The following story is about one of these women and her children – to show whom this book intends to help, and why. It is also a preview of my next anthology: stories of those who have survived and escaped from abusive relationships.*

*– Eric Bowen*

# Independence Day
## Susan Harmon

*A brave mother acts to rescue her children from abuse*

"You don't understand how bad my life is cause you just sit here with the kids doing nothing," my husband, Randy*, said.

"Well, a lot of people have to work every day and I don't understand why you are so stressed. I mean, you have a good paying job, a wife who respects you, and three beautiful, healthy children. You know, some people would die to be in your shoes," I replied.

Randy drank everyday and chased his misery down with an assortment of painkillers, sleeping pills, and anti-anxiety medication. Randy blamed his misery on his easy job at Potlatch where he worked alternating shift work, but made more than a sufficient amount of money.

"Yeah, but everyone doesn't understand what is going on inside my head," Randy said making me feel uneasy.

I wondered if his previous references to the ghostly little girl he claimed laughed at him or his sightings of an unknown woman in the mirror were from the alcohol and pills or from a mental disorder.

I had dealt with his intermittent hurtful words and belligerent attitude for 11 years. Honestly, I couldn't count the times I was accused of adultery while a gun was held to my temple or was raped during my second pregnancy which, due to complications, left me bedridden and unable to move, much less have consensual sex, in order to save my unborn son's life. Randy had induced a consuming fear in me which caused me to attempt to leave him at one point, but was cut short when my hands were bound with a rope while I slept. I was adorned with red cuts and blue bruises, but despite the long shirts worn in summer I appeared to be a happy, young woman. As a mother, I felt it was one thing to hurt me and a completely different thing to harm my children. I never thought he would turn on his own children, but my assumptions proved wrong in 2004.

While I was anticipating a small family fireworks display in our backyard, Randy was outside gulping down Budweisers like a parched vagabond.

"C'mon boys, let's go out and shoot some firecrackers," Randy shouted drunkenly from outside the front door.

My 4-year-old son, Reece, and 7-year-old, Max, slowly walked outside into the yard while my 7-month-old daughter, Kelly, and I stayed inside to prevent exposure to the suffocating July heat. I stirred the peas cooking on the stove and decided to look through the screen door to check on the boys. To my dismay, I witnessed Reece dodging back and forth frantically while his father threw smoke bombs at him.

"What the heck are you doing?" I yelled as I shoved open the door.

"Oh, the boy and I are just playing," Randy snickered while I observed the tears welling up in Reece's eyes.

"He doesn't seem to be having a good time to me," I screamed with a livid demeanor.

"Watch then," Randy demanded loudly.

As I stood at the door, Randy threw the lit smoke bomb at Reece suddenly striking him in the face.

"Oh my God, Randy, what did you do?" I asked while attempting to see if Reece was hurt, but was stopped by threatening words before I could reach him.

"Hell, go inside. He should've just dodged a little better. You don't need to come out here and be nosy. This ain't got nothin' to do with you," Randy said with his eyebrows furrowed.

I cautiously went back inside to check on Kelly who slept quietly in her playpen. I snuck around the house and peeped through windows trying to catch a glimpse of what was happening. To my astonishment, Randy placed the firecrackers in both boys hand and lit them. Reece was fearful to refuse his father's request, so he grimaced each time a firecracker would explode in his hand. On the other hand, I knew my sensitive older son wanted no part in playing with something loud and harmful, so I sat and waited for the inevitable explosion. Not from the firecracker, but from Randy's temper.

Suddenly, the front door swung open so hard it knocked a hole in the wall while Randy pushed Max into the house.

"Here is your little pussy boy," Randy said to me breathing hard.

"You act like a damn girl," he told Max.

Randy turned and hit the wall with his fist while screaming for Reece to come inside the house. My blood boiled with anger towards Randy, but at the same time my heart felt like it would burst out of my chest from fear. I scooped up my sleeping daughter out of the playpen in the living room and placed her in her crib for safety. While I walked down the hall with my baby in my arms, I could hear Randy asking the boys a question. After laying Kelly in her crib, I walked back down the hall and hesitantly stood in the kitchen, out of sight, listening to the fermented asshole verbally attack our sons.

"Y'all act like fuckin' little girls. Are y'all girls?" Randy asked our sons.

"Pull your pants down. I want to check if y'all have a dick or not," Randy said.

I supposed at this point my innocent children stood pantless in the living room while Randy inspected their genitals. Then Randy asked the boys to come to him while he started to sit in his recliner. Randy heard me take a few steps in the kitchen and demanded for me to come into the living room. I reluctantly sat in my recliner next to Randy while Max stood frightened in front of his father and Reece sat silent on the couch.

"Prove to me you aren't a pussy. A real man can take pain," Randy said to Max while lighting a cigarette with his lighter.

"Give me your hand, boy," Randy demanded while grabbing Max's unblemished hand.

Randy held Max's hand tightly as he twisted and turned the lit cigarette into Max's tender flesh. Max fought back his tears hoping his punishment would end while Randy maliciously took his lighter and lit it so the metal would become hot. A single tear trickled down Max's face when his own father pushed the hot lighter forcibly into the skin on his hand. Max proved his "manhood," and was demanded to take Reece's place on the couch. Now, it was Reece's turn.

"Reece, are you a boy or a girl?" Randy asked.

"A boy," Reece said quietly, afraid to say the wrong word.

"What's that? You are a girl? Is that what you said?" asked Randy.

"No daddy, I am a boy. I'm tough," Reece said hoping to deter the contact of the glowing red lighter.

Randy's buzz had heightened because of his anger with Reece's uncertain response so he dug the lighter in even harder to Reece's small, chubby hand. While I sat in fear and oppression, the boys looked at me, but I could tell by the persecuted look in their eyes they knew I couldn't defend them. The boys sat quietly and tried to avoid Randy at all costs, only sitting close to him at dinner. Thankfully, soon after dinner Randy drifted into a deep slumber in his recliner while the shock of the horrific event still played on in my thoughts.

I cleaned the table of dishes and glasses and began to wash them when Reece asked me why his daddy burned him. I stopped washing and knelt down, looked into his blue-gray eyes and told him I wasn't sure, but I assured him it wouldn't ever happen again. At that moment, I began to arrange my thoughts and propose different angles in order to save my children from further abuse. Kelly awoke from her nap and the boys went to their room to watch television. I stopped washing dishes to get Kelly from her crib then quietly tiptoed past the sleeping piece of shit in the recliner to get the phonebook to write down some numbers for help. I wrote down various emergency abuse hotline numbers because I knew I would have the opportunity to seek help sooner or later. Then I remembered some movies we rented from the Movie Gallery were due back the next day and usually I was the one to return them. With anticipation, I folded the paper with the listed phone numbers into a tiny square and hid it among bills piled on top of the computer desk.

The rest of the evening went smoothly as well as the night. Morning rose and I awoke. Randy sat awake in his recliner when I entered the living room. His quiet demeanor led me to think he knew he had fucked up big this time. I ignored him most of the morning while I let the children stay asleep as long as possible. Finally, I broke the silence.

"I am going to take those movies back in a minute," I said.

"Uh huh," Randy replied.

"I'll take Kelly with me," I said, knowing his two seat truck wouldn't fit all three children.

With Randy helpless from a hangover, I awoke Kelly, grabbed the diaper bag, the movies, and went out the door to the truck.

As soon as I strapped Kelly into her car seat and backed out the driveway, I began calling the numbers I had written down. No one answered because on July 4th none of the government type offices were open. In a panic, I called my daddy.

"Daddy, can you meet me at the Movie Gallery?" I quickly asked.

"Sure, but why?" he asked as if he knew something was wrong.

"I can't get into it now, but something really bad has happened," I said.

Kelly and I finally arrive at the Movie Gallery where my daddy waited. I explained what happened while wailing, "The boys are still with him!"

After several failed phone calls while inside the Movie Gallery, Daddy decided to simply call the police. I feared Randy may have killed them since he always told me that if he couldn't be with them, neither would I. My father and I arrived at the police station where I tried to tell the story in between the panic and tears. After about five hours of the police calling other agencies, one police officer entered the room and told me I could go home because Randy was in custody. My father and I drove up to my house where Randy sat handcuffed in the backseat of a police car. Even then, I feared he would escape and hurt us, but he didn't, but only because he couldn't. I didn't even look at him for fear his glare would invoke the familiar mind-numbing fear. I exited the car and entered the house with Kelly on my hip to find my two sons telling the story to a Child Protection worker while my daddy talked to the police officers.

"They told us the same story you reported to the police, Mrs. Harmon," the worker said.

"I won't have a daddy anymore, Momma," Reece cried.

"Sweetheart, you'll always have a father," I assured him.

"He isn't going to hurt us anymore is he, Momma?" Max asked.

"No baby, today truly is our Independence Day," I said.

*Name changed

*About the Editor*

*Born in Renton, Washington State in 1953, Eric Bowen uses his day job as an accountant to support his family and his various hobbies and social activities, including Toastmasters, the Unitarians, hiking, taekwondo, linguistics, singing, and of course writing. His first book,* An American View of Wales, *chronicled his decade of volunteering for the Welsh home rule and language restoration movement.*

Made in the USA
Charleston, SC
30 August 2010